"From irresistible yet approachable recipes to the story of how John Kanell traded hurried city life for centered farmhouse living, *Preppy Kitchen* invites us into a world where we can shift our priorities back to family, passion, and everything else that's most important, all with amazing food on our supper tables."

—JOCELYN DELK ADAMS,
award-winning author of *Grandbaby Cakes: Modern Recipes, Vintage Charm, Soulful Memories*

"My family and I were instantly drawn to John's food. Everything he bakes and cooks is as delicious as it is perfect to look at. That's why *Preppy Kitchen* is a must-have!"

—KATHERINE SCHWARZENEGGER PRATT,
New York Times bestselling author

preppy kitchen

preppy kitchen

RECIPES FOR SEASONAL DISHES
AND SIMPLE PLEASURES

JOHN KANELL
WITH RACHEL HOLTZMAN

PHOTOGRAPHS BY DAVID MALOSH
WITH ADDITIONAL PHOTOGRAPHS BY JOHN KANELL AND JOHN GRUEN

SIMON ELEMENT
NEW YORK LONDON TORONTO SYDNEY NEW DELHI

SIMON
ELEMENT

An Imprint of Simon & Schuster, Inc.
1230 Avenue of the Americas
New York, NY 10020

First Simon Element hardcover edition
October 2022

SIMON ELEMENT is a trademark
of Simon & Schuster, Inc.

For information about special discounts for bulk
purchases, please contact Simon & Schuster
Special Sales at 1-866-506-1949 or
business@simonandschuster.com.

The Simon & Schuster Speakers Bureau can
bring authors to your live event. For more
information or to book an event, contact
the Simon & Schuster Speakers Bureau
at 1-866-248-3049 or visit our website at
www.simonspeakers.com.

Design by Jennifer K. Beal Davis

Food Photography Copyright © 2022 by
David Malosh
Additional Photography Copyright © 2022 by
Food Media and Commerce, LLC
Food Styling by Simon Andrews

Manufactured in China

10 9 8 7 6 5 4 3 2 1

Library of Congress Cataloging-in-Publication
Data has been applied for.

ISBN 978-1-9821-7837-6
ISBN 978-1-9821-7838-3 (ebook)

Dedicated to my loving,
supportive husband, Brian,
and our beautiful boys,
Lachlan and George

contents

WELCOME TO PREPPY KITCHEN

I didn't set out to be the guy who makes beautiful dinners and portrait-ready desserts for millions of people on Instagram and YouTube. Nor did I think I'd be making Reese Witherspoon's birthday cake (confetti cake with hand-painted butterflies), and it never occurred to me that I might find myself raising a flock of Nigerian dwarf goats on the grounds of my Connecticut farmhouse with my husband, Brian, and our five-year-old twin boys. And I certainly didn't expect that my recipes would be a powerful salve for so many people during a global pandemic. After all, until six years ago, I was a middle school math and science teacher who just happened to love to cook, bake, and feed people something special whenever we got together.

Up until that point, every big decision I'd made had been to move closer to a life that put those values at the center—the kind of life that I grew up having, and the kind of life I want my sons to experience. It may sound a little unlikely that a first-generation American, his husband, and two kids would embody that kind of Norman Rockwell sentiment, but as Brian (the husband) likes to say, we are the most traditional untraditional family there is. And when it came to preserving the things that matter most to us—being together, having children, devoting as much time as we could to them, giving them wide-open spaces to explore, and filling all of our lives with rich memories—we have made the choices that have brought Preppy Kitchen into existence.

In 2015, I had been living and working in Los Angeles, commuting back and forth to New York with Brian, who at the time was part of the 24-7 Hollywood agent grind. In order to have more flexibility to travel for work, and to spend more time with Brian—as well as in anticipation of one day having kids and wanting to be home with them as much as possible—I made the wrenching decision to leave my position as a schoolteacher. But I wanted something just as satisfying to do. When people say there is a moment in their lives when they know they need to "follow their passion" and make a change—this one was mine.

Luckily, I had something that I truly was already in love with: cooking and creating recipes. One of my proudest childhood memories is of making a flourless chestnut torte using chestnuts that I'd roasted and milled myself. (I was thirteen.) When the other kids in high school were going out to parties, my friends and I were making tiramisu with candied violets. The one time my friends and I ever ditched class, we were all dressed up in eighteenth-century French court regalia (it's a long story) and went to the Westwood Marquis for afternoon tea. (It's worth pointing out that Brian, on the other hand, had barely attended a full day of school and graduated with a 1.9 GPA—to say opposites attract is an understatement.)

Mine was a love born of being in the kitchen from an early age. My mother was an intuitive home cook who regularly made new dishes for us kids to try. She was raised in a small village in Mexico where she made from-scratch tortillas every morning, and there were no canned goods, prepared foods, or shortcuts under her watch. It was always fresh, high-quality ingredients combined with techniques and flavor influences from all over the world—a curiosity that was further stoked by marrying my Greek and French Canadian father and, eventually, by discovering Julia Child. From the time she and my father met in the United States after having emigrated from Mexico and Montreal respectively, she made a point to create new, meaningful traditions to go with their new American life. Easter, Thanksgiving, Christmas Eve, Christmas Day, and New Year's Eve were giant feasts featuring a mash-up of cultures with Greek-style roasted lamb and herbed rice sharing the table with duck à l'orange and flan. Every Sunday was reserved for a big extended-family supper, and every weeknight our attendance was required at the dinner table, where we enjoyed three-course dinners whose leftovers often became breakfast the next morning (usually cake; my favorite was German chocolate). Even though my mom juggled studying for her master's and doctoral degrees in teaching with taking care of all of us, her love for cooking and her desire to create strong connective tissue in our family meant making it all work, and I was there by her side for as much of it as possible. Being a teacher by trade, she was a natural mentor to me in the kitchen.

So I started to cook and bake with an eye toward doing just that for other people—giving them the nurturing and confidence to take on their own culinary feats in the name of making memories. From light-as-air lemon cake to surprisingly elegant French toast casserole to a perfect and simple savory heirloom tomato tart to afternoon tea sandwiches (naturally!), I started sending my recipes out into the world. I knew that putting my fine arts degree to use creating this visual finesse was what would elevate these dishes from "I made it because I had to" to "I made it because I

wanted to." These were not twenty-minute meals, they didn't follow diet fads, and there was nothing trendy about them. No, these were refined—though highly achievable—dishes destined to be at the center of birthdays, anniversaries, Thanksgivings, Easters, barbecues, and picnics—the kind of gracious, timeless cooking that is perfectly summed up by the name: Preppy Kitchen. It became clear that people all over the country—from both coasts to the Midwest to the South—love these "want to" dishes as much as I do. And they especially love that they come with my promise of: "If I can teach twelve-year-olds how to do algebra, I can teach you how to master Swiss meringue buttercream/poach an egg/conquer roast chicken." Which, of course, is exactly what this book is all about.

But while I'd certainly found my own kitchen, I still needed a home to go with it. In early 2019, our lives were increasingly defined by traffic, brown buildings (West Coast), tall gray buildings (East Coast), and more and more traffic. Brian and I had successfully navigated the surrogacy process and had been graced with our twin boys, Lachlan and George. Yet Brian was lucky if he could carve out any time to see them before he had to leave for work in the morning or make it back home again before their bedtime—and believe me, two gay men don't wind up with kids as an afterthought. We didn't like the life we were living, so we set out to build the one we wanted. Which is when Brian decided to leave his job and put in an offer—yes! Sight unseen—on a house. In Connecticut.

We'd had an on-again-off-again love affair with Litchfield County for years after a friend had invited us up for a visit. From Manhattan we'd taken the Saw Mill River Parkway up through the Bronx, and as if by some

heaven-ordained miracle, the traffic parted, all that gray of the city gave way to the greens and blues of trees and lakes, and within an hour and a half, we had arrived in a different place completely. And it was *love*. The white clapboard churches with their quintessentially New England steeples, the lush stretches of land that hadn't been developed (and wouldn't be thanks to centuries-old land trusts), the historical homes frozen in (adorable, perfectly styled) time, the spotty cell service–induced time-warp vibes—it was a long way from the strip malls and freeways we'd both grown up with in LA, and it was a slice of straight-out-of-an-L.L.-Bean-catalog Americana that we hadn't experienced before.

WEST MEETS EAST

To say that making Connecticut our new home has been a leap into the unknown is not an exaggeration. We are two LA guys who knew *nothing* about rural life. Who knew that you couldn't put your mini ponies in your barn with your goats because those ponies make trouble? Or that in the country you can't have your Christmas tree delivered the way you do when you're living in a big city—you have to go to the farm, saw it down, then schlep it home. Well, slowly but surely, we've been figuring it out. And along the way, we've refurbished our farmhouse and named it Hedge Hill Farm. With our boys by our side, we planted our own apple saplings, watched them blossom in the spring, and baked pies with the fruit in the fall. We opened a farm stand, selling our very own fresh honey, flavored chèvre, meringue kisses made with eggs from our chickens, and bundles of our peonies, dahlias, and tulips. We found a small dairy down the road that raises happy, stress-free cows with the delicious, creamy milk to show for it—which the boys have every morning with their breakfast. We learned never to turn up at a neighbor's place empty-handed, whether you're bringing a bouquet of flowers from your garden, a basket of tomatoes from your harvest, or strawberry jam you've just put up. (Or, in our initially garden-less case, truffles from the cow-spa dairy down the road.) And yes, we've added more goats to our flock and sorted out their drama with the mini ponies.

We've also gotten to see our boys find their place. They didn't waste any time embracing the natural cycle of things, greeting each season as it came. They watched with awe as our bare apple trees burst with pink and white blossoms in the spring, and have since been fascinated with the bees that come from our apiary to buzz around the garden. Our first summer, we could take the boys on a proper picnic, surrounded by the wildflowers that had exploded from the dormant soil. When Lachlan picked bouquets for me and Brian, it was the ultimate *I'm glad we're here* moment. They know that our two Great Pyrenees, Bobo and Charlie, are tasked with "keeping the coyotes and bears away" from the chickens, and they love feeding the birds and the goats blades of grass. They know what it's like to eat a sun-ripened tomato from the vine, having watched it grow from a tiny bud. And for the time being, they'll never know a life filled with traffic and city noise. Knowing that we're surrounding them with all these incredible sensory experiences and are giving them a hands-on education about how the natural world works and all its simple pleasures has erased any doubt about whether we've made the right move.

That's why this magical place where we live is just as much a part of this book as the recipes. Because there's nothing like finding pleasure and happiness in the everyday. There's no better medicine than looking out the window at a meticulously plotted cut-flower garden, vegetable garden, or herb garden (no huge expanse of land required); bundling parcels of treats to drop off at the door for long-missed neighbors and loved ones; setting the table with a few special touches (like expertly curated vintage linens and china—we're total collecting junkies, like little old ladies), or treating yourself to handmade compound chèvre (no goat rearing required).

The scenic Connecticut backdrop is also why I've decided to divide this book into seasons to showcase the recipes, because with each shift in the weather comes those dependable, feel-it-in-your-bones traditions, ingredients, and flavors that Preppy Kitchen is all about embracing and celebrating. As sure as the weather turns cooler, our sweaters come out of storage, and the oven goes back on after what seems like an entire summer in hibernation. You can find us and our sons at our pumpkin patch or picking pears in our orchard, then coming home to spend a lazy afternoon fixing something hearty and soul-warming. There's Dutch Oven Chicken Pot Roast with Fingerling Potatoes, Shallots, and Olives and Charred Vegetable Lasagna to roast, and Sweet Potato and Toasted Marshmallow Pie and Apple Cake with Maple Buttercream to bake. The winter holidays, whether they're a quiet but cozy evening with the four of us or an occasion we can share with friends, family, and neighbors, call for Crab Cake Latkes with Garlic-Caper Aioli, Beef Tenderloin with Miso-Honey Caramel, and Orange Linzer Cookie Wreaths. And maybe some Spiked Eggnog Crème Brûlées for the grown-ups. (Did I say maybe? Definitely.) Spring and its much-needed warmth creeping between the slats in our barn means the animals—like us—know there's a new beginning in the air as we make big plans for the upcoming season. Gardens get plotted out, projects around the house get dreamt up, and the recipes take advantage of all the new greenness coming out of the ground. Silky Spring Greens Soup with Parmesan-Kale Crisps and Champagne-Butter Clams with Herby Sourdough Toasts are worthy of this celebration; and Breakfast-for-Dinner Tart with Farm Eggs, Asparagus, and Radishes; Lemon-Elderflower Tea Cake; and Vanilla Bean Panna Cotta with Rosé Rhubarb are what all spring recipes should be: a simple canvas for fresh, bright flavors. And then there's summer—the grand finale with its fireworks, fireflies, unrelenting heat, and saltwater-soaked everything. When we're not harvesting tomatoes, cucumbers, peppers, and beans by the armload, we're thinking up new ways to cook and share the bounty—preferably quickly, and preferably on the grill. Even the most casual of cookouts can become a noteworthy affair with breezy effort thanks to Chilled Elote Soup, Grilled Halloumi and Figs with Toasty Pitas, or Chorizo-Beef Burgers with Queso and Avocado. And the sweets need a respite from the heat, too, which is when I reach for Brambleberry Icebox Pie with Biscoff-Almond Crust and Summer Trifle with Grilled Peaches, Cherries, and Boozy Pound Cake.

BRINGING HOME PREPPY KITCHEN

These are recipes that create their own special moments because of the consideration and care that so clearly goes into making them, regardless of whether it's a weeknight meal, holiday, or milestone celebration. And yet, there's also nothing too complicated or difficult required. Remember earlier when I said that I used to teach tweens math and science? That same attention to detail that goes into guaranteeing success in the classroom applies to getting set up in the kitchen (prep, prep, prep is the name of the game). Sure, I have a soft spot for the frillier indulgences like decorative flowers, all day, every day, but I'm also a big fan of realist shortcuts like using Russian piping tips to make them (it's seriously like riding a cake-decorating bike with training wheels). Or using yogurt containers as custom cake-shaping tools. And while I'll be sharing plenty of chemistry-nerd know-how about things, such as what happens when you add acid to milk (DIY buttermilk, which helps leaven your cake!) or insulating your cake pans with fabric cake strips (perfectly flat, moist cake layers!), my ultimate goal is simplicity, accessibility, and a beautiful and tasty end product.

I find solace in knowing that my recipes will be reached for again and again as indispensable and dependable, but always stylish, staples. Because Preppy Kitchen, like all that is good and classic and timeless, is about preserving a generosity of spirit. So that the people who are able to be at our table know they're going to feel special there. And, more important, like family.

THE RECIPE
FOR TRADITION

When I was growing up, my family traditions didn't look like a lot of my friends'. Our turkey didn't sit next to piles of mashed potatoes and candied yams. There was no Christmas ham, and there definitely wasn't an American flag sheet cake on the Fourth of July. This wasn't because my brother and I were deprived or that my parents didn't care enough about these things. In fact, it was the opposite. For my mother, who came to the States from a small village in Mexico, and my father, who came from Montreal but was part of a Greek family, their lives here were a fresh start. They saw their emigration as an opportunity to not only combine the traditions that they each loved most from their respective cultures but also to define new ones. Because while they didn't have an emotional connection to many of these new American experiences (and, frankly, found many of them too commercial), they did understand the power of gathering as a family. And at the center of that, of course, was food. Food was the common place where we all could meet in the middle; it was the language we all spoke with the same accent.

Our big family gatherings—Christmas Eve, Christmas, New Year's Eve, Greek Easter, every Sunday with my father's parents and my great-uncle Steve—were special celebrations complete with special feasts. The menus reflected the make-your-own-way, do-what-brings-you-joy spirit that my mother in particular embraced. Tired of having made tortillas from scratch for her twelve brothers and sisters every single morning for as long as she could remember, she was ready for something new. She embraced the Greek flavors from my father's side, jostling with her mother-in-law in a little friendly competition to make the most tender leg of lamb (braised with lemon, garlic, and rosemary), flaky *spanakopita* (Greek spinach pie), and *galaktoboureko* (custard-filled phyllo drizzled with orange syrup). And just as she had taught herself to speak English from a dictionary, so, too, did she teach herself to cook from books—first from an encyclopedic series about how to make everything from scratch (even aspic, including boiling down the cow bones) and then from the godmother of French cooking herself, Julia Child. "She has an *insouciance*," my mom would like to say of Julia, admiring the way she could bring laid-back enjoyment into the kitchen, along with ingredients that were fresh and lovely—an ethos that my mom very much embodied. It was also so very '70s chic, which was just frosting on the Harvey Wallbanger cake. Dishes like duck à l'orange, baba au rhum, bûche de Noël, and fillet of sole with spinach, cheese, and caramelized shallots were revelations for my mom. They continue to be among her most requested dishes when we're together (particularly a bûche de Noël on my birthday, never mind the fact that it's in September), and one of my proudest moments was making that sole recipe with her on my YouTube channel. But even though she ventured away from her Mexican cooking roots, when her family would come to visit us, our kitchen would suddenly shift energies, filled with traditional deep-fried tacos, pozole, and Mexican wedding cookies.

My mother's new culinary traditions weren't just reserved for special occasions, though. They trickled down into the daily rituals that she forged for our family. Every night was family dinner night, often involving at least three courses with a salad or appetizer, entrée, and dessert—which we'd always end up eating again for breakfast the next morning because there always was so much food. If it was a week- end, there would be from- scratch yeasted doughnuts or homemade yogurt. There was always a timer going for some- thing in the oven or resting on the counter, and there was always a schedule—something that hasn't changed a bit, even when Mom comes to visit me in Connecticut. Providing these meals for us was, in no uncertain terms, an expression of love. And, in turn, they gave us the stability, secu- rity, and predictability that imparts the soul-warming reassurance that you're cared for, that you're thought of, and that everything is going to be okay. Oh, and she still managed to go to night school and get master's and doctoral degrees in teaching.

> "We may not always experience that same level of sheer joy every time we eat a meal, how- ever delicious, but somewhere deep down, those feelings still stir."

Now, years after I've left home and started a family of my own, those meals have stayed with me. They planted the seed of fervent curiosity about food, flavors, and ingredients, along with the deep desire to bring people together around a table. There were moments between high school and getting married when those traditions started to atrophy, as they often do when we first become adults. But after having our sons, Brian and I knew we wanted to dust off the traditions we have both carried with us and forge them together to make new, authentic-for-us rituals for our own family. There is, of course, the completely over-the-top Christmas including a second outdoor tree that we swirl with lights so the boys can see it from their room, way too many gifts, and a (more seasonally appropriate) bûche de Noël; and Thanksgiving with all the classic dishes— Brian's mashed potatoes and sweet potato casserole (the dessert-in-disguise kind) and my mother's herbed rice and simply poached asparagus (controversial addi- tions for some . . . ahem, Brian). But, like in my house growing up, we don't just want special-feeling family gatherings to be relegated to the holidays.

Now, we make an effort to come together for daily meals—one of the main reasons we have moved to the country to spend more time with our kids. They know that Papa makes "treats" in the kitchen all day, and that they can taste whatever they like (which Dada is also a big fan of). They know that they're welcome to help whisk, stir, and pour (within reason; we don't get too crazy), and that with each new exploration in the kitchen they're experiencing new flavors and widening their little worlds. Seeing the looks on their faces when they find something new that they love—from the expected (pumpkin muffins) to the slightly less so (my mom's pineapple chicken curry)—is like watching them opening their Christmas presents.

We may not always experience that same level of sheer joy every time we eat a meal, however delicious, but somewhere deep down, those feelings still stir. They speak to us of feeling cared for and everything being okay. And when you think of meals this way, they become so much bigger than what you're putting on the plate or how pretty it turns out. It's about creating the traditions for your family that make memories, that make lasting impressions for generations, and that make people feel the kind of love to which words sometimes can't do justice.

FALL

Fall was our first "we're not in LA anymore" seasonal experience. We weren't used to seeing a gradual shift toward (slightly) cooler weather until January or February, and the only changing leaves we'd see were on the few non-palm trees dotted around the city. We've come to love this abrupt turn; there being no question that it's time to leave behind the cookouts and picnics for the cozy warmth of boot socks and the indoors. We get to watch the wave of color that spreads over the trees, until all the leaves have dropped except for little sprinklings of evergreens. We explain to the kids how the trees are resting and, come spring, will wake back up again. Before that big tree nap, we round up apples and pears for pies, tarts, muffins, and cakes. We watch as the farm stands dotting the road transition from selling berries, corn, and peaches to pumpkins and squash, picking up everything we'll need for our Halloween decorations on a cash honor system. And we spend our mornings doing our chores around the farm, tending to the animals, mending what needs mending—or just digging holes in the mud—but, as quickly as we can, come back inside to surround ourselves in the singular warmth that only a fire in the fireplace and an oven heating something delicious can provide.

The recipes in this chapter are exactly what these fall afternoons call for: cozy, slow, and indulgent. Because let's be honest: we have the next six months to be cocooned in layers of sweaters and overcoats, so we may as well enjoy ourselves.

RECECIPES

SPECIAL PROJECTS

RECIPES

Chai Babka

FOR THE BREAD

¼ cup (60ml) whole milk

1½ teaspoons finely ground black tea leaves (from about 1 tea bag)

2¼ cups (300g) all-purpose flour

¼ cup (50g) granulated sugar

2¼ teaspoons (¼-ounce envelope/7g) instant yeast

2 large eggs, room temperature and lightly beaten

1 teaspoon kosher salt

6 tablespoons (85g) unsalted butter, room temperature, plus more for the bowl and pan

FOR THE FILLING

½ cup (110g) firmly packed dark brown sugar

3 tablespoons all-purpose flour

2 teaspoons ground ginger

1 teaspoon ground cardamom

1 teaspoon ground cinnamon

½ teaspoon freshly ground black pepper

¼ teaspoon kosher salt

¼ cup (57g) unsalted butter, melted

1 tablespoon water

FOR THE HONEY SYRUP

¼ cup (60ml) water

¼ cup (85g) honey

1 cinnamon stick

A freshly baked sweet bread in the morning is a comforting season staple. My biggest pet peeve is a dry cinnamon roll or babka, so I've made it my mission to create a version that is a rich yeasted pillow sent from heaven. To do that, I've packed this recipe full of butter and cream, steeping black tea in the milk for the dough, and combined brown sugar and chai spices to create the perfect autumnal flavor. This goes particularly well with a warm cup of coffee or tea and a nest of soft blankets.

MAKES 1 (9 X 5-INCH) LOAF

MAKE THE BREAD: In a microwave-safe measuring cup, microwave the milk to 110°F to 120°F, about 30 seconds. Stir in the black tea and let the mixture steep for 5 minutes.

In the bowl of a stand mixer, whisk together the flour, sugar, and yeast. Add the milk and tea mixture, followed by the eggs and salt. Attach the dough hook and set the mixer to low speed. Beat the mixture until a dough starts to form but still looks crumbly, about 2 minutes. With the mixer running, add the butter 1 tablespoon at a time, letting each tablespoon fully incorporate before adding the next. Once all the butter is added, continue beating on low until the dough is sticky and elastic, 8 to 10 minutes.

Grease a large bowl with butter and add the dough, turning it a few times to coat. Cover and let rise in a warm spot until doubled in size, 1 to 2 hours.

Lightly butter a 9x5-inch loaf pan and line it with parchment paper, letting the excess fall over the sides of the pan.

MAKE THE FILLING: When the dough is done rising, in a medium bowl, whisk together the brown sugar, flour, ginger, cardamom, cinnamon, black pepper, and salt. Add the melted butter and 1 tablespoon of water and stir until well combined and pasty.

Turn out the dough on a clean work surface and gently roll it out to a 12x20-inch rectangle. Spread the filling on the dough all the way to the edge on three sides, leaving a 1-inch border on one short side. (The dough may pull a little bit while you spread the filling, but it shouldn't

continued

tear.) Starting at the short side opposite the border, roll the dough into a tight coil and pinch the seam to seal. Using a large sharp knife, cut the dough in half lengthwise. Position each half parallel to each other with the cut sides facing up. Twist the halves together, keeping the cut sides facing up, and tuck the ends under. Gently place in the prepared loaf pan.

Cover and let the dough rise until the loaf has risen almost to the top of the pan, about 1 hour.

MAKE THE HONEY SYRUP: In a small saucepan over medium heat, combine ¼ cup of water with the honey and cinnamon stick. Bring to a simmer and cook, stirring frequently, for 5 minutes or until thickened. Remove from the heat and let cool. Discard the cinnamon stick.

Preheat the oven to 350°F.

Uncover the loaf pan, set it on a rimmed baking sheet, and bake for 50 to 55 minutes, until deep golden brown. After about 40 minutes, if you find the bread is browning too quickly, you can cover it with foil for the remaining time. Immediately pour or brush the Honey Syrup over the bread. Let the bread cool in the pan for at least an hour before removing and slicing.

TIPS & TRICKS

Yeast is greatly affected by the temperature of the room when it's rising. If you're making this bread in warmer months, it may rise in half the time on your counter. If making this recipe in cooler months, preheat the oven to 200ºF for 5 minutes. Then, turn the oven off and place the dough or shaped loaf inside the oven to rise. If your oven has a light inside, you can also leave that on to help maintain a little bit of warmth.

Don't flour your work surface when rolling out the dough. It's oily enough to not stick to the counter or rolling pin, and flour will cause it to slip. However, if the dough starts to wrinkle when rolling, gently lift the dough and stretch it slightly to release it from the counter.

Leek *and* Potato Breakfast Quiche

FOR THE SAVORY PIE DOUGH

1½ cups (180g) all-purpose flour, plus more for rolling

1 teaspoon dried thyme

½ teaspoon kosher salt

¼ teaspoon garlic powder

⅛ teaspoon cayenne pepper

½ cup (1 stick/113g) cold unsalted butter, cubed

5 to 7 tablespoons (60 to 90ml) ice water

FOR THE FILLING

4 slices thick-cut bacon, chopped

1 tablespoon extra-virgin olive oil

1½ cups (375g) sliced leeks (see Tips & Tricks)

1 cup (150g) Yukon gold potatoes, peeled and thinly sliced ⅛-inch thick

¾ teaspoon kosher salt

2 garlic cloves, minced

4 large eggs

1½ cups (150g) shredded Gruyère cheese

1¼ cups (300ml) heavy whipping cream

¼ teaspoon freshly ground black pepper

I frequently reach for leeks in the fall because their flavor is more subtle than onions but still brings an earthy, aromatic quality to a dish. In this quiche, the leek's flavor is front and center as a play on the potato-leek soup my mom would make for us growing up. It's every bit as buttery and comforting as the original and perfect for breakfast, lunch, dinner, or all three.

SERVES 6 TO 8

MAKE THE SAVORY PIE DOUGH: In a large bowl, whisk together the flour, thyme, salt, garlic powder, and cayenne pepper. Add the butter and toss it gently in the flour to coat completely. Cut in the butter using a pastry blender, or briefly squeeze the pieces of butter between your thumb and forefinger until the biggest pieces are the size of almonds and the smallest are about the size of peas. Using a fork, mix in half the water. Continue adding the water a tablespoon at a time until the mixture forms a shaggy dough. Gently knead the dough together in the bowl until it clumps together. Shape it into a disk and wrap tightly in plastic wrap. Chill for 1 hour or up to 3 days.

Preheat the oven to 425°F.

On a lightly floured surface, roll the chilled pie dough into a 13-inch circle. Transfer the dough to a 9-inch pie pan and trim the excess dough to an inch from the edge of the pan. Tuck under any excess dough and crimp around the edge as desired. Poke the bottom of the crust all over with a fork. Freeze for 15 minutes. Set a piece of parchment paper inside the pie crust and fill with pie weights or dried beans. Place the pie pan on a rimmed baking sheet and bake for 15 to 18 minutes, until the edges are just golden brown. Carefully remove the parchment and weights and return the crust to the oven, baking for 3 to 5 more minutes or until the bottom of the crust looks set. Set aside to cool. Reduce the oven temperature to 350°F.

MAKE THE FILLING: In a large frying pan, add the bacon and olive oil. Set the pan over medium heat and cook, stirring occasionally, until the bacon is lightly browned, about 5 minutes. Add the leeks, potatoes, and ½ teaspoon of the salt, stirring to coat everything in the bacon fat. Cook,

continued

Leeks are grown in sandy soil, so it's really important to wash them thoroughly before cooking. I like to split them lengthwise, then I separate the layers as I rinse them under cold running water. Dry them thoroughly, of course. While the whole leek is edible, I like to stick to the white parts and about 2 inches of the green parts for this recipe.

Don't skip a step when it comes to parbaking the piecrust—it's essential to make sure the bottom of your quiche is crispy instead of soggy. Crimp the edges any way you like; use your fingers for a rustic, handmade look, or press with the tines of a fork for a more classic look.

stirring occasionally, until the leeks have softened and the potatoes are lightly browned, 5 to 7 minutes. (The potatoes will not be tender at this point; that's okay.) Add the garlic and cook for 2 minutes more. Remove the pan from the heat.

In a medium bowl, whisk together the eggs, 1 cup of the Gruyère, cream, pepper, and the remaining $1/4$ teaspoon of salt until well combined. Add three-quarters of the potato-leek mixture to the parbaked crust and pour the egg mixture on top. Scatter the remaining potato-leek mixture on top of the eggs, followed by the remaining $1/2$ cup of Gruyère.

Bake until the top is golden brown and the center is set, 40 to 45 minutes. If the crust is getting too dark before the filling is cooked, cover the edges of the pie pan with foil to prevent burning. Let the quiche cool for 10 minutes before serving.

Mexican Egg Bake

3 tablespoons extra-virgin olive oil

½ pound (225g) fresh Mexican chorizo

3 cups (375g) sweet potato, peeled and cut into ½-inch cubes

½ teaspoon kosher salt

½ teaspoon ground cumin

¼ teaspoon freshly ground black pepper

1 cup (150g) diced red onion

¼ cup (60ml) water

1 cup (150g) thinly sliced sweet red bell pepper

5 or 6 large eggs

¼ cup fresh cilantro leaves, for serving

Crushed red pepper (optional), for serving

1 jalapeño, stemmed, deseeded, and sliced, for serving

½ cup (60g) crumbled queso fresco, for serving

½ cup (120ml) salsa, for serving

8 to 12 corn tortillas, for serving

TIPS & TRICKS

Chorizo Smarts: When shopping for chorizo, be sure to look for fresh Mexican chorizo, which is uncooked (like breakfast sausage) instead of Spanish chorizo, which is dried and cured. If you can't find chorizo, simply use regular or spicy Italian sausage and stir in a teaspoon of smoked paprika during cooking. Also, not all Mexican chorizo is created equal; it can vary in spiciness and fat content. If your skillet is looking a little dry, add a little extra olive oil. If the cooked chorizo doesn't taste spicy enough, hit it with a dash of chile powder or red pepper.

Runny vs. Firm: Some folks adore a runny egg yolk; others get squeamish at the sight of it. I've given a range here so you can please all diners, but I recommend checking your oven after 10 minutes; you can always add a little more time for firmer yolks.

For breakfast, my mom would cook chorizo and potatoes in a skillet with a chili-flecked tomato sauce, then serve them with scrambled eggs. I wanted to combine this idea with another favorite breakfast dish of mine, shakshuka, where eggs are baked in the sauce along with garlic and cheeses. The result: this gloriously hearty morning dish. SERVES 4 TO 6

Preheat the oven to 350°F.

In a large (12-inch) oven-safe skillet over medium heat, heat the olive oil. Crumble in the chorizo and cook, stirring occasionally, until the chorizo is crumbly and begins to render, 5 to 7 minutes. Push the chorizo to the edges of the skillet to create a well in the center. Add the sweet potatoes, ¼ teaspoon of the salt, the cumin, and pepper and stir to coat the sweet potatoes in the rendered chorizo fat. Cook until the sweet potatoes are slightly tender, 5 to 7 minutes, stirring occasionally and gradually incorporating chorizo from the edges.

Add the onion, the remaining ¼ teaspoon salt, and ¼ cup of water, and stir to release any browned bits from the bottom of the pan. Cook, stirring often, until the onion is slightly softened, about 3 minutes. Stir in the red bell pepper and cook for 2 minutes more. Remove the skillet from the heat.

Use the back of a spoon to make five or six wells in the sweet potato mixture, spacing evenly. Gently crack one egg into each well and season with salt to taste.

Bake until the eggs are cooked to your desired degree of doneness, 13 to 15 minutes for set whites and runny yolks. Let cool for 5 minutes before serving. Garnish with cilantro, red pepper (if desired), and jalapeño, and serve with queso fresco, salsa, and tortillas.

Apple Butter

8 pounds (3,620g) mixed varieties of apples, such as Honeycrisp, Opal, and Granny Smith, washed, cored, and chopped into 1-inch chunks

2 navel oranges, peel and pith removed, cut into 1-inch chunks

1½ cups (330g) firmly packed light brown sugar

1½ cups (300g) granulated sugar

1 tablespoon ground cinnamon

2 teaspoons ground ginger

½ teaspoon ground allspice

½ teaspoon ground cardamom

⅛ teaspoon kosher salt

2 cups (480ml) apple cider or water

⅓ cup (80ml) fresh lemon juice

¼ cup (60ml) bourbon (optional)

TIPS & TRICKS

If you don't have a food mill and are pureeing the roasted apples with a blender or food processor, you can press the pureed apple mixture through a fine mesh sieve before returning it to the pans. This will catch any small pieces of apple skin left in the mixture and produce a velvety smooth butter.

Have fun with the flavors in the apple butter. You can add your favorite baking spices or vanilla bean for added flavor, or swap the bourbon for a fruit liqueur, like Kirsch or applejack, or a sweet wine, like Madeira.

As much as I love being in the kitchen, there are some special recipes that are just as rewarding to make as it is to enjoy them. I know that when I pull out my big roasting pan in the fall, I'm going to be making batch after batch of this apple butter through the winter, just tossing in heaps of apples with warming spices and citrus. The whole house smells like freshly baked apple pie, and then for months we enjoy this butter swirled into yogurt, slathered between cake layers, or simply spread on toast.

MAKES ABOUT 2 QUARTS/9 (8-OUNCE) JARS

Preheat the oven to 400°F.

In a large roasting pan, add the apples, oranges, brown sugar, granulated sugar, cinnamon, ginger, allspice, cardamom, and salt. Toss thoroughly to combine. Cover the pan with foil, sealing the edges tightly, and lift up one corner to create a steam vent.

Roast for 1 hour or until the apples are very soft and mash easily with a fork. Remove from the oven. Carefully remove the foil and let the apple mixture cool for 20 minutes, stirring occasionally.

Reduce the oven temperature to 300°F.

Carefully process the apples through a food mill or, working in batches, blend the apples in a food processor or blender on medium speed until very smooth. Transfer the pureed apples back to the roasting pan and stir in the cider or water, lemon juice, and bourbon, if using.

Bake, stirring every 30 minutes, until the mixture is very thick and velvety and the color deepens to a dark golden brown, 3 to 4 hours.

From here, the hot apple butter can be transferred to jars and kept refrigerated for up to 2 months, or it can be placed in sterilized 8-ounce canning jars and processed in a water bath for 12 minutes (see Pickling, page 308, for sterilizing and canning instructions).

Spiced Pumpkin Soup *with* Garlic-Chili Oil

Pumpkin has the advantage of being able to play sweet or savory. So while we all love pumpkin muffins and pancakes, don't forget that with the addition of warm spices like ginger and garam masala, pumpkin also majorly delivers when pureed into a rich, flavorful soup—especially when drizzled with a garlic- and chili-infused oil. SERVES 6 TO 8

FOR THE GARLIC-CHILI OIL

1 to 2 tablespoons gochugaru or red chili flakes

2 teaspoons brown sugar

½ cup (120ml) peanut or vegetable oil

¼ cup minced sweet onion

6 garlic cloves, minced

½ teaspoon kosher salt

FOR THE PUMPKIN SOUP

4½ to 5 pounds (2 to 2½kg) sweet baking pumpkins or winter squash, such as butternut, candy roaster, or kuri

3 tablespoons unsalted butter or vegetable oil

1 sweet onion, chopped

1 (2-inch) piece ginger, grated

6 garlic cloves, grated

1 teaspoon ground ginger

1 teaspoon garam masala

¾ teaspoon freshly ground black pepper

½ teaspoon ground cinnamon

2 tablespoons sherry vinegar

4 cups (960ml) unsalted or low-sodium vegetable broth

3 tablespoons light brown sugar

½ cup (120ml) heavy whipping cream, plus more for serving

Kosher salt

MAKE THE GARLIC-CHILI OIL: In a medium heatproof metal or ceramic bowl, stir together the chili flakes and brown sugar.

Heat the oil in a small saucepan over medium-high heat until very hot, about 5 minutes. Carefully add the minced onion and fry, stirring frequently, until the onion pieces start to brown on the edges, about 5 minutes. Add the minced garlic and cook, stirring constantly, until the onions and garlic are lightly golden brown, 1 to 2 minutes more. Quickly and carefully pour the hot oil mixture into the bowl of chili flakes. The mixture will bubble in the bowl. When the bubbling subsides, stir in the salt and set aside to cool completely.

MAKE THE PUMPKIN SOUP: Preheat the oven to 375°F. Line a baking sheet with heavy duty foil.

Place the whole pumpkins or squash on the foil and pierce them all over with the tip of a sharp knife. Roast for about 1 hour or until the skin looks puffed or wrinkled and the squash is very easily pierced with a fork. Let cool for 1 hour.

Use a fork to perforate the skin all around the stem of the pumpkin to remove it, or pry open the squash in half lengthwise to reveal the seeds. Scoop out the seeds and any fibrous portions with a spoon and discard. Scoop the cooked pumpkin into a large bowl and discard the skins.

In a large Dutch oven or stockpot over medium heat, heat the butter or olive oil. Add the onion and cook, stirring frequently, until the onion browns, about 12 minutes. Stir in the ginger and garlic and cook for 1 to 2 minutes, until very fragrant. Add the ground ginger, garam masala, black pepper, and cinnamon and cook, stirring constantly, for another minute. Stir in the vinegar and scrape the bottom of the pot with a wooden spoon to deglaze it.

TIPS & TRICKS

Garlic-Chili Oil is an excellent condiment to have in your pantry. Drizzle it on eggs, leftover rice, or anywhere a little extra heat is desired. It's especially good slathered over fried chicken!

Add the roasted pumpkin, vegetable stock, and brown sugar to the Dutch oven. Bring to a boil and cook for 15 minutes, stirring occasionally and breaking up any large chunks of pumpkin with the back of the spoon.

Use an immersion blender to puree the soup until smooth. Alternatively, you can carefully ladle the hot soup into a blender with the center of the top removed, then return the pureed soup to the pot. Stir in the cream and salt to taste. Serve with a drizzle of cream and garlic-chili oil.

Persimmon-Fennel Salad

Juice of 2 Meyer lemons

1 medium shallot, finely chopped

2 strips duck or thick-cut applewood smoked bacon, roughly chopped

1 tablespoon honey

¼ teaspoon kosher salt

¼ cup (60ml) extra-virgin olive oil

2 large fennel bulbs, trimmed, halved, cored, and thinly sliced, fronds reserved for garnish

3 firm but ripe Fuyu persimmons, peeled, halved through the stem end, and thinly sliced

2 ounces (60g) aged Manchego cheese

Freshly ground black pepper, for serving

TIPS & TRICKS

Regular lemons can be used in place of Meyer lemons if they are unavailable.

See the tip for the Persimmon-Pecan Galettes (page 83) for picking out the perfect persimmon. Make sure you use the Fuyu variety and not Hachiya or honey persimmons.

What tends to keep people from loving persimmons as much as I do is realizing there are two types, and they're each suited for different types of preparations. Most people know about Hachiya persimmons because they're what are used for things like pudding and baking. These are the oblong guys that need to ripen until they're almost liquefied before they'll work for you because that's when their tannins—astringent, bitter compounds—start to dissipate. If you've ever taken a bite of an unripe Hachiya, you know that it's like eating chalk. Fuyus, on the other hand, are the shorter, more squat-looking versions of the fruit, and they're meant to be crunchy like an apple but still have that signature persimmon custardy flavor. *That's* what we're going for here. Their flavor pairs really well with fresh, subtle fennel and some bacon for a salty, savory crunch. I prefer duck bacon, which has a more restrained flavor than pork, but if you can't find it at your market or online, feel free to use any bacon of your choice—or leave it out for a salad that is still wonderfully delicious.

SERVES 6

In a large bowl, combine the Meyer lemon juice and shallots and set aside. (This will soften the shallots' bite.)

In a large skillet over medium-high heat, add the bacon and cook until the fat has rendered and the bacon pieces are crispy, 8 to 10 minutes. Transfer the bacon to a paper towel–lined plate and set aside to cool.

In the bowl with the lemon juice and shallots, whisk in the honey and salt. Slowly add the olive oil and continue whisking until the dressing is emulsified and smooth.

Add the sliced fennel and persimmons to the dressing and toss very gently to coat. Transfer the salad to a large serving plate and use a vegetable peeler to shave large strips of the Manchego over the salad. Scatter the cooked bacon on top and finish with freshly ground black pepper and the reserved fennel fronds.

Delicata Squash Gratin

¼ cup plus 2 tablespoons (85g) unsalted butter, plus more for the pan

2 large sweet onions, halved and thinly sliced root-to-stem

1¼ teaspoons kosher salt

1 teaspoon light brown sugar

1½-pounds (680g) delicata squash, halved, deseeded, and cut into ¼-inch semicircles

3 tablespoons all-purpose flour

1½ cups (360ml) warm whole milk

4 ounces (115g) herbed goat cheese, crumbled

1 cup (100g) shredded Fontina cheese

½ cup (25g) grated Asiago or Parmesan cheese, plus more for finishing

½ teaspoon freshly ground black pepper, plus more for finishing

1 teaspoon chopped fresh thyme, plus more for finishing

1½ cups fresh bread crumbs

TIPS & TRICKS

If you can't find delicata squash, acorn squash or peeled, sliced butternut squash will be a good substitute. Thanks to delicata's thin skin, which becomes tender with heat, you don't need to peel it before cooking.

To speed up the assembly for this dish if you're adding it to a holiday menu, the caramelized onions can be made up to 3 days in advance and refrigerated. The squash can be cut the day before and refrigerated in an airtight container or zip-top bag.

Give this decadent gratin the perfect finishing touch by using the buttery bread crumbs from the Asparagus Spears with Poached Eggs and Butter-Fried Bread Crumbs (page 188) on top.

Winter squash often get passed over for their cold-weather-produce counterparts because, and I get it, they can be intimidating to prepare. But these seemingly impenetrable gourds are good for so much more than front-porch decoration and are actually very simple to incorporate into familiar recipes. One of my favorite ways to take advantage of their meaty sweetness is by making this deeply savory, deeply filling vegetarian main dish. It's proof that you need not be afraid of winter squash, and also that you don't need meat or tons of cheese to make comfort food. SERVES 6 TO 8

Preheat the oven to 375°F. Lightly butter a 2-quart baking dish or spray with nonstick cooking spray and set aside.

In a large skillet over medium heat, melt 2 tablespoons of the butter. Add the onions and cook, stirring occasionally, for about 5 minutes. Add ¼ teaspoon of the salt and continue cooking until the onions are very soft and just starting to turn golden, about 20 minutes. Stir in the brown sugar. Continue cooking, stirring every 2 to 3 minutes, until onions are very soft and deep amber in color, about 20 minutes more. You can add a tablespoon of water at a time as needed to unstick any onions and scrape the brown bits off the bottom of the pan. Spread the caramelized onions evenly on the bottom of the prepared baking dish. Arrange the squash slices on top.

In the same skillet, melt the remaining ¼ cup of butter over medium heat. Whisk in the flour and cook until it smells nutty, about 2 minutes. Slowly whisk in the warm milk and continue cooking, whisking constantly, until the mixture is slightly thickened and bubbling, 3 to 5 more minutes. Remove the pan from the heat and whisk in the goat cheese until the sauce is smooth. Add the Fontina and Asiago a few tablespoons at a time, whisking until the cheese is fully incorporated before adding more. Whisk in the pepper, thyme, and remaining teaspoon of salt. Pour the sauce evenly over the squash and cover the dish with foil.

Bake for 60 minutes, until the squash is slightly softened. Remove the foil and sprinkle with the bread crumbs. Bake for an additional 15 to 20 minutes, until the top is golden brown and squash is tender. Let the gratin cool for 15 minutes and sprinkle with additional black pepper, Asiago, and thyme before serving.

Sunchoke Risotto *with* Fried Sage

6 cups low-sodium or unsalted chicken or vegetable broth

1 Parmesan rind

1 fresh sage sprig

¼ cup (60ml) olive oil

12 fresh sage leaves

1 pound (450g) fresh sunchokes, scrubbed, 2 thinly sliced, remaining diced

Fine sea salt, for sprinkling

2 tablespoons unsalted butter

1 large shallot, chopped

4 garlic cloves, minced

1 teaspoon kosher salt

¾ teaspoon freshly ground black pepper, plus more for serving

1½ cups (270g) Arborio or short-grain white rice

½ cup (120ml) dry white wine, such as Sauvignon Blanc

¾ cup (60g) freshly grated Parmesan cheese, plus more for garnish

TIPS & TRICKS

Sunchokes are typically found in the refrigerated produce section during the winter and early spring months.

Using broth versus stock will lend a lighter color to the finished risotto, but either one will give you delicious results.

I've always adored the flavor of artichokes, so when I discovered sunchokes or Jerusalem artichokes, I was enchanted. They're knobby root vegetables that look like ginger, and when trimmed, roasted, and pureed, they're like the silky love child of a potato and an artichoke. There's nothing complicated about making risotto; it's simply about cooking rice with confidence and good timing. SERVES ABOUT 6

In a medium saucepan over medium-high heat, add the broth, Parmesan rind, and sage sprig and bring to a boil. Reduce the heat to medium-low and simmer for 15 minutes. Remove and discard the Parmesan rind and sage. Reduce the heat to low and cover the stock to keep warm.

In a Dutch oven over medium heat, heat the olive oil until shimmering. Add the sage leaves and fry until they turn dark and crispy, about 1 minute. Remove with a slotted spoon and let drain on a paper towel–lined plate.

Add the sliced sunchokes to the pot and fry until golden brown and crispy, about 5 minutes. Remove with a slotted spoon and let drain on the paper towel with the sage leaves. Sprinkle lightly with the fine sea salt, if desired.

Add the butter to the pot and let it melt into the olive oil. Add the diced sunchokes and cook, stirring occasionally, until the sunchokes are soft and translucent, about 10 minutes. Add the shallot, garlic, kosher salt, and black pepper and cook for another 5 minutes, stirring frequently, until the sunchokes start to brown on the edges.

Add the rice and cook, stirring occasionally, until the rice is toasted and smells nutty, about 2 minutes. Add the wine and scrape the bottom of the pot with a wooden spoon to release any browned bits. Simmer until the wine is mostly absorbed, 1 to 2 minutes. Reduce the heat to medium-low and ladle in about 1 cup of the warm stock. Cook, stirring constantly, until the stock is mostly evaporated. Continue adding the stock, about a cup at a time, stirring very frequently until the liquid is mostly absorbed before the next addition, and cook until the rice is tender, about 40 minutes.

Remove the pot from the heat. Stir in the Parmesan, taste, and add more salt if desired. Divide the risotto among bowls and top each serving with the fried sage and sunchoke chips, black pepper, and additional Parmesan as desired.

Charred Vegetable Lasagna

FOR THE CHARRED VEGETABLES

8 ounces (225g) cremini or baby bella mushrooms, cleaned and halved

4 large carrots, peeled, halved, and cut into 1-inch pieces

3 stalks celery, halved and cut into 1-inch pieces

1 large sweet onion, peeled and cut into 8 wedges

1 garlic head, cloves separated but not peeled

¼ cup (60ml) extra-virgin olive oil

1 teaspoon kosher salt

1 teaspoon freshly ground black pepper

1 teaspoon fennel seeds

¼ teaspoon crushed red pepper

2 tablespoons tomato paste

2 tablespoons balsamic vinegar

FOR THE EASY TOMATO SAUCE

1 (15-ounce/425g) can tomato sauce

1 (14.5-ounce/411g) can crushed fire-roasted tomatoes

1 tablespoon Italian seasoning

¾ teaspoon garlic powder

½ teaspoon kosher salt

½ teaspoon freshly ground black pepper

We all love lasagna in theory, but in practice, it can be . . . not so great. It seems like it should be this incredibly comforting, delicious dish (I mean, all that cheese!), but then it's kind of *eh*. My solution was to keep all the things you love—the noodles, the sauce, and yes, the cheese—then introduce more flavor with charred, caramelized vegetables like mushrooms and carrots. The dish is still its signature hearty self, but the veg helps lighten things up while keeping the lasagna from tasting one-note.

SERVES 8 TO 10

MAKE THE CHARRED VEGETABLES: Position an oven rack in the upper third of the oven. Preheat the oven to low broil (450°F).

On a baking sheet, toss the mushrooms, carrots, celery, onion, and garlic cloves with 3 tablespoons of the oil, plus the salt, pepper, fennel seeds, and red pepper. Broil for 12 minutes.

In a small bowl, whisk together the tomato paste, vinegar, and the remaining tablespoon of oil. Drizzle the mixture over the broiled vegetables and toss to coat. Return the vegetables to the oven and broil until tender and slightly charred, about 10 minutes more. Let cool slightly.

Squeeze the roasted garlic cloves out of the skins and discard the skins. Transfer the vegetable mixture and garlic to a food processor and pulse 15 to 20 times, until coarsely chopped, stopping to scrape down the sides as needed. Set the mixture aside.

MAKE THE EASY TOMATO SAUCE: In a large bowl, add the tomato sauce, crushed tomatoes, Italian seasoning, garlic powder, salt, and pepper and stir to combine. Cover and set aside until ready to use.

ASSEMBLE THE LASAGNA: In a medium bowl, whisk together the ricotta, egg, ¼ cup of the Parmesan, basil, salt, and pepper until combined. Cover and chill until ready to use.

Bring a large pot of water to a boil over high heat and season well with salt. Add the lasagna noodles and cook until tender and pliable but not fully cooked, about 7 minutes. Drain and set aside.

Preheat the oven to 375°F.

In a deep 13x9-inch baking dish, spread 1 cup of the tomato sauce evenly over the bottom of the dish. Top with a layer of noodles (about five),

FOR THE LASAGNA

2 cups (500g) ricotta cheese

1 large egg

1¼ cups (113g) grated Parmesan cheese

¼ cup finely chopped fresh basil

½ teaspoon kosher salt, plus more for the pasta

½ teaspoon freshly ground black pepper

1 (16-ounce/454g) box dried lasagna noodles

16 ounces (450g) fresh mozzarella, sliced

3 cups (340g) shredded mozzarella cheese

Fresh basil leaves, for garnish

TIPS & TRICKS

Feel free to use whatever vegetables you like, such as fresh fennel, shallots, parsnips, or bell peppers of any color. Just be sure to cut them in similar-sized pieces so they cook evenly.

Be sure to leave the garlic peels on during broiling to keep the cloves from burning. To make squeezing out the roasted garlic cloves easier, cut off the hard "root" end from each clove before roasting.

Since lasagna noodles can vary slightly in size and can break during cooking, I like to have a few extra cooked noodles on hand to make sure there are plenty for this recipe. Do not use no-boil noodles.

I definitely recommend making the Easy Tomato Sauce, but if you have a favorite jarred sauce or just want to save a few minutes in prep, I recommend Rao's and Newman's Own.

If you want to freeze the unbaked lasagna, cover tightly with plastic wrap, then with foil. Freeze up to 3 months. Thaw in refrigerator overnight. Remove plastic wrap and bake covered, at 350ºF, for 20 minutes. Uncover and bake at 375ºF until heated through and top is browned and bubbly, 30 to 45 minutes more.

tearing any noodles to cover gaps, if needed. Spread 1 cup of the ricotta mixture over noodles and scatter half the vegetable mixture on top. Dollop with about 1 cup of the tomato sauce and scatter about a third of the fresh mozzarella slices on top. Sprinkle with 1 cup of the shredded mozzarella and 2 tablespoons of the Parmesan. Repeat the layers, starting with the lasagna noodles. Top with another layer of noodles (you may have extra) and the remaining tomato sauce, ricotta mixture, fresh mozzarella, shredded mozzarella, and Parmesan. Set the baking dish on a rimmed baking sheet to catch any drips.

Bake for about 1 hour, until the top is golden brown and bubbly. Let cool for 10 minutes and garnish with the basil.

Rustic Chicken Potpie *with* Roasted Root Vegetables

I'm pretty sure when the idea of comfort food was invented, chicken potpie was the first dish to be considered for the category. For this version, I'm particularly fond of how the traditionally rich, creamy filling is studded with deeply sweet roasted root vegetables, capped off with homey (as in simple) crust that gets baked right over the top. SERVES ABOUT 8

FOR THE ROASTED CHICKEN / VEGETABLES

3 tablespoons extra-virgin olive oil

2 pounds (900g) chicken quarters

Kosher salt and freshly ground black pepper

2 fresh sage sprigs

1 turnip root, peeled and cut into ½-inch pieces

1 pound (450g) Yukon gold potatoes, peeled and cut into ½-inch pieces

3 large carrots, peeled and cut into ½-inch pieces

FOR THE POTPIE

2 tablespoons unsalted butter

1 tablespoon extra-virgin olive oil

½ large sweet onion, chopped

5 garlic cloves, minced

1 tablespoon finely chopped fresh sage

3 tablespoons all-purpose flour, plus more for dusting

2 cups (480ml) warm whole milk

½ cup (120ml) warm chicken stock or broth

½ cup (120ml) dry white wine, such as Sauvignon Blanc

Grated zest of ½ lemon

½ teaspoon kosher salt

½ teaspoon freshly ground black pepper

1 recipe Savory Pie Dough (page 27)

1 large egg, beaten

MAKE THE ROASTED CHICKEN AND VEGETABLES: Preheat the oven to 400°F. Brush a large rimmed baking sheet with 1 tablespoon of the olive oil.

Place the chicken quarters on one side of the sheet pan and brush them all over with 1 tablespoon of the olive oil. Season generously with salt and pepper and tuck a sprig of sage under the skin of each quarter. Roast for 15 minutes.

In a large bowl, toss the turnips, potatoes, and carrots with the remaining tablespoon of olive oil and salt and pepper to taste. Add the vegetables in an even layer on the other half of the baking sheet and return the pan to the oven. Continue roasting for about 20 minutes, stirring the vegetables halfway through, until the chicken registers 165°F on an instant-read thermometer when inserted into the thickest portion.

Let cool until the chicken is cool enough to handle, about 20 minutes. Remove the skin, discard the sage, and shred the meat, saving the bones for stock if you like.

MAKE THE POTPIE: Preheat the oven to 400°F.

In a large skillet over medium-high heat, heat the butter and olive oil. Add the onions and cook, stirring occasionally, until they turn translucent, about 8 minutes. Stir in the garlic and sage and cook for 1 minute. Sprinkle the flour over the vegetables and stir for 1 minute more. Reduce the heat to medium-low.

While stirring constantly, slowly add the warm milk until combined. Stir in the stock, wine, lemon zest, salt, and pepper. Bring to a simmer, stirring occasionally, and cook until the sauce has thickened and coats the back of a spoon, about 10 minutes. Stir in the roasted vegetables and shredded chicken. Taste and season with more salt and pepper if needed. Transfer the mixture to a 2-quart baking dish and place the dish on a rimmed baking sheet.

TIPS & TRICKS

For the Savory Pie Dough, you can substitute the dried thyme with dried sage or 1 tablespoon minced fresh sage.

On a lightly floured surface, roll the pie dough to ⅛-inch thick. Use a round cookie cutter to cut circles out of the dough and place them over the filling. Brush lightly with the beaten egg. Bake for 35 minutes, or until the crust is a deep golden brown and the filling is bubbling. Let cool for 15 minutes before serving.

Dutch Oven Chicken Pot Roast *with* Fingerling Potatoes, Shallots, *and* Olives

1 (5- to 6-pound/2.2 to 2.7kg) whole chicken

1 tablespoon plus 2 teaspoons kosher salt

1 tablespoon freshly ground black pepper

2 teaspoons dried oregano

½ teaspoon crushed red pepper

2 lemons

1½ pounds (675g) fingerling potatoes

6 shallots, halved lengthwise

2 heads of garlic, halved widthwise

½ cup (120ml) dry white wine, such as Sauvignon Blanc

¼ cup (60ml) olive brine (from jarred olives)

2 tablespoons extra-virgin olive oil

1½ cups (270g) jarred pitted olives, such as Kalamata and/or Castelvetrano

Chopped fresh oregano or parsley, for garnish (optional)

Few things are more comforting than the smell of a chicken roasting in the oven, promising a delicious dinner to come, especially on a crisp fall day. This Greek-inspired version of the dish reminds me of cooking with my mom, both because of the flavors she embraced on behalf of my Greek dad, and because I like to cook it in a large cast iron pot, just like the ones my mom saved up for and that have lasted for decades in her kitchen. While I know you've seen (many) recipes for roast chicken before, this version adds two noteworthy updates into the mix, which make it a robustly flavored one-pot meal. First, it calls for roasting the chicken on a bed of petite fingerling potatoes, which get tender and buttery as they soak up the juices from the roasting bird. Then, in true Greek fashion, I turn to leftover olive brine—yes, the juice from the olive jar—to infuse the vegetables with its rich, salty flavor. SERVES 4 TO 6

Preheat the oven to 375°F.

Remove and discard any giblets from the chicken; check to be sure that the cavity is empty. Set the chicken aside.

In a small bowl, stir together the salt, pepper, oregano, and red pepper. Zest the lemons and add the zest to the salt mixture. Rub the mixture with your fingers to combine.

Halve the lemons and set aside. In a large Dutch oven, combine 2 of the lemon halves with the potatoes, shallots, and 1 head of the garlic. Pour in the wine and olive brine.

Sprinkle 2 teaspoons of the salt mixture into the chicken cavity. Add the remaining 2 lemon halves and head of garlic to the cavity as well. Drizzle the chicken with the olive oil and sprinkle the outside with the remaining salt mixture. Truss the chicken with butcher's twine (see Tips & Tricks).

Place the chicken on top of the potatoes in the pot and arrange the shallots around the chicken. Cover the pot and roast for 1 hour. Uncover, scatter the olives around the chicken, and roast uncovered until the chicken is browned and crispy and the internal temperature has reached 165°F, 30 to 40 minutes more.

continued

Pick up the best possible bird you can find for this recipe. I try to find organic, antibiotic-free, free-range chickens whenever possible. Any chicken will work with this recipe, but the better the bird, the more tender and delicious your dinner will be. If the weight is under 5 pounds, uncover the pot after 45 minutes of roasting.

If you can't find fingerling potatoes, don't worry—any small potatoes will work fine. For best results, use potatoes that are no bigger than 1½ to 2 inches thick. If all you have are larger potatoes, cut them into chunky pieces to help them cook evenly.

Trussing a chicken with twine keeps the items you stuffed into the cavity in place and helps the chicken legs roast evenly. Here's my preferred method for doing it; use cotton butcher's twine for best results:

Cut an approximately 3-foot length of twine. Find the center of the twine and evenly drape the ends over the chicken. Loop the twine under the wings so that when you pull up, the chicken "stands up." Cross the ends of the twine over the breast side of the chicken and then again around the back so the wings are held tight to the body. Next, wrap the twine over each leg from the outside in so that both strands are now between the legs. Loop each strand back to the outside of the legs, pushing the legs close to the body, and tightening the twine to remove any slack. Bring the ends of the twine together over the tail, pull them tight, and tie them into a knot. Cut any excess twine.

Remove the chicken from the pot and let it rest for 10 to 15 minutes before serving. Discard the lemons, transfer the potatoes, olives, and shallots to a bowl, leaving the drippings in the pot, and cover to keep warm. Squeeze the garlic cloves into the drippings, mash with a fork, and stir to combine. Place the pot over medium-low heat to keep the drippings warm.

Carve the chicken (or pull it apart with your hands!) and serve with potatoes, shallots, and warm pan juices. Garnish with herbs, if desired.

Herb-Stuffed Pork Roast

3 cups (about 1 big bunch/180g) packed fresh parsley, large stems removed

½ cup (70g) pine nuts

2 garlic cloves, peeled and left whole

2¾ teaspoons kosher salt

⅓ cup plus 3 tablespoons (110ml) extra-virgin olive oil

Zest of 1 orange

2 teaspoons ground fennel seed

1¼ teaspoons freshly ground black pepper

½ teaspoon dried oregano

¼ teaspoon crushed red pepper

1 (3-pound/1.3kg) boneless pork loin roast

1½ pounds (675g) fingerling potatoes

5 fresh rosemary sprigs, plus more for garnish

Before you say, "OMG, I could never make something this beautiful," let me reassure you that *yes you can*. These gorgeous spirals of herb-stuffed pork are a cinch to pull off when you follow a few easy steps. It all starts with flattening the pork loin, which, I might add, is a great way to pound out your frustrations! If that seems like too much for you, ask your butcher to flatten the roast for you. Then all you have to do is season it, slather on the pesto, then rock and roll your way to an easy and elegant supper.

SERVES 6 TO 8

In the bowl of a food processor, add the parsley, pine nuts, garlic, and ¼ teaspoon of the salt. Pulse until chopped, about 10 times. With the processor running, add ⅓ cup of the oil in a steady stream, pulsing until combined. (The texture will be slightly chunky.) Taste and add additional salt if needed. Set aside.

In a small bowl, stir together 2 teaspoons of the salt, the orange zest, fennel seed, 1 teaspoon of the black pepper, oregano, and red pepper. Set aside.

Place the pork on a cutting board. If it has a fat cap (a thicker layer of fat on one long side), use a sharp knife to score a diamond-shaped pattern in the fat. Flip the pork over so the fat cap is on the cutting board. With a very sharp knife, cut down the center of the pork, lengthwise, stopping about ½ inch from the bottom so as to not cut all the way through the loin. You should be able to open the pork like a book. Make the same lengthwise center cut on the left half of the pork. Repeat on the right half.

Open the pork so it lays mostly flat and cover it with plastic wrap. Use a meat mallet or rolling pin to pound the pork into an even ½-inch thickness. Remove the plastic wrap and sprinkle 2 teaspoons of the spice mixture over the flattened pork. Set the remaining spice mixture aside.

Spread the pesto mixture over the pork. Starting with one long end, tightly roll up the pork as you would a jelly roll. Using butcher's twine, tightly tie the pork in 2-inch intervals. Sprinkle all sides with the remaining spice mixture.

Preheat the oven to 350°F.

continued

First things first: be sure to get the right cut of pork for this recipe. You're looking for pork loin—not tenderloin. Pork loin is wider, shorter, and typically a little less lean than tenderloin. While delicious and totally stuffable, pork tenderloin is not the best choice for this recipe.

The flattened pork doesn't have to be perfectly even. You want to aim for a fairly uniform ½-inch thickness, but don't stress about it. The more important goal is to have a basic flattish rectangle of pork that you can roll up tightly and evenly.

Cotton butcher's twine is available at most markets and is important for this recipe. First, you have to tie the pork so it doesn't unroll in the oven. Second, it's important to use twine made from natural materials (like cotton) instead of synthetics, which will melt in the oven's heat.

Feel free to make this pesto your own: swap grated lemon zest for orange zest, pecans or walnuts for pine nuts, and throw in a cup of your favorite soft herbs for 1 cup of the parsley (think mint, chives, or even tarragon). Or, if you want to skip a step, you can jazz up store-bought pesto with grated orange zest and forgo making homemade pesto.

On a rimmed baking sheet or roasting pan, toss the potatoes with 1 tablespoon of the oil, the remaining ½ teaspoon salt, and the remaining ¼ teaspoon black pepper. Push the potatoes to the edges to make a space for the pork in the center and nestle the rosemary sprigs among the potatoes.

In a 12-inch cast iron skillet over medium-high heat, heat the remaining 2 tablespoons of oil. Add the tied pork, fat cap side down, and cook until well browned, 3 to 4 minutes. Turn and brown the remaining sides, about 2 minutes each. Transfer the pork to the roasting pan.

Roast until the potatoes are tender and the pork is cooked through, 40 to 50 minutes. Let the pork rest for 10 minutes, remove the twine, and slice as desired. Transfer the pork to a serving platter and surround it with the potatoes. Garnish with additional rosemary sprigs.

Chive *and* Parmesan Buttermilk Biscuits

¾ cup (180g) cold unsalted European-style butter, cubed

4 cups (530g) all-purpose flour

1 cup (80g) grated Parmesan cheese

1 tablespoon baking powder

1 tablespoon granulated sugar

1½ teaspoons kosher salt

1 teaspoon freshly ground black or white pepper

¼ teaspoon baking soda

¼ cup (9g) minced fresh chives or scallions

1½ cups (360ml) cold whole cultured buttermilk

2 tablespoons unsalted European-style butter, melted

Flaky sea salt (optional)

TIPS & TRICKS

When you start shaping and folding the biscuit dough, the mixture will still be very crumbly and may not fully hold together. Don't be tempted to add more liquid—the dough will come together as you continue folding, stacking, and patting it out.

The repeated process of folding, stacking, and patting out the biscuit dough not only brings the dough together but creates those signature, irresistible layers in the baked biscuits.

If you don't have buttermilk, stir together 1⅓ cups whole milk and 4 teaspoons lemon juice or white vinegar. Let stand for 5 minutes before using.

Even though fall is when we start thinking less about cooking with "fresh" flavors and more about using hearty, soul-warming ingredients, I love reaching for chives to lend a pop of nice green flavor (and color) to these biscuits.

You could, of course, omit the chives, which would leave you with an otherwise perfectly classic, flaky buttermilk biscuit that gets a salty tang from the Parmesan. Either way, these are everything you could want on a cool fall day, whether you're enjoying them on their own or using them to sop up a hearty stew.

MAKES 8 BISCUITS

Place the cubed butter in the freezer for 10 minutes to chill. Line a rimmed baking sheet with parchment paper and set aside.

In a large bowl, whisk together the flour, cheese, baking powder, sugar, salt, pepper, and baking soda. Add the cold butter and toss to coat the pieces with flour. Using a pastry blender or briefly squeezing the pieces of butter between your thumb and forefinger, cut the butter into the flour mixture until the butter pieces are between the size of peas and almonds. Stir in the chives.

Add the buttermilk and fold the mixture together with a silicone spatula until the dough is mostly combined but still crumbly. Turn out the dough on a clean work surface and pat it into a 1-inch-thick square.

Using a bench scraper or large knife, fold the dough in half like a book. (It may still be very crumbly, and that's okay.) Cut the dough in half and stack the two halves on top of each other. Pat the dough back into a 1-inch-thick square. Repeat this process three more times, folding, stacking, and patting back down. Use a 3½-inch round cookie cutter dipped in flour to cut out the biscuits. Reroll and cut any scraps as needed. Place the biscuits on the prepared baking sheet 1 inch apart and freeze for 10 minutes or refrigerate for 30 minutes.

Preheat the oven to 425°F.

Brush the chilled biscuits with the melted butter and sprinkle with the flaky salt, if desired. Bake for 18 to 20 minutes, until the tops are golden brown and the sides are very flaky. Serve warm with butter.

Apple Butter *and* Marzipan Bread

FOR THE CLOVE DOUGH

¾ cup (180ml) whole milk

3 tablespoons granulated sugar

2¼ teaspoons (¼-ounce envelope/7g) active dry yeast

2¾ cups (330g) all-purpose flour, plus more as needed

1 teaspoon kosher salt

½ teaspoon ground cloves

5 tablespoons (70g) unsalted butter, melted

1 large egg, room temperature and lightly beaten

1 teaspoon vegetable oil

FOR THE CRANBERRY COMPOTE

½ cup (55g) fresh or thawed frozen cranberries

¼ cup (50g) granulated sugar

1 teaspoon ground ginger

FOR THE EASY FRANGIPANE

¼ cup (50g) granulated sugar

1 large egg

2 tablespoons (28g) unsalted butter, softened

¼ teaspoon almond extract

1 cup (96g) blanched almond flour

1 tablespoon all-purpose flour

TO ASSEMBLE

3 tablespoons Apple Butter (page 32), or store-bought

1 large egg, beaten

Sparkling or granulated sugar, for sprinkling

½ cup (60g) powdered sugar

2 to 3 teaspoons whole milk

I had a friend in high school who would make these little marzipan fruits and airbrush them to look like miniature versions of the real thing. It was my introduction to marzipan, its versatility, and its unique almond flavor, and I was smitten. I was also raised with a lot of ground-nut desserts thanks to my mom's vintage nut grinder that she got as a wedding gift in the '70s. So when I think of a great cold-weather sweet bread that ticks all the boxes of things I love (marzipan, nuts, warm apple desserts), this is the first recipe that comes to mind.   MAKES 1 (16-INCH) LOAF

MAKE THE CLOVE DOUGH: Heat the milk in the microwave or on the stove until it is just warm to the touch (110°F to 120°F). Stir in 1 teaspoon of the sugar and sprinkle the yeast over the top. Stir to combine and let the mixture stand until foamy, 5 to 10 minutes.

In the bowl of a stand mixer, whisk together the flour, the remaining sugar, salt, and ground cloves. Attach the dough hook to the mixer and add the melted butter, egg, and yeast mixture. Mix on medium-low until a sticky dough forms, about 4 minutes, adding more flour a tablespoon at a time if needed. (The dough won't form a smooth ball or pull away from the bottom of the bowl. It should feel tacky but not stick to a clean finger.)

Coat a large bowl with the oil and transfer the dough to the bowl, turning to coat. Shape into a ball, cover, and let rise at room temperature until doubled in size, about 1 hour.

MAKE THE CRANBERRY COMPOTE: In a small saucepan over medium heat, add the cranberries, sugar, ginger, and 1 tablespoon of water. Cover and cook, stirring occasionally, until the berries have burst and are very soft, about 7 minutes. Mash the cranberries with the back of a spoon and continue cooking until the compote is very thick, about 5 minutes. Transfer the compote to a bowl and let cool completely, or cover and chill until ready to use.

MAKE THE EASY FRANGIPANE: In a medium bowl, add the sugar, egg, butter, and almond extract and beat with a handheld electric mixer on medium speed until fluffy, about 1 minute. Add the almond flour and all-purpose flour, beating just until combined. Cover and set aside.

ASSEMBLE THE BREAD: Preheat the oven to 350°F.

continued

This bread is a great way to use up leftover cranberry sauce. Just skip the compote and use an equal amount of homemade or even canned cranberry sauce.

For a twist, try finely grinding pecans or walnuts in the food processor and using them in place of the almond flour in the frangipane.

Slice and freeze any leftover bread for a quick breakfast treat. Frozen slices will keep wrapped in plastic and stored in an airtight freezer bag for up to 2 months.

Transfer the risen dough to a lightly floured piece of parchment paper and gently press it into a square. Roll the dough into a 16x11-inch rectangle and trim if needed to straighten the edges.

Spread the frangipane down the center of the dough in a 3-inch-wide strip, leaving a 1-inch gap on each short end. Top with the apple butter and cranberry compote and smooth with a spatula.

Starting at each corner, measure 1 inch down each long edge. Make a small cut from each 1-inch mark to the edge of the filling. Make a small perpendicular cut and remove each of the corner pieces. Working down each long edge, make twelve cuts about an inch apart starting at the edge of the dough and stopping at the filling. (This will create strips of dough or "fringe" down each side.) Fold 1-inch ends of the center dough over the filling. Starting at one end, fold the cut strips over the filling on a diagonal, alternating between sides, to create a braided pattern. Cover loosely and let rise for 15 minutes or until noticeably puffed.

Set the risen braid and the parchment on a rimmed baking sheet. Brush with the beaten egg and sprinkle with the sparkling sugar. Bake for 30 to 35 minutes, until the bread is golden brown. Let the bread cool for at least 20 minutes. Whisk together the powdered sugar and milk to the desired consistency and drizzle over the bread.

Pecan Shortbread *and* Rosemary Caramel Bars

Rosemary has the type of earthy, piney flavor that calls to mind afternoon walks in the woods. While it's delicious in savory dishes, it's equally lovely balanced with sweeter notes and makes for a sophisticated offering, especially when sent home with guests after dinner. MAKES ABOUT 18 BARS

FOR THE PECAN SHORTBREAD

1½ cups (170g) pecan halves

1 cup (2 sticks/226g) unsalted butter, room temperature

½ cup (100g) granulated sugar

½ teaspoon kosher salt

1 large egg yolk

1 teaspoon vanilla extract

2 cups (240g) all-purpose flour

FOR THE ROSEMARY CARAMEL

1 (14-ounce/397g) can sweetened condensed milk

¾ cup (165g) firmly packed light brown sugar

½ cup (1 stick/113g) unsalted butter, cubed

¼ cup (60ml) light corn syrup

1 teaspoon vanilla extract

½ teaspoon kosher salt

¾ teaspoon powdered rosemary (see Tips & Tricks)

FOR THE GANACHE

2 ounces (56g) high-quality semisweet chocolate, chopped

1 tablespoon plus 1 teaspoon heavy whipping cream

Flaky sea salt (optional)

MAKE THE PECAN SHORTBREAD: Preheat the oven to 350°F. Line a 9-inch square cake pan with parchment paper or foil, letting the excess hang over the edges of the pan. Set aside.

Spread the pecans on a baking sheet and bake for 12 to 15 minutes, stirring every 5 minutes, until fragrant and slightly darkened. Transfer the pecans to a cutting board to let cool. Reserve ½ cup of the toasted pecans and roughly chop the remaining pecans.

In the bowl of a stand mixer fitted with the paddle attachment, add the butter and beat on medium speed until creamy, about 1 minute. Add the sugar and salt and continue beating until light and fluffy, about 3 minutes. Add the egg yolk and vanilla and beat just until combined. Reduce the mixer speed to low and add the flour a few tablespoons at a time, mixing just until combined. Add the chopped pecans and mix just until incorporated. Transfer the mixture to the prepared pan and press into an even layer.

Bake for 20 to 25 minutes, until the edges are golden brown. Set aside and let cool.

MAKE THE ROSEMARY CARAMEL: In a small saucepan over medium heat, whisk together the condensed milk, brown sugar, butter, corn syrup, vanilla, and salt. Cook, whisking constantly, until the mixture comes to a boil. Continue whisking until it reaches 225°F on an instant-read or candy thermometer, about 5 minutes. The mixture will darken slightly in color, begin to thicken, and pull away from the edge. Remove the pan from the heat and immediately whisk in the rosemary. Pour the caramel over the shortbread base and use a spatula to smooth it out to the edges. Set aside to cool.

MAKE THE GANACHE: In a small saucepan over medium heat, bring 2 inches of water to a simmer. In a heatproof bowl, add the chocolate and cream and place the bowl over the pot, making sure the bowl doesn't

continued

Powdered rosemary can sometimes be found in the spice section of the grocery store or specialty spice shops, but it's easy to make your own. Process 1 tablespoon dried rosemary leaves in a clean coffee or spice grinder into a fine powder. Store in an airtight container in the pantry. It's best if used within 3 months.

The shortbread base can be baked in advance and left to completely cool. Make sure the caramel and the chocolate steps are done together. If the bars are left to fully chill after you add the caramel, the melted chocolate will be difficult to spread into a thin layer before setting up.

You can mix up the flavor of the caramel by substituting the rosemary for cinnamon, pumpkin pie spice, or vanilla bean paste.

touch the water. Reduce the heat to low and stir until the chocolate is fully melted and the mixture is smooth, 3 to 5 minutes.

Pour the ganache over the caramel and smooth into an even layer. Break the reserved toasted pecans into pieces over the top and sprinkle with the flaky salt, if desired. Refrigerate for at least 4 hours or overnight. Cut into bars using a warm knife. Store bars in an airtight container in the refrigerator for up to 2 weeks.

Apple Cake *with* Maple Buttercream

FOR THE APPLE CAKE

1 cup (2 sticks/226g) unsalted butter, softened, plus more for the pan

3 cups (360g) all-purpose flour, plus more for the pan

2 teaspoons baking powder

1 teaspoon kosher salt

1 teaspoon ground cinnamon

½ teaspoon ground allspice

1¼ cups (250g) granulated sugar

1 cup (220g) firmly packed light brown sugar

4 large eggs, room temperature

2 teaspoons vanilla extract

2 teaspoons fresh thyme leaves, chopped

3 medium Honeycrisp apples, peeled and grated (should yield about 2 cups/400g)

FOR THE MAPLE BUTTERCREAM

2 cups (4 sticks/454g) unsalted butter

1 tablespoon vanilla bean paste or 1 vanilla bean, scraped

¼ cup (60ml) Grade A maple syrup

1 teaspoon kosher salt

6 cups (1½ pounds/675g) powdered sugar, sifted

6 to 8 tablespoons (90 to 120ml) heavy whipping cream

FOR THE ASSEMBLY

12 thyme sprigs

1 cup (200g) granulated sugar

⅓ cup Apple Butter (page 32), or store-bought

Adding fresh robust herbs, such as thyme or rosemary, to a dessert is one of the easiest ways to add interest and depth of flavor to an otherwise sweet-on-sweet recipe. But one of the fatal errors that people often make is adding too much or over-steeping, which can take things in an overpowering, medicinal direction. So know that when I call for adding thyme to the apple mixture, it's using a light hand on purpose. You just want a little dance on the palate that makes your brain go "that was nice," before getting enveloped by the rich notes of baked apple and maple.

MAKES 1 (2-LAYER, 9-INCH ROUND) CAKE

MAKE THE APPLE CAKE: Preheat the oven to 350°F. Butter and flour two (9-inch) round cake pans or spray with baking spray. Line the bottoms of the pans with parchment paper rounds.

In a large bowl, sift together the flour, baking powder, salt, cinnamon, and allspice. Set aside.

In the bowl of a stand mixer fitted with the paddle attachment, add the butter and beat on medium-low speed until smooth. Add the sugars and beat on medium speed until light and fluffy, about 5 minutes. Add the eggs one at a time, beating until fully incorporated before adding the next one. Stop to scrape down the bowl as needed. Add vanilla and thyme and beat until just combined.

Reduce the mixer speed to low and add the flour mixture in three portions, alternating with the grated apple. Beat just until combined, stopping to scrape down the bowl as needed. Divide the batter among the cake pans and smooth the tops with a spatula.

Bake for 30 to 35 minutes, until a wooden pick inserted in the center comes out with a few moist crumbs. Let the cakes cool completely in the pans.

MAKE THE MAPLE BUTTERCREAM: In a small saucepan over medium heat, melt the butter. Bring to a simmer and continue cooking, stirring occasionally, until the butter smells nutty and the milk solids begin to brown, 12 to 15 minutes. (The butter will become very foamy when it's almost done.) Transfer the browned butter to a heatproof bowl and whisk

continued

For perfectly even cake layers, wrap the outside of greased cake pans with water-soaked fabric baking strips. These are specifically designed for using in the oven and can be found in the cake decorating section of craft or specialty baking stores.

I prefer Honeycrisp apples for their sweet flavor and great texture, but your favorite apple variety will work great in this cake.

Not a fan of thyme? Simply omit it from the recipe or substitute it with another flavorful ingredient like grated lemon zest or minced rosemary.

If you prefer to store your cakes in the fridge and enjoy them cold, try using a butter with a higher fat content like Kerrygold or Land-o-Lakes European-Style butter. These butters will make a superbly tender cake, even when it's chilled, but they are more delicate at room temperature, so handle them with care when assembling the cake.

in the vanilla bean paste. Let cool at room temperature until the butter is firm but still spreadable, about 4 hours, or freeze for 30 minutes, stirring halfway through chilling.

In the bowl of a stand mixer fitted with the paddle attachment, add the cooled browned butter, maple syrup, and salt and beat on medium speed until combined. Reduce the mixer speed to low and gradually add the powdered sugar a cup or two at a time, alternating with the cream, until fully incorporated. Increase the mixer speed to medium and beat for 1 more minute. Switch to the whip attachment, return the mixer to medium speed, and beat until light and fluffy, about 3 minutes.

ASSEMBLE THE CAKE: In a small saucepan over medium heat, combine $\frac{1}{2}$ cup of the sugar with $\frac{1}{2}$ cup water. Heat, stirring frequently, until the sugar is just dissolved. Let cool for a few minutes. Dip each thyme sprig in the simple syrup and gently shake to remove excess. Sprinkle with the remaining sugar until well coated and place on a plate to dry.

On a cake stand, place one of the cake layers and spread 1 cup of the buttercream on top. Spread the apple butter in a thin, even layer over the buttercream. Top with the remaining cake layer and cover the top and sides with the remaining buttercream. Top with the sugared thyme.

The cake can be stored covered at room temperature for up to 3 days or refrigerated for 1 week.

Spiced Apple Pie *with* Brandy Crème Anglaise

FOR THE BRANDY CRÈME ANGLAISE

3 large egg yolks, room temperature

¼ cup plus 2 tablespoons (75g) granulated sugar

1½ cups (360ml) half-and-half

2 teaspoons vanilla bean paste, or ½ vanilla bean

2 tablespoons apple brandy

FOR THE CINNAMON PIE DOUGH

3¼ cups (390g) all-purpose flour, plus more for dusting

2 tablespoons granulated sugar

2 teaspoons ground cinnamon

½ teaspoon kosher salt

1 cup (2 sticks/226g) cold unsalted butter, cubed

½ cup (120ml) ice water

¼ cup (60ml) apple brandy

FOR THE FILLING

3½ pounds (1,500g) apples, peeled, cored, and cut into ⅛-inch slices

Grated zest and juice of 2 mandarin oranges

½ cup (100g) granulated sugar

½ cup (110g) firmly packed light brown sugar

1½ teaspoons ground cinnamon

1½ teaspoons ground ginger

½ teaspoon freshly ground black pepper

½ teaspoon ground allspice

¼ teaspoon freshly grated nutmeg

¼ teaspoon ground cardamom

¼ cup plus 2 tablespoons (45g) tapioca flour or cornstarch

1 large egg, beaten

All through my childhood, my mother and my dad's mother had a friendly competition with their apple pies. My mom was always distraught because she felt her crust was never crispy or flaky enough, and my grandmother wasn't exactly forthcoming with her secrets. Well, after wanting to continue the family tradition of making a really great spiced apple pie, I realized her secret was lard. Even so, that route wasn't for me—I prefer butter. I had to figure out another way to achieve crust perfection, which was to eliminate the nemesis of flaky crust: soggy baked apples. The solution, I found, was to macerate the apples and then reduce any liquid they give off into a thick syrup that you can then add to the filling. You get more concentrated flavor in the filling, and a much crispier crust—all the better vehicle for brandy crème anglaise and an obscene amount of whipped cream.

MAKES 1 (9-INCH) DEEP-DISH PIE

MAKE THE BRANDY CRÈME ANGLAISE: Place a fine mesh sieve over a heatproof bowl. In a separate heatproof bowl, whisk together the egg yolks and sugar and set aside.

In a small saucepan over medium heat, combine the half-and-half and vanilla bean. Heat until the mixture is very steamy but not boiling. Remove the pan from the heat and discard any skin that may have formed on top. Slowly whisk a couple of ladles of the hot half-and-half mixture into the egg yolks. Whisk the egg yolk mixture back into the saucepan and add the brandy.

Cook the custard over medium heat, stirring constantly, for 3 to 5 minutes until it is thickened and coats the back of the spoon but does not boil. Pour the mixture through the prepared sieve and scrape the vanilla bean into the custard, discarding the pod. Chill until ready to serve.

MAKE THE CINNAMON PIE DOUGH: In a large bowl, whisk together the flour, sugar, cinnamon, and salt. Add the butter, tossing to coat it with the flour. Cut in the butter using a pastry blender or squeeze the pieces between your fingers until the biggest pieces are the size of almonds and the smallest are about the size of peas.

continued

If you can't find apple brandy, substitute an aged or spiced rum. You can also replace the brandy with apple cider in the crème anglaise and the pie dough.

If you want to serve the pie with a crème anglaise but don't have time to make one, try this easy trick: Set a pint of vanilla bean ice cream in your refrigerator for a few hours to melt. Stir in a tablespoon of brandy, if desired, and serve the melted ice cream over the pie servings. Crème anglaise is often used as the base for ice cream, so by melting ice cream, you're essentially returning it back to a crème anglaise!

In a small bowl, stir together the ice water and brandy. Add half of the brandy mixture to the dough mixture and fold in using a fork. Continue adding the brandy mixture a tablespoon at a time, as needed, until a shaggy dough forms. Gently knead it together in the bowl just until the dough holds together in a loose ball. Cut dough in half and shape into two disks. Wrap the disks tightly in plastic wrap and chill for at least 2 hours or up to 3 days.

MAKE THE FILLING: In a large bowl, toss together the apple slices and the mandarin orange zest and juice. Add the sugars, cinnamon, ginger, pepper, allspice, nutmeg, and cardamom and toss again until well combined. Cover and let the apples stand for at least 1 hour or up to 3 hours.

Drain the apples, reserving the liquid. Toss the drained apple slices with the tapioca flour and set aside.

Add the reserved liquid to a small saucepan over medium heat. Bring to a boil and cook, stirring occasionally, until thick and syrupy, about 15 minutes. Remove the pan from the heat.

Preheat the oven to 425°F. Line a sheet pan with parchment paper.

On a lightly floured surface, roll out one disk of pie dough to ⅛ inch. Using a small leaf-shaped cookie cutter, cut the dough and place the shapes in a single layer on the prepared sheet pan. (Top the cutouts with additional paper to create multiple layers if needed.) Freeze the cutouts until firm, about 15 minutes.

Roll the remaining disk of pie dough into a 14-inch circle. Transfer to a 9-inch deep-dish pie pan. Trim the excess dough to 1 inch from the edge of the pie pan. Tuck the ends under and crimp as desired. Add the apple slices and press down gently to even out the filling and minimize any gaps. Pour the reduced apple liquid over the top of the filling and top with the frozen pie dough cutouts. Set the pie on a rimmed baking sheet and brush the dough with the beaten egg.

Bake for 15 minutes. Reduce the oven temperature to 375°F and continue baking for 50 to 60 minutes, until the crust is a deep golden brown and the filling is bubbling. Let cool for at least 2 hours before slicing. Serve with the chilled brandy crème anglaise, if desired. The pie and crème anglaise can be stored, refrigerated, for up to 4 days.

Browned Butter Apple-Pecan Crostata

Crostatas are for when you want all the flavor of a pie but in a foolproof, free-form package. I often keep rounds of this pastry dough in the fridge or freezer—made more interesting with cinnamon, allspice, and cardamom—so any time I have extra fruit lying around (which is often), I can whip together one of these in just a few minutes. **MAKES 1 (10-INCH) CROSTATA**

FOR THE SUGARED PECANS

¾ cup plus 2 tablespoons (1¾ sticks/198g) unsalted butter

1 cup (95g) pecan halves

1 tablespoon granulated sugar

¼ teaspoon ground allspice

FOR THE SPICED DOUGH

¼ cup plus 2 tablespoons (90ml) cold whole milk

1 large egg

2¼ cups (270g) all-purpose flour, plus more for rolling

3 tablespoons granulated sugar

1 teaspoon ground cinnamon

½ teaspoon ground allspice

½ teaspoon kosher salt

¼ teaspoon ground cardamom

FOR THE APPLE FILLING

½ cup (100g) granulated sugar, plus more for sprinkling

1 tablespoon cornstarch

1 teaspoon ground cinnamon

2 pounds Honeycrisp apples (900g), peeled, cored, and cut into ⅛-inch slices

1 large egg, lightly beaten

Vanilla ice cream, for serving

MAKE THE SUGARED PECANS: Line a small sheet pan with parchment paper.

In a small saucepan over medium heat, melt the butter. Cook, stirring occasionally, until the butter smells nutty and the milk solids begin to brown, about 12 to 15 minutes. The butter will become very foamy and quiet when it's almost done. Remove the pan from the heat and place 1 tablespoon of the browned butter in a small bowl. (You'll use the rest of the browned butter in the dough.) Add the pecans and toss to coat. Add the sugar and allspice and toss once more to coat. Spread the pecans on the prepared sheet pan and freeze until ready to use.

MAKE THE SPICED DOUGH: Line a medium bowl with foil. Pour the remaining 13 tablespoons of browned butter into the bowl and freeze for 1 hour or until firm. Remove the butter from the foil, cut it into cubes, and set aside.

In a medium bowl, whisk together the milk and egg and set aside.

In a food processor, add the flour, sugar, cinnamon, allspice, salt, and cardamom and pulse to combine. Add the cubed butter and pulse four times. Slowly add the milk mixture as you continue pulsing, and process until the dough starts to clump together. Turn out the dough onto a floured work surface and gently knead it into a ball. Shape the dough ball into a disk, wrap it tightly in plastic wrap, and chill for at least 30 minutes or up to 2 days.

Preheat the oven to 400°F. Line a baking sheet with parchment paper.

On a lightly floured surface, roll the dough into an ⅛-inch-thick circle. If desired, you can trim any uneven edges to make a clean circle. Carefully transfer the dough to the parchment paper.

MAKE THE APPLE FILLING: In a large bowl, whisk together the sugar, cornstarch, and cinnamon. Add the apples and toss until well coated. Mound the apples in the center of the dough, leaving a 3-inch border. Scatter the sugared pecans over the apples and fold the edges of the dough up over the filling toward the center. Brush the top of the crust with the egg and sprinkle with sugar, if desired.

Bake for 45 to 50 minutes, until the crust is deep golden brown and the filling is bubbly. After 30 minutes, cover loosely with foil to prevent the pecans from burning. Let cool for 30 minutes before serving and serve with vanilla ice cream. Store the crostata covered in the refrigerator for up to 4 days.

TIPS & TRICKS

This would be absolutely delicious served with boozy or spiced whipped cream. To make the whipped cream, simply beat 1 cup heavy whipping cream with 2 tablespoons powdered sugar, ¼ teaspoon of any of the spices used in this recipe, or a tablespoon of liquor like bourbon until soft peaks form.

I chose Honeycrisp for their great flavor and how well they keep their texture when baked, but Granny Smith, Cortland, or Fuji would work great alongside them, and in any combination.

Don't have all these individual spices in your cabinet? That's okay! Use 2¼ teaspoons of apple pie spice, pumpkin pie spice, or your favorite baking spice blend in the crust.

The pecans and browned butter can be made several days in advance and kept frozen until ready to use.

Poached Pear Tarte Tatin

FOR THE ROUGH PUFF PASTRY

1½ cups (180g) all-purpose flour

1 tablespoon granulated sugar

¼ teaspoon kosher salt

¾ cup (1½ sticks/170g) unsalted butter, frozen and grated

6 to 7 tablespoons (90 to 105ml) cold water

FOR THE POACHED PEARS

1 (750ml) bottle fruity white wine, such as Pinot Grigio

½ cup (100g) granulated sugar

1 (2-inch) piece fresh ginger, peeled and sliced

1 cinnamon stick

½ vanilla bean, split lengthwise

1 large orange peel

6 whole cloves

4 large (about 985g) firm D'Anjou pears, peeled, cored, and cut into quarters

FOR THE MULLED WINE CARAMEL SAUCE

1½ cups (300g) granulated sugar

½ cup (1 stick/113g) unsalted butter, cubed

FOR ASSEMBLY

1 sheet thawed frozen puff pastry (if not using Rough Puff Pastry)

½ cup (100g) granulated sugar

3 tablespoons (42g) cold unsalted butter, cubed

1 cup (240ml) heavy whipping cream

¼ teaspoon ground ginger

Dash of ground cinnamon

We have a few pear trees, so we get to watch as the fruit begins to develop in the spring after the blossoms have been pollinated. And of course, I start dreaming about all the desserts that those pears will become (and praying that the animals don't get them all!). This recipe was born from one of those daydreams and showcases poached pears as an updated, autumnal mash-up of the undeniably timeless tarte tatin. There are few desserts more dramatic—poaching the fruit, layering puff pastry over the top, and then flipping the pan upside down to reveal a beautiful fruit-studded tarte. It's a magical moment made even more special by the pears' being poached in mulled white wine, which also happens to transform into a butter-caramel sauce you can drizzle over the top alongside a dollop of gingery whipped cream.

While this tarte is typically baked in a cast iron skillet or tarte tatin pan, if you don't have one, you can make the sugar base in a saucepan and pour it into a 9- or 10-inch cake pan for baking. You are also welcome to substitute one sheet of thawed frozen puff pastry for the Rough Puff Pastry called for in the recipe.   MAKES 1 (10-INCH) TARTE

MAKE THE ROUGH PUFF PASTRY: In a large bowl, whisk together the flour, sugar, and salt. Add the grated butter and toss to coat with the flour. Add the water a couple of tablespoons at a time, folding in with a fork or your hands until a shaggy dough forms, 3 to 4 minutes. Gently knead the dough in the bowl until it comes together in a solid mass. (Some parts may still be a little crumbly.) Shape the dough into a 5-inch square. Wrap it tightly in plastic wrap and chill for 2 hours.

On a lightly floured surface, roll the dough into a 12x6-inch rectangle. Fold the dough in thirds like a letter starting with the short sides. Rewrap and chill for another 30 minutes.

Place the dough on a lightly floured surface seam side up with the short sides at the top and bottom. Roll the dough into a 12x6-inch rectangle. Fold into thirds again and wrap and chill for another 30 minutes. Repeat rolling, folding, and chilling two more times. Chill after the final roll for at least 2 hours or overnight.

continued

The pear variety for this tarte can be changed based on what you have available. Avoid very crisp varieties like Asian pears or southern yard pears. D'Anjou, Bosc, Tosca, and firm Bartlett pears are the best varieties to use.

When picking a wine to poach the pears, a mid-range quality bottle will do. It doesn't need to be a special-occasion bottle; an everyday drinking wine is perfect.

To grate frozen butter, use your food processor with the larger grating blade attached. Or, grate by hand with a box grater and grip the frozen sticks of butter with a dry paper towel. Just finely chop the end that you can't grate.

MAKE THE POACHED PEARS: Cut a round of parchment to the diameter of a large saucepan and cut a 1-inch hole in the center.

In a large saucepan, combine the wine, sugar, ginger, cinnamon, vanilla bean, orange peel, and cloves. Bring the mixture to a simmer over medium heat, stirring occasionally, until the sugar is dissolved. Add the pears and reduce the heat to medium-low. Place the parchment round directly on top of the pears. Continue simmering until the pears are firm but tender, about 15 to 20 minutes.

Discard the parchment. Using a slotted spoon, transfer the pears to a shallow dish to cool, returning any whole spices back to the poaching liquid.

MAKE THE MULLED WINE CARAMEL SAUCE: In the same saucepan you used for poaching the pears, bring the poaching liquid to a boil over medium-high heat. Boil until the liquid is reduced to about $3/4$ cup, about 25 minutes. Strain the sauce through a fine-mesh sieve and discard the spices.

Return $1/2$ cup of the reduced poaching liquid to the same saucepan. Sprinkle the sugar evenly over the bottom of the pan and bring the mixture to a boil over medium heat. Let the sauce cook without stirring until the sugar turns a deep amber color, 10 to 12 minutes. (The mixture will bubble up to fill about half of the pan.) Whisk the mixture and remove the pan from the heat.

Carefully add the butter in two parts, whisking until completely melted and combined after each addition. The mixture will foam. Whisk in the remaining $1/4$ cup poaching liquid until incorporated. Transfer the sauce to a heatproof container and let it cool. The caramel sauce will keep refrigerated for up to 2 weeks. Warm before serving.

ASSEMBLE THE TARTE: Preheat the oven to 400°F. Line a baking sheet with parchment paper and set aside.

On a lightly floured surface, roll out the pastry into an 11- to 12-inch circle. Place it on the lined baking sheet and chill until ready to use.

Sprinkle the sugar evenly over the bottom of a 10-inch cast iron skillet. Place the pan over medium heat and cook without stirring until the sugar starts to bubble and turn a dark amber color, about 4 minutes. Whisk to combine any unmelted sugar. Remove the pan from the heat and whisk in the butter until completely combined.

Arrange the cooled poached pears, cut side down, over the caramel layer. Discard any juice the pears have released while cooling. Place the pastry over the top of the pears and carefully fold the edges under until the pastry fits snugly in the skillet. Place the skillet on a rimmed baking sheet.

Bake for about 35 minutes, until the pastry is puffed and very golden brown and the caramel is bubbling on the sides. Transfer the pan to a cooling rack and let the tarte rest in the pan for 30 to 40 minutes. (If baked in a cake pan, cool for 10 to 15 minutes.)

Meanwhile, in a large bowl with a whisk, beat together the cream, ginger, and cinnamon until soft peaks form.

When the tarte is done resting, carefully invert it onto a rimmed serving plate. Serve with the Mulled Wine Caramel Sauce and whipped cream.

Maple Pumpkin Pie

FOR THE GINGER PIE DOUGH

1½ cups (180g) all-purpose flour

1 tablespoon granulated sugar

1 tablespoon ground ginger

¼ teaspoon kosher salt

½ cup (113g) cold unsalted butter, cubed

5 to 7 tablespoons (60 to 90ml) ice water

FOR THE MAPLE PUMPKIN FILLING

½ cup plus 2 tablespoons (85g)
all-purpose flour

¼ cup (50g) granulated sugar

½ teaspoon cinnamon

¼ teaspoon ground allspice

¼ teaspoon fresh grated nutmeg

1¼ cups (300g) canned pumpkin puree

1 cup (240ml) Grade A pure maple syrup

1 cup (240ml) heavy whipping cream

1 teaspoon orange zest

1 teaspoon vanilla extract

¾ teaspoon kosher salt

Powdered sugar, for dusting

Maple syrup has always had a special place in my heart, and now that we're living in the Northeast, it's like I'm in some kind of maple fantasy. Around here, the maple trees are the crowning glory of the season; their vibrant leaves are like stained glass windows in the sky. And by late winter, we get to help our neighbors tap their maples so they can bottle their own syrup—and, thankfully, share it with us. Maple is also close to my heart because it speaks to my father's French Canadian heritage. To celebrate this love, I've given the classic pumpkin pie recipe a maple twist, along with adding my favorite baking spices and a perfectly crisp crust (because soggy bottoms are unacceptable).

MAKES 1 (9-INCH) PIE

MAKE THE GINGER PIE DOUGH: In a large bowl, whisk together the flour, sugar, ginger, and salt. Add the butter and toss to coat. Cut in the butter using a pastry blender or squeeze the pieces between your fingers until the biggest pieces are the size of almonds and small ones are about the size of peas. Add half of the water and fold in using a fork. Continue adding water a tablespoon at a time until the mixture forms a shaggy dough. Gently knead it together in the bowl until the dough clumps together. Shape it into a disk and wrap tightly in plastic wrap. Chill for 1 hour or up to 3 days.

Preheat the oven to 425°F.

On a lightly floured surface, roll the chilled pie dough into a 14-inch circle. Transfer to a 9-inch pie pan. Trim the excess dough to 1 inch from the edge of the pan, tuck the excess under, and crimp around the edge as desired. Poke the bottom of the crust all over with a fork. Freeze for 15 minutes. Place a piece of parchment paper inside the pie crust and fill with pie weights or dried beans.

Set the pie plate on a rimmed baking sheet and bake for 15 to 18 minutes, until the edges start to turn golden brown. Carefully remove the parchment and weights. Continue baking for 3 to 5 minutes more or until the bottom of the crust looks dry and set. Let cool while you make the filling.

continued

For an impressive but easy decoration, place a piece of lace, a doily, or other lightweight patterned item over the top of the pie before dusting with powdered sugar. Carefully remove the item to reveal the sugar design.

I recommend sticking to canned pumpkin for this recipe instead of using a homemade roasted pumpkin puree. The canned version contains more liquid than most homemade purees, which affects how the pie bakes and sets.

MAKE THE MAPLE PUMPKIN FILLING: Reduce the oven temperature to 375°F.

In a large bowl, sift together the flour, sugar, cinnamon, allspice, and nutmeg. In another bowl, whisk together the pumpkin, maple syrup, cream, orange zest, vanilla, and salt. Whisk the pumpkin mixture into the flour mixture until well combined. Pour the filling into the cooled pie crust.

Bake for 35 to 40 minutes, until the edges are set and the center is slightly wobbly when gently nudged. Let the pie cool completely at room temperature, then refrigerate for at least 2 hours. (The pie can be chilled for up to 2 days in advance.) Dust with powdered sugar just before serving.

Sweet Potato *and* Toasted Marshmallow Pie

FOR THE CLASSIC PIE DOUGH

1½ cups (180g) all-purpose flour, plus more for dusting

1 tablespoon granulated sugar

¼ teaspoon kosher salt

½ cup (113g) cold unsalted butter, cubed

4 to 6 tablespoons (60 to 90ml) ice water

1 tablespoon heavy whipping cream

FOR THE SWEET POTATO FILLING

2½ pounds (1,134g) sweet potatoes, roasted and peeled

1 cup (220g) firmly packed dark brown sugar

½ cup (135ml) heavy whipping cream

2 large eggs

3 large egg yolks

2 teaspoons vanilla extract

1½ teaspoons ground ginger

1 teaspoon ground cinnamon

¼ teaspoon freshly grated nutmeg

FOR THE MARSHMALLOW TOPPING

1 (¼-ounce) packet unflavored gelatin

⅓ cup (80ml) cold water

3 large egg whites

¾ cup (150g) granulated sugar

2 teaspoons vanilla extract or vanilla bean paste

As the child of immigrants, I often celebrated American holidays through the lens of my parents' Mexican and Greek cultures. Thanksgiving in particular was a mash-up—a roasted turkey, but with my mom's herbed rice, a few vegetable sides, a nice salad, and a sweet potato "casserole" that was pretty much just baked potatoes layered with thinly sliced apples, a tiny sprinkle of sugar, and a few little dabs of butter. After Brian and I got married and we merged our traditions, though, I realized that this wasn't really the norm for most people in this country. So when I tried a "real" sweet potato casserole—toasted marshmallows and all—as an adult, it felt like some kind of naughty experiment . . . and I liked it. I decided to rev up those flavors and turn them into a decadent, gooey pie.   MAKES 1 (9-INCH) PIE

MAKE THE CLASSIC PIE DOUGH: In a large bowl, whisk together the flour, sugar, and salt. Add the butter and toss to coat with the flour mixture. Use a pastry blender or your fingers to cut or squeeze the butter pieces until the biggest ones are the size of almonds and the smallest are about the size of peas. Add half of the water and fold in with a fork. Continue adding the water 1 tablespoon at a time until the mixture forms a shaggy dough. Gently knead it together in the bowl until the dough clumps together, sprinkling more water on any very dry and crumbly areas. Shape the dough into a disk and wrap tightly in plastic wrap. Chill for 1 hour or up to 3 days.

Preheat the oven to 425°F.

On a lightly floured surface, roll the chilled pie dough into a 13-inch circle. Transfer to a 9-inch deep-dish pie pan. Trim the dough to a 1-inch overhang, tuck the excess under, and crimp around the edge as desired. Poke the bottom of the crust all over with a fork. Freeze for 15 minutes. Brush the edges with the cream. Place a piece of parchment paper inside the crust and fill it with pie weights or dried beans.

Set the pie plate on a rimmed baking sheet and bake for 18 minutes. Reduce the oven temperature to 375°F. Carefully remove the parchment and weights and continue baking for 5 minutes more. Set aside to cool completely and leave the oven on.

continued

For the perfect roasted sweet potatoes, preheat the oven to 375ºF. Pierce the sweet potatoes several times with a knife and place them on an aluminum foil-lined baking sheet. Cover the potatoes loosely with foil and bake for 60 to 90 minutes, or until they soften and the skin is starting to wrinkle. Let them cool completely and remove the skin.

If you don't have gelatin or would prefer not to use it, the topping can be made without it. It will be lighter in texture than marshmallow-like, but it will still be delicious!

MAKE THE SWEET POTATO FILLING: In a food processor, add the roasted sweet potatoes and brown sugar and process until very smooth, about 1 minute. Add the cream, eggs, egg yolks, vanilla, ginger, cinnamon, and nutmeg and process until combined. Pour the filling into the cooled pie crust and smooth with a spatula. Cover only the pie crust with foil by folding long pieces of foil in half and wrapping them around the side of the pie pan and just over the edges.

Bake for 45 to 50 minutes, until the edges are set and the center is slightly wobbly when nudged. Let cool completely. The pie can be chilled for up to 2 days before topping and serving.

MAKE THE MARSHMALLOW TOPPING: Fill a small saucepan with 1 inch of water and set over medium heat. Bring to a simmer.

In a small bowl, add the cold water and sprinkle the gelatin on top. Set aside to hydrate.

In the bowl of a stand mixer fitted with the whisk attachment, add the egg whites and sugar and beat on medium speed until combined. Set the mixing bowl over the saucepan, making sure the bowl doesn't touch the water. Stirring frequently with a silicone spatula, cook until the mixture reaches 160°F to 165°F, 4 to 6 minutes. (If you don't have a thermometer, you can rub the mixture between your fingers. It should feel smooth and very warm to the touch.) Remove the bowl from the pot and stir in the gelatin until dissolved.

Return the bowl to the mixer and beat on medium-high speed until the bowl feels barely warm and the mixture has thick, glossy peaks, about 10 minutes. Add the vanilla and beat on low speed until just combined. Working quickly, spread the marshmallow over the pie, all the way out to the crust. If desired, toast the marshmallow with a kitchen torch. Let the pie stand for at least 30 minutes before slicing.

Vanilla Bean *and* Fresh Fig Cake

We had incredible trees in the backyard of our childhood home, and one of them was an ancient fig tree that had the most delicious fruit that would get heavy with honey-like syrup. My brother and I would always be out back, digging holes, climbing, causing mischief—with our mouths full of figs. This cake, with its subtle vanilla canvas, is an homage to that flavor. SERVES 8

FOR THE VANILLA BEAN CAKE

¾ cup (1½ sticks/170g) unsalted European-style butter, such as Kerrygold, room temperature, plus more for the pan

1⅔ cups (200g) all-purpose flour, plus more for the pan

¾ teaspoon baking powder

¾ cup (150g) granulated sugar

½ cup (110g) firmly packed light brown sugar

¼ teaspoon kosher salt

1 vanilla bean, scraped, or 1 tablespoon vanilla bean paste

2 large eggs, room temperature

½ cup (120g) sour cream, room temperature

FOR THE SOUR CREAM BUTTERCREAM

¼ cup (57g) unsalted European-style butter, room temperature

1⅔ to 2 cups (200 to 240g) powdered sugar

¼ cup (60g) sour cream, room temperature

½ teaspoon vanilla extract

8 fresh figs, halved

TIPS & TRICKS

European-style butter gives a soft and tender texture to this cake loaf, even when refrigerated, because it has a higher fat content than most other standard stick butter. If you can't find European-style butter, regular butter can be used.

MAKE THE VANILLA BEAN CAKE: Preheat the oven to 350°F. Butter and flour a 9x5-inch loaf pan or spray with cooking spray. Line the pan with parchment paper, letting any excess hang over the edges. Set aside.

In a medium bowl, whisk together the flour and baking powder and set aside.

In the bowl of a stand mixer fitted with the paddle attachment, beat the butter on medium speed until creamy, about 1 minute. Add the sugars and salt and continue beating on medium speed until light and fluffy, about 5 minutes. Scrape down the sides of the bowl. Add the vanilla and beat until combined. Add the eggs, one at a time, beating until well combined and fluffy after each addition.

Reduce the mixer speed to low and slowly add about a third of the flour mixture, followed by half of the sour cream. Repeat, finishing with the final third of the flour mixture, and beat until just combined. Pour the batter into the prepared pan and smooth the top with a spatula.

Bake for 1 hour to 1 hour and 10 minutes, or until the cake is golden brown and a toothpick inserted into the center comes out with a few moist crumbs. Let the cake cool in the pan for 20 minutes. Use the parchment as handles and transfer the cake to a wire rack to cool completely.

MAKE THE SOUR CREAM BUTTERCREAM: In the bowl of a stand mixer fitted with the whisk attachment, beat the butter on medium speed until fluffy, about 1 minute. Add 1⅔ cups of the powdered sugar, sour cream, and vanilla and beat on low speed until combined. If the mixture looks too soft to spread and hold its shape, add the additional ⅓ cup powdered sugar. Increase the speed to medium and beat until the mixture is smooth and fluffy, about 2 minutes. Spread the buttercream on top of the cooled cake and top with the fresh figs. Store any leftover cake in the refrigerator for up to 4 days.

Persimmon-Pecan Galettes

I'd like to let you in on a little secret: a galette is just a crostata's French cousin. It's the same free-form pie crust that you can fill with just about anything, sweet or savory. While galettes are in heavy rotation in my kitchen during the summer because I'm constantly coming home with more fruit than I can eat, they're also really nice in the fall rotation, too, especially when you hit that ideal moment in the season when there are persimmons at the market. And for all those other moments, you can use apples.

MAKES 5 (5-INCH) GALETTES

FOR THE GALETTE DOUGH

2 cups (240g) all-purpose flour, plus more for dusting

2 tablespoons granulated sugar

½ teaspoon kosher salt

½ cup plus 2 tablespoons (140g) cold unsalted butter, cubed

6 to 8 (90 to 120ml) tablespoons ice water

FOR THE GALETTES

2 firm but ripe Fuyu persimmons, peeled, halved, and sliced in ⅛-inch half rounds

2 teaspoons granulated sugar

½ cup (60g) raw pecan pieces

3 tablespoons firmly packed light brown sugar

2 tablespoons unsalted butter, softened

2 tablespoons all-purpose flour

1 large egg yolk

2 tablespoons half-and-half or heavy whipping cream

1 teaspoon ground cinnamon

1 teaspoon vanilla extract

⅛ teaspoon kosher salt

Sparkling or granulated sugar

MAKE THE GALETTE DOUGH: In a large bowl, add the flour, sugar, and salt and whisk to combine. Add the butter and toss to coat it with the flour mixture. Cut in the butter using a pastry blender or squeeze the butter pieces between your fingers until the biggest pieces are the size of almonds and small ones are about the size of peas. Add half of the water and fold in with a fork. Continue adding the water 1 tablespoon at a time until the mixture forms a shaggy dough. Gently knead it together in the bowl until the dough clumps together. Shape the dough into a disk and wrap tightly in plastic wrap. Chill for 1 hour or up to 3 days.

MAKE THE GALETTES: In a medium bowl, layer the persimmon slices with the sparkling sugar, sprinkling more with each layer. Set aside.

In a food processor, add the pecans and brown sugar and process until the nuts are very finely ground and just starting to clump but are not yet a paste. Add the butter, flour, egg yolk, 1 tablespoon of the half-and-half, the cinnamon, vanilla, and salt. Process until a paste forms, about 1 minute, stopping to scrape down the bowl if needed. Transfer the mixture to a bowl and set aside.

Preheat the oven to 425°F. Line a rimmed baking sheet with parchment paper and set aside.

On a lightly floured surface, roll the dough to an ⅛-inch thickness. Cut five (6- to 7-inch) circles out of the dough, rerolling the dough scraps as needed. (Turn a cereal bowl upside down as a guide, if needed. See Tips & Tricks.) Transfer the dough rounds to the prepared baking sheet. Divide the pecan mixture between the dough rounds, leaving a 2-inch border. Shingle five or six persimmon slices over the pecan mixture. Fold and crimp the edges of the dough up over the persimmons toward the center. Brush the dough with the remaining tablespoon of half-and-half and sprinkle lightly with the sparkling sugar. Freeze for 15 minutes or refrigerate for 30 minutes.

Bake for 20 to 25 minutes, until the crust is a deep golden brown and the filling has puffed up a bit. Let cool for at least 20 minutes before serving.

TIPS & TRICKS

When purchasing persimmons, there are two main varieties to know: Fuyu and Hachiya. While they are both related, they have very different eating experiences when ripe. Hachiyas are tear-drop shaped and must be eaten when very soft. If eaten when they are hard, they are very astringent. Fuyus are tomato-like in shape, and ripe and edible when they are still firm. Look for Fuyus that have a rich orange color but are still firm when gently squeezed. If they maintain indentations when pressed, they are too soft to use for these galettes but are delicious eaten over ice cream or oatmeal.

Firm Fuyu persimmons can be peeled like an apple with a vegetable peeler.

Other unroasted nuts can be used in place of pecans for the filling. Try cashews, blanched almonds, or walnuts for variety or if you don't have pecans in your pantry.

You don't need a special 6- or 7-inch round cutter for these pastries. Simply flip over a cereal bowl or place a round lid on the rolled dough and cut around it with a pastry wheel or small sharp knife.

Swedish Apple Cake

FOR THE POACHED APPLES

2 cups (480ml) cold water

½ cup (100g) granulated sugar

½ lemon

4 large apples, such as Golden Delicious, Pink Lady, or Honeycrisp, peeled, halved, and cored

FOR THE ALMOND TOPPING

½ cup (1 stick/113g) unsalted butter, room temperature, plus more for the pan

⅔ cup (133g) granulated sugar

3 large egg yolks, room temperature

½ cup (56g) blanched almond flour

Grated zest and juice of ½ lemon

⅛ teaspoon kosher salt

3 large egg whites, room temperature

Vanilla ice cream, for serving

TIPS & TRICKS

Use a variety of apple that will hold up well to poaching and baking. Honeycrisp is my preferred apple, but a fresh Golden Delicious or Pink Lady works well, too. This is also beautiful made with Hidden Rose apples for a surprising pop of pink.

My parents were always reading and learning. History books lined the shelves of our living room, and there were just as many cookbooks in the kitchen. My mom loved immersing herself in other cultures, especially through their food. One of her discoveries was this Swedish apple cake called *äppelkaka*, which she would always make for us come the fall. There are layers of poached apples suspended in a fluffy, meringue-like cloud that gets filled with ground almonds. After it bakes, it develops a wonderful crust on top but the inside stays moist and fluffy, like apple clouds. SERVES 8

MAKE THE POACHED APPLES: Place a wire rack inside a rimmed baking sheet and set aside.

In a large saucepan, combine the water and sugar. Squeeze the lemon juice into the water and add the rind. Add the apples and stir to coat any unsubmerged portions of the apples. Set the pot over medium-high heat and bring to a boil, stirring occasionally. Reduce the heat to medium-low and simmer for 6 to 8 minutes, until the apples are soft enough to pierce with a fork but with some resistance. Transfer the apples to the prepared rack to drain and cool completely.

MAKE THE ALMOND TOPPING: Preheat the oven to 350°F. Lightly butter a 2-quart or 12-inch round baking dish. Place the cooled poached apples in the baking dish cut side down and set aside.

In a large mixing bowl, add the butter and use a handheld electric mixer to beat at medium speed until creamy, about 1 minute. While beating, slowly add the sugar until fully incorporated. Add the egg yolks one at a time, beating until well combined before adding the next. Mix in the almond flour, lemon zest and juice, and salt.

In a separate bowl with clean beaters, add the egg whites and beat on high speed until they form stiff peaks, about 5 minutes. Gently fold the egg whites into the butter mixture in two additions. Spread the topping over the prepared apples.

Bake for 35 to 40 minutes, until the top is golden brown. Serve warm with vanilla ice cream.

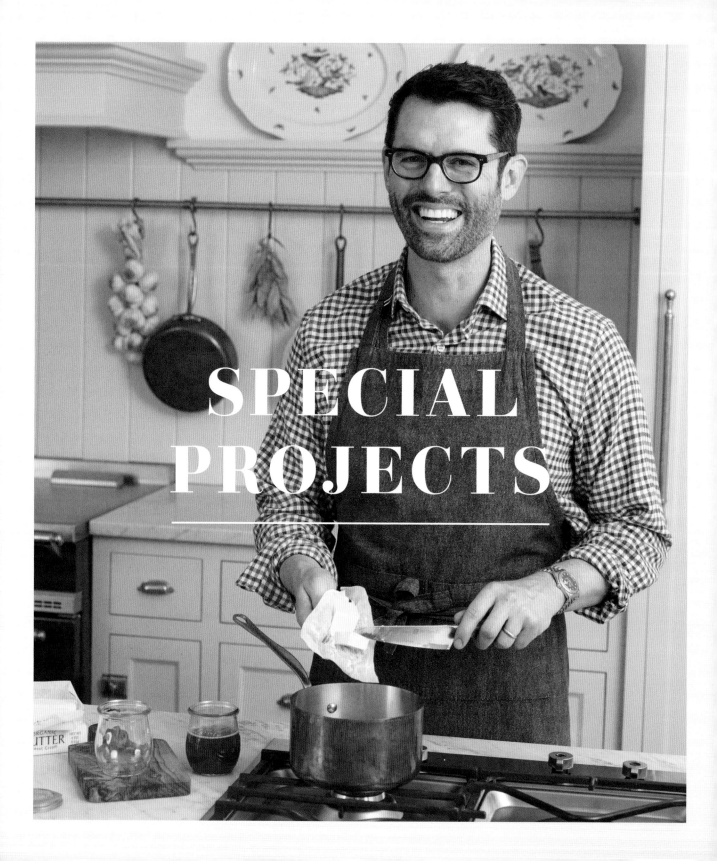

SPECIAL
PROJECTS

Brown Butter

1 cup (2 sticks/226g) unsalted butter

Brown butter, or butter that's been gently warmed until all of its milk solids have turned a deep, nutty, caramelly brown, is one of the easiest ways to add a little something extra to a recipe (did I hear brown butter buttercream?). In the fall I'll brown big batches and store it in the fridge so it's always on hand to use for baking or cooking. This is also advantageous because brown butter takes forever to cool, so you're much more likely to reach for it if there's a room-temperature batch at your fingertips. You can use it any time you see butter called for in a baking recipe as 1:1 sub, or even when cooking meats or root vegetables.

Like caramel, there are different levels of brownness that you can go for: light and blond for subtle nuttiness, or dark to the edge of burnt for a hint of bitterness, which is my personal preference.   MAKES 1 CUP

In a small saucepan over medium heat, melt the butter. Bring to a simmer and continue cooking, stirring occasionally, until the butter smells nutty and the milk solids begin to brown, 12 to 15 minutes. (The butter will become very foamy and make less noise when it's almost done.) For darker butter, keep cooking until the desired color is reached, up to 7 minutes more. (Watch it carefully and stir often so it doesn't burn.)

Transfer the browned butter to a container and let it cool until spreadable for using in recipes where softened butter is used. Or chill until firm and use in recipes where cold butter is used.

SETTING A
SPECIAL TABLE

Part of the reason why I love making beautifully deco-rated desserts is because when your food looks inviting and special, it's creating a moment for someone. It lets them know that you care about them, and that you spent time on them. It also happens to be a blank canvas upon which you can create compositions of colors, shapes, and pattern to express yourself. A nicely set table is much the same. I got an early lesson in this because my parents always made a point of making the holiday table a special place to be. There would be my grandmother's tablecloths, flowers, and, most important, a wonderful meal. That little bit of extra thoughtfulness went a long way in making us all feel welcome, safe, and loved.

> "What can I do to make my guests feel welcome… How do I want my guests to feel?"

That's why when I'm setting a table for a special occasion, I always start with *What can I do to make my guests feel welcome?* Or, similarly, *How do I want my guests to feel?* I also think about layers, similar to the layers and depth of flavor I'm adding to a dish. In the case of the table, those layers can be linens like tablecloths and napkins, chargers, and place mats. You don't necessar-ily need all of these elements, but using some of them helps warm up a table.

I also like to ask myself *What does everyone need?* These items are functional in nature—water glasses, wineglasses, salt cellars, butter dishes—but when added to a table in anticipation of a guest reaching for them, it creates a warm, hospitable feel.

Additionally, I consider small, inviting gestures. Place cards are one of the easiest ones to include. When I was younger, I didn't have any fancy dishes or linens, but I always put out place cards for my guests.

They can just be folded pieces of paper with your best handwriting attempt, or as I've graduated to, actual place card holders. Centerpieces or floral arrangements are another special touch, depending on the season and occasion. (I've included my favorite ways to do this in each of the seasons.) I like to create one larger focal piece in the middle, and then scatter smaller arrangements over the table. There's all manner of other ways you can add other bits of personality and embellishment—adorned napkin rings, individualized butter molds, you name it. Make things as simple or as formal as you please.

COLLECTING
CHINA

One of the loveliest ways to bring your personality and hospitality to a table is through china or vintage place settings that you've collected. As I said earlier, Brian and I are like little old ladies—we love picking up new trea-sures for our collection whenever we can. It began back when we first got married and visited the little shops and antique stores in France and Austria and were so taken by the artistry that went into fine china. As an art major, I deeply appreciated the painting and composition, and we both have a love for things that are handmade. So we dipped our toes in, picking up pieces whenever we'd travel; and we haven't really stopped since, scouring auctions, sales, and antique stores whenever we can.

These treasures have brought us so much joy because they not only remind us of the places we've been but also lend themselves to creating beautiful moments every day. Something as simple as an afternoon cup of tea or a cookie becomes that much more special when served on china. The same goes for larger gatherings.

The only guidance I'll give you is to collect what you like. If you love pink, look for pink. If you love roses, seek them out. And don't feel as though every-thing has to match. If you find a slew of random plates that make you happy, over time you'll have a unique composition that you've created based on your choices and memories. And whatever you do, don't only use them for company or "special occasions." These gems were meant to be used and bring you joy every day.

DECORATING WITH NATURE

To me, fall is all about nature's one last hurrah before everything goes to sleep. So I like to take advantage of that bounty before it disappears until summer. Besides cooking with seasonal ingredients, I also like decorating with things that grow outside and bringing the outdoors in as much as possible to mark this time. Here are some of my favorite ways to do that:

- Pumpkins. We're living our dream and finally have a patch of our own, but you can find pumpkins at pretty much any market. They're festive in all their different colors and shapes and refreshingly hardy, meaning your hard work will pay off because these things live pretty much forever. I like to make a big arrangement by the front door, another on the table where we eat all of our meals, and another in the kitchen.

- Apples. Or even better, apples and their branches straight from the orchard. I like to snip them off whole and lay them over the table. I especially like when the fruit is a little pocked and imperfect—it's what real apples look like! Not like their waxy, Botoxed friends from the supermarket.

- Branches, brush, and greenery. I always joke that my mom has the stickiest fingers when she's out for a walk. She's notorious for grabbing a bundle of this or a snipping of that whenever she passes by something that catches her eye. This approach is perfect for the fall when there are evergreen branches, winter berries, pine cones, leaves, and other natural treasures begging to be plucked for an organic centerpiece or mantel arrangement.

WINTER

Brian and I thought we had it all figured out with the fall in New England—it was chilly, but nothing unmanageable. All that bundling up was charming and cozy. We could totally handle the cold weather. But by December, those days were a memory. The bundling up was now for survival. Gone were the Barbour coats, and in their place were triple-layer down jackets with fur-lined hoods, scarves, and mittens. Wool sweaters that we once laughed at in LA department stores as completely ridiculous were now one of multiple layers. Instead of getting caught in those delightful flurries of unexpected autumn snow, we were hurrying out for errands before the winter storms rolled in. I lost count of the number of times I'd run into a store, only to come out to about a foot of snow. The roads would be empty, of course, because everyone with more sense had already gone home. And while the drive home would be peaceful and quiet, all I could think about were the brakes and how I hoped nothing would go amiss.

But the winter has also become one of our favorite seasons. It's the beginning of the holidays, for one—a time that we've begun to fill with a mix of our favorite traditions and new ones we're making with the kids. And all that cold and howling wind also makes us feel that much more warm and safe inside. It prompts us to look for the warmth, comfort, and light. Since those first winter days in our new home, we've realized what a treat it is to have our oven on as much as possible, making the kitchen the snuggest room in the house. It makes me want to stay there all day, tending to long-braised meats, hearty vegetables, soups, and stews, in addition to baked goods with all manner of deep, rich flavors. The shorter days when it's hard to tell whether it's time to eat dinner or go to bed make it seem even more important to prepare things that feel a little special.

RECIPES

SPECIAL PROJECTS

RECIPES

Goat Cheese Shakshuka

2 tablespoons extra-virgin olive oil

1 small white onion, halved and thinly sliced

4 garlic cloves, thinly sliced

½ teaspoon ground fennel seed

2 to 3 tablespoons harissa

1 (28-ounce/793g) can diced or crushed fire-roasted tomatoes

1 (12-ounce/340g) jar roasted red bell peppers, drained and thinly sliced

¾ teaspoon kosher salt

1 tablespoon chopped fresh dill, plus more for serving

½ lemon, seeds removed

4 ounces (112g) goat cheese

6 large eggs

Freshly ground black pepper, for serving

Crusty bread, for serving (optional)

TIPS & TRICKS

Feta cheese can be used in place of goat cheese if you prefer something different.

Harissa can be found at Mediterranean specialty stores or in the international foods section of some grocery stores. If you can't find it, use 3 tablespoons tomato paste and ¼ teaspoon crushed red pepper as a substitute.

Feel free to add herbs of your choice, like parsley or basil.

While my Mexican Egg Bake is a riff on shakshuka, this is even closer to a traditional version of the Tunisian dish. The foundation is a flavorful tomato sauce in which the eggs get gently poached, then I've added goat cheese to bring a little bit of our farm to the mix. While we make our own, if you don't have the time or inclination, a store-bought chèvre will still get you the same great creamy tanginess that plays so nicely with the egg-enriched sauce and tons of fresh herbs. It's an easy, comforting dish that's just as good for breakfast as it is for lunch or dinner.

SERVES 6

Preheat the oven to 375°F.

In a 12- to 14-inch skillet over medium heat, heat the olive oil. Add the onion and cook until soft, about 7 minutes, stirring frequently. Stir in the garlic and fennel seed and cook for 1 to 2 minutes, just until fragrant. Add the harissa and continue stirring until fragrant, 1 to 2 minutes. Stir in the tomatoes, roasted peppers, salt, and dill. Add ¼ cup of water to the tomato can, swish it around, and add it to the skillet. Squeeze in the juice from the lemon half and add the rind as well. Bring the mixture to a simmer, stirring occasionally, and cook until the tomato sauce is slightly reduced, about 10 minutes. Reduce the heat to low and discard the lemon rind.

Crumble half of the goat cheese over the tomato sauce. Using the back of a wooden spoon, make six small wells in the tomato sauce and crack an egg into each well. Crumble the remaining goat cheese over the top.

Transfer the pan to the oven and bake until the egg whites are cooked through and the yolks are done to your liking, about 10 minutes for runny yolks and up to 16 minutes for set yolks. Sprinkle with black pepper and dill before serving. This is best served with crusty bread to soak up the tomato sauce.

Caramelized Garlic *and* Chard Quiche

FOR THE BLACK PEPPER PIE DOUGH

1½ cups (180g) all-purpose flour, plus more for rolling

1 tablespoon minced fresh thyme leaves or 1 teaspoon dried thyme leaves

¾ teaspoon kosher salt

½ teaspoon freshly ground black pepper

½ cup (1 stick/113g) cold unsalted butter, cubed

5 to 7 tablespoons (60 to 90ml) ice water

FOR THE FILLING

2 tablespoons unsalted butter

2 tablespoons extra-virgin olive oil

7 garlic cloves, thinly sliced

1 bunch (450g) rainbow chard, stems cut into ½-inch pieces and leaves roughly chopped (about 5 packed cups leaves and 1 cup stems)

¾ teaspoon kosher salt

½ teaspoon freshly ground black pepper, plus more for serving

4 large eggs

1¼ cups (360ml) heavy whipping cream

1 cup (113g) shredded aged cheddar cheese

Fresh thyme leaves, for garnish

Whenever my mom would visit us in LA, she would bring a big batch of rainbow chard from her garden. I instantly fell in love with its vibrant color and earthy flavor, not to mention the fact that cooking with it reminds me of my mom (aww). It's also the perfect addition to a quiche that goes big on rich flavors, without relying on bacon to get there thanks to plenty of caramelized garlic. A slice of quiche, a simple salad, and a glass of wine? That's called a good day.   SERVES 6 TO 8

MAKE THE BLACK PEPPER PIE DOUGH: In a large bowl, whisk together the flour, thyme, salt, and pepper. Add the butter and toss gently to coat the pieces with flour. Cut in the butter using a pastry blender or squeeze the pieces between your fingers until the biggest ones are the size of almonds and the smallest are about the size of peas. Add half of the water and work it in with a fork. Continue adding the water a tablespoon at a time as needed until the mixture forms a shaggy dough. Gently knead the dough together in the bowl until it clumps together. Shape the dough into a disk and wrap it tightly in plastic wrap. Chill for 1 hour or up to 3 days.

Preheat the oven to 425°F.

On a lightly floured surface, roll the chilled pie dough into a 13-inch circle. Transfer to a 9-inch pie pan. Trim the excess dough to about an inch from the edge of the pan, tuck the excess under, and crimp around the edge as desired. Poke the bottom of the crust all over with a fork and freeze for 15 minutes.

Set a piece of parchment paper inside the pie crust and fill the pan with pie weights or dried beans. Place the pie pan on a rimmed baking sheet and bake for 15 to 18 minutes, until the edges are starting to turn golden brown. Carefully remove the parchment and weights. Return the pan to the oven and bake for 3 to 5 more minutes, until the bottom of the crust looks matte and set. Set the crust aside to cool and reduce the oven temperature to 350°F.

MAKE THE FILLING: In a large skillet over medium heat, heat the butter and olive oil. Add the garlic and cook, stirring often, until light golden brown, about 5 minutes. Remove the garlic from the skillet and set aside. Add the chard stems and ¼ teaspoon of salt and cook, stirring occasionally, until the stems have softened slightly, about 3 minutes. Add the

TIPS & TRICKS

Keep a close eye on the garlic while it's cooking. The name of the game here is to cook it gently, until it's just lightly toasted. Because of its high sugar content, garlic will turn on you quickly and burn, resulting in a bitter taste. Cook it low and slow to tame its spicy heat and tease out the garlic's sweet flavor.

Swiss chard falls in between kale and spinach on the hardiness scale; it doesn't wilt down to nothing like spinach, but it doesn't need to cook as long as kale. Be sure to chop the stems and start cooking them first to help them get a head start on getting tender.

chard leaves, ¼ teaspoon of the salt, and ¼ teaspoon of the pepper and cook, stirring frequently, until the leaves are wilted, 2 to 3 minutes more. Remove the pan from the heat and stir in the caramelized garlic.

In a medium bowl, whisk together the eggs, cream, ½ cup of the cheese, and the remaining ¼ teaspoon each of the salt and pepper. Add ¾ of the chard mixture to the parbaked crust in an even layer and pour the egg mixture over the chard. Scatter the remaining chard mixture over the eggs and sprinkle the remaining ½ cup of the cheese on top.

Bake the quiche until the top is brown and the center is set, 35 to 40 minutes. If the crust is browning too quickly, you can cover the edges of the crust with foil to prevent burning. Let the quiche cool for 10 minutes before serving. Garnish with the thyme and more ground black pepper.

Sun-Dried Tomato *and* Sausage Strata

Normally, I don't need much of an excuse to eat slices upon slices of sourdough bread, but the combination of its signature umami sourness plus savory-salty sausage, olives, tomatoes, and creamy mozzarella is like a breakfast—or brunch or dinner—invitation from heaven. This is a particularly great dish to make if you're making a special-occasion breakfast because you can assemble it in the evening and bake it off in the morning. SERVES 8

Unsalted butter or nonstick cooking spray, for the pan

1 cup (3 ounces/85g) sun-dried tomatoes, julienned

½ cup (120ml) boiling water

1 tablespoon extra-virgin olive oil

1 pound (450g) ground breakfast sausage

½ large sweet onion, diced

6 large eggs

2 cups (480ml) whole milk

½ cup (120ml) heavy whipping cream or half-and-half

2 teaspoons kosher salt

1 teaspoon Italian seasoning

½ teaspoon freshly ground black pepper

1 (1-pound/450g) loaf crusty sourdough bread, cut into 1-inch cubes

1 (6-ounce/170g) jar pitted green olives, drained and cut in half

1 pound (450g) fresh mozzarella, drained and cut into ½-inch chunks, or use mozzarella pearls

Fresh basil, thinly sliced, for serving

Preheat the oven to 350°F. Butter a 13x9-inch or 3-quart baking dish or spray with nonstick cooking spray and set aside.

In a medium bowl, cover the sun-dried tomatoes with the boiling water and set aside to soften.

Heat the olive oil in a large skillet over medium-high heat. Add the sausage and cook, breaking up the sausage with the back of a spoon, until it is just browned, about 5 minutes. Add the onion and continue cooking for 5 minutes, stirring occasionally. Remove the pan from the heat. If the sausage is especially greasy, drain off the fat.

In a large mixing bowl, whisk together the eggs, milk, cream, salt, Italian seasoning, and pepper. Add the bread cubes and toss to coat the bread completely. Let stand for 5 minutes, tossing occasionally to help the bread absorb the liquid evenly.

Drain the sun-dried tomatoes thoroughly and add them to the bread mixture. Add the olives, cooked sausage and onion, and mozzarella. Pour the mixture into the prepared baking dish, gently pressing down with your hands to evenly distribute the mixture. Cover the dish loosely with foil and bake for 35 minutes. Remove the foil and continue baking until the top is golden brown and the center is set, about 30 more minutes. Let cool for 15 minutes and top with the fresh basil before serving. Refrigerate any leftovers for up to 3 days.

TIPS & TRICKS

You can also use a 7-ounce (205ml) jar of oil-packed sun-dried tomatoes. Just drain the tomatoes well and skip soaking them in boiling water. The drained oil is great for frying eggs or using in salad dressings!

This strata is best when enjoyed freshly baked, but to prep ahead, the casserole can be assembled and chilled for several hours or overnight. Just let it sit at room temperature for 30 minutes before baking.

Orange Pecan Cinnamon Rolls

FOR THE DOUGH

4 cups (480g) all-purpose flour, plus more for dusting

⅔ cup (133g) granulated sugar

2¼ teaspoons (¼-ounce envelope/7g) active dry yeast

1 cup (240ml) whole milk

6 tablespoons (85g) unsalted butter

1 tablespoon vanilla extract

1 teaspoon kosher salt

1 large egg, room temperature

1 teaspoon vegetable oil, for the bowl

FOR THE FILLING

5 tablespoons granulated sugar

Grated zest of ½ orange (about 1 teaspoon)

4 tablespoons firmly packed light brown sugar

1 tablespoon ground cinnamon

¼ cup plus 2 tablespoons (85g) unsalted butter, melted, plus more for the pan

½ cup (60g) pecans, finely chopped

FOR THE GLAZE

4 ounces (114g) cream cheese, room temperature

2 tablespoons unsalted butter, room temperature

1 pinch kosher salt

1½ cups (180g) powdered sugar

Zest of ½ orange

1 tablespoon fresh orange juice

1 teaspoon vanilla extract

Brian is obsessed with cinnamon rolls. So when we moved to Connecticut, we went on a hunt for the very best ones. Long story short, we had so many dry, disappointing rolls that I had to develop my own. The key is making a very, very enriched dough (meaning added fat; in this case butter), which does require a longer rise time, but it's absolutely worth it and can be done overnight. One of my favorite things to do is stay up a little late putting together a batch, then baking them off in the morning, which lends itself to the Ultimate Amazing Dad moment the next day. **MAKES 12 ROLLS**

MAKE THE DOUGH: In the bowl of a stand mixer fitted with the dough hook attachment, combine 3¾ cups (450g) of the flour, plus the sugar and yeast.

In a glass measuring cup, combine the milk and butter. Microwave on high for about 2 minutes, until the butter is mostly melted and the milk is warm to the touch (110°F to 120°F). Add the vanilla and salt and stir until the butter is fully melted. Pour the milk mixture into the flour mixture and add the egg.

Mix on low speed until the dough is smooth and tacky, about 15 minutes, gradually adding the remaining ¼ cup (30g) of flour a tablespoon at a time if the dough still sticks to your finger when touched. Turn out the dough onto a lightly floured surface and shape it into a ball. Place the dough in a lightly oiled bowl, turning to coat it in oil. Cover and let rise in a warm place until doubled in size, about 1 hour.

MAKE THE FILLING: In a small bowl, combine the granulated sugar and orange zest. Rub the mixture with your fingers until the sugar is fragrant and is pale orange in color. Stir in the brown sugar and cinnamon. Add the melted butter and stir until smooth.

Butter or spray a 9x13-inch baking dish with nonstick baking spray.

Punch down the risen dough and turn it out onto a lightly floured surface. Roll the dough into a 12x18-inch rectangle. Spread the sugar mixture onto the dough, leaving a 1-inch border on one short side. Scatter the pecans evenly over the filling. Starting at the short end opposite the

continued

For perfectly round and cleanly cut rolls, use unwaxed, unflavored dental floss! Simply slip the floss under the cinnamon roll log, cross the ends over the top of the roll, and pull in opposite directions, slicing through the log.

The unbaked rolls can be chilled overnight for ready-to-bake treats the next morning. Simply complete through step 6, skipping the second rise. Tightly wrap the pan in plastic wrap and chill overnight or up to 12 hours. Preheat the oven and let the rolls stand at room temperature for 30 minutes before baking. Bake as directed!

border, tightly roll up the dough and pinch the seam to seal. Cut the dough into twelve rolls (see Tips & Tricks) and place in the prepared baking dish, cut side down. Cover and let rise in a warm place until noticeably puffed, about 45 minutes.

Preheat the oven to 350°F.

Bake the rolls for 25 to 30 minutes, until the tops are golden brown. Let cool for 10 minutes.

MAKE THE GLAZE: In a medium bowl, add the cream cheese, butter, and salt. Beat with an electric mixer on medium speed until smooth. Add the powdered sugar, zest, orange juice, and vanilla and beat on low speed until combined. Increase the mixer speed to high and beat until smooth and fluffy, about 2 minutes. Spread the glaze over the hot rolls and serve warm. Any leftovers can be covered and stored at room temperature for 2 days.

Citrus Confetti Marmalade

2 pounds (900g) citrus rinds
(see Tips & Tricks), roughly chopped
or quartered

8 cups (1,920ml) water or fresh citrus juice

6¾ cups (1,350g) granulated sugar

Additional flavorings or spices of your
choice (see Tips & Tricks)

¼ teaspoon kosher salt

TIPS & TRICKS

Citrus marmalade is delicious in its simplest form with only rinds, sugar, and water, but you can add spices or flavorings for a twist. My favorite combinations are lemons with ½ teaspoon ground cardamom, oranges with 1 vanilla bean split, and grapefruits with 4 dried star anise pods.

Whenever a recipe calls for citrus juice, save the rinds by freezing them in a zip-top bag. Once the bag is full or you have 2 pounds' worth of rinds, make marmalade! Just thaw the rinds before chopping them.

If you want to start with fresh fruit, purchase 4½ to 5 pounds of fresh citrus. Juice the citrus, then process the rinds according to the recipe.

Any variety of orange works for this recipe, as well as grapefruit, lemons, or Meyer lemons. Grapefruit has the most bitter rind and is perfect for true marmalade lovers. Lime rinds become hard when cooked in sugar syrup, so I recommend avoiding them, or only using the juice.

In my opinion, it doesn't get better than the bittersweet combination of a citrus marmalade. That's why in the winter, when the best fresh fruit is going to be citrus, I'm always making batches to enjoy on toast or scones. Luckily, that doesn't entail much more than taking whatever oranges, grapefruits, or lemons I have on hand, tossing them into the food processor—rinds and all—and pulsing it up. I balance the natural bitterness of the rinds with just enough sweetness for the spread to not be overbearing, and perhaps just sweet enough to convince Brian, who is Scottish by descent, that this quintessentially Scottish invention is just as delicious as his favorite strawberry jam.

MAKES ABOUT 9 CUPS OR 10 (8-OUNCE) JARS

Working in batches, add a few handfuls of the citrus rinds to the bowl of a food processor and pulse until finely chopped. Transfer the processed citrus rinds to a large Dutch oven or heavy-bottomed pot and add the water or citrus juice.

Set the pot over medium-high heat and bring to a boil, about 20 minutes, stirring occasionally. Continue boiling for 10 minutes, stirring occasionally. Stir in the sugar, any flavorings, if using, and the salt. Place a candy thermometer in the pot, if you have one. Reduce the heat to medium.

Continue boiling the mixture, stirring frequently, until it reaches 215°F to 220°F, about 45 minutes. At this point, the liquid should be thick and syrupy and the pieces of rind should appear translucent.

From here, the hot marmalade can be transferred to jars and kept refrigerated for up to 3 months, or it can be placed in 10 sterilized 8-ounce canning jars and processed in a water bath for 12 minutes (see Pickling, page 308, for sterilizing and canning instructions).

Browned Butter *and* Sage Cornbread

2 cups (270g) stone-ground or medium-grind cornmeal

1 cup (120g) all-purpose flour

2½ teaspoons baking powder

2½ teaspoons kosher salt

2 cups (480ml) whole cultured buttermilk

2 large eggs

¼ cup (55g) firmly packed light brown sugar

¼ cup (57g) unsalted butter

2 fresh sage sprigs

1 tablespoon finely chopped sage leaves

1 tablespoon vegetable oil

TIPS & TRICKS

Finely ground cornmeal will also work in this recipe. The stone-ground or medium-grind variety is a bit coarser, so it adds texture to the baked loaf. Just avoid a cornbread mix and self-rising cornmeal, as they have added leaveners, as well as corn flour (masa harina), as it is too fine and will bake a dense, dry loaf.

White, yellow, blue, or the new varieties like red or "unicorn" cornmeals can all be used.

If you don't love sage or want to mix up the flavor, fresh rosemary is a nice substitute.

It's no accident that I call for using fried sage in more than one recipe in this book. There's an almost mystical transformation that happens when this pungent herb crisps up in oil, becoming deeply flavorful and savory. To me, that's the perfect fleck of flavor to lace throughout this cornbread. Unlike some of the sweet cornbread "cake" recipes floating around out there, this one stays true to its traditional southern roots. The trick is to get a cast iron skillet screaming hot, add some oil, then add the batter. The result is a savory bread with a crispy fried bottom infused with the nutty flavor of browned butter. And most important: it's *not* dry.   MAKES 1 (10-INCH) LOAF

Preheat the oven to 425°F. Line a small plate with a paper towel and set aside.

In a large bowl, whisk together the cornmeal, flour, baking powder, and salt. In a separate bowl, whisk together the buttermilk, eggs, and brown sugar. Add the buttermilk mixture to the cornmeal mixture and stir gently until smooth. Set aside.

In a 10-inch cast iron skillet over medium-high heat, add the butter and swirl the pan occasionally until the butter is foamy and just starts to smell nutty, about 5 minutes. Add the sage sprigs and fry until they turn slightly translucent and crisp, about 30 seconds. Transfer the sprigs to the paper towel–lined plate to drain. Add the chopped sage to the skillet and fry, stirring constantly, until crisp, about 15 seconds. Immediately add the browned butter and sage to the batter and whisk quickly to combine.

Wipe the skillet clean and return to medium heat. Add the oil, swirl it around a few times and heat until shimmering, and pour the batter into the hot skillet. (The batter should sizzle.) Transfer the skillet to the oven and bake for 20 to 25 minutes, until a wooden pick inserted in the center comes out clean. Let the cornbread cool in the skillet for 5 minutes, then transfer to a wire rack for at least 10 minutes before serving. Top with the fried sage. Store any leftovers in an airtight container. The cornbread is best if consumed within a day or two.

White Cheddar *and* Rosemary Dinner Rolls

1 cup (240ml) warm whole milk, 110ºF to 120ºF

2¼ teaspoons (¼-ounce envelope/7g) active dry yeast

¼ cup plus ¼ teaspoon (54g) granulated sugar

½ cup (1 stick/113g) unsalted butter, melted, plus more for brushing

2 large eggs, room temperature

4¾ cups (570g) bread flour, plus more for dusting

1 teaspoon kosher salt

2 cups (227g) shredded sharp white cheddar cheese

1 tablespoon minced fresh rosemary, plus more for garnish

½ teaspoon vegetable oil

1 large egg, beaten

Flaky sea salt, for garnish

TIPS & TRICKS

Swap out the cheese or herb to your liking. Any shredded cheese, such as Gouda, Pepper Jack, or low-moisture mozzarella will work in these rolls. You can also leave out the cheese and herbs for very delicious, classic yeast rolls.

While I love the idea of spending all day creating the perfect loaf of bread to be the warm, doughy accompaniment to a meal, sometimes I want things to come together a little bit faster. And when I do, these pan-made rolls are just the thing. With salty cheese and savory herbs, they have the unique ability to elevate even the most thrown-together meals. The secret to taking these from good to great is generously brushing them with melted butter at the end of baking. They really do wake up and say, "Hello."

MAKES 12 ROLLS

In the bowl of a stand mixer, stir together the warm milk, yeast, and ¼ teaspoon of the sugar. Let the mixture stand until it's very foamy, about 5 minutes.

Add the melted butter, eggs, and the remaining ¼ cup sugar. Attach the paddle to the mixer and mix on low speed until mostly combined. Add 2 cups of the flour and the salt. Continue mixing on low speed until the mixture is fully combined and smooth, about 1 minute.

Switch to the dough hook attachment and add the remaining 2¾ cups of flour, ¼ cup at a time, kneading until a smooth dough ball forms and pulls away from the sides of the bowl, about 12 minutes. (The dough may still feel slightly sticky. Add a tablespoon of flour as needed if the dough is too sticky and isn't pulling away from the bowl.) Add the cheese and rosemary and mix just until well combined, about 1 minute.

Coat a large bowl with the oil and transfer the dough to the bowl, turning to coat. Shape the dough into a ball, cover, and let rise in a warm spot until doubled in size, about 45 minutes.

Butter a 9x13-inch baking pan and set aside.

Turn the dough out onto a lightly floured surface. Cut into twelve equal pieces. Shape each piece into a ball and place in the prepared baking pan. Cover and let rise until doubled in size, about 30 to 45 minutes.

Preheat the oven to 350ºF.

Brush the tops of the rolls with the beaten egg and bake for 25 minutes, until the tops are golden brown. Immediately brush the warm rolls with melted butter. Sprinkle with the flaky salt and rosemary. Let the rolls cool for 10 minutes before removing or serving.

Crab Cake Latkes *with* Garlic-Caper Aioli

Brian and I share an obsession with crab cakes, which means we've also shared no shortage of heartbreak. Because while crab cakes have potential for greatness, they can often be too dense, too under-seasoned, or too skimpy on big lumps of crab meat. To make sure that we're forever protected from that disappointment, and to have a dish in my rotation that's just as lovely for company as it is for nights in, I've created the perfect recipe for crispy, creamy-but-light crab cakes. With their shredded potato and onion, they're sort of a latke–crab cake mash-up, and I serve them with a bright, briny aioli that reminds us that sunshine and warmth are only a few more months away.

MAKES ABOUT 24 LATKES

FOR THE GARLIC-CAPER AIOLI

2 large egg yolks

2 garlic cloves, grated

1 tablespoon plus 1 teaspoon caper brine

Zest and juice of ½ lemon

½ cup (120ml) extra-virgin olive oil

½ cup (120ml) grapeseed or sunflower oil

2 tablespoons brined capers, drained

1 tablespoon fresh parsley leaves, minced

FOR THE CRAB CAKE LATKES

1 large russet potato (about ¾ pound/338g), scrubbed and peeled

3 yellow or Yukon gold potatoes (about 1 pound/450g), scrubbed and peeled

½ sweet onion, minced

2 large eggs

2 tablespoons Dijon mustard

1 tablespoon Worcestershire sauce

Zest and juice of ½ lemon

¾ teaspoon kosher salt

½ teaspoon freshly ground black pepper

1 cup (108g) panko bread crumbs

2 tablespoons all-purpose flour

2 tablespoons fresh parsley, chopped, plus more for serving

1 pound (450g) lump crab meat, drained and picked free of any shells

Grapeseed or sunflower oil, for frying

Lemon wedges, for serving

MAKE THE GARLIC-CAPER AIOLI: In a large mixing bowl, whisk the egg yolks, garlic, caper brine, and lemon zest and juice until smooth. In a liquid measuring cup, combine the olive and grapeseed oils. While whisking, very slowly stream the oils into the egg yolk mixture, continuing to whisk until thickened and very creamy, about 5 minutes. Stir in the capers and parsley. Cover and chill until ready to serve or up to 5 days.

MAKE THE CRAB CAKE LATKES: In a food processor with the grater attachment, shred the potatoes. (You can also use a box grater for this.) Transfer the potatoes to a large piece of cheesecloth or a thin kitchen towel and add the onions. Gather the cloth and twist, squeezing out as much liquid as possible.

In a large bowl, add the eggs, mustard, Worcestershire, lemon zest and juice, salt, pepper, and 2 tablespoons of the Garlic-Caper Aioli and whisk until smooth. Add the squeezed potato-onion mixture, bread crumbs, flour, and parsley and stir to combine. Add the crab meat and gently toss with your hands to combine.

Set a wire rack inside a rimmed baking sheet and place it near the stove.

In a large cast iron skillet over medium-high heat, heat about ¼ inch of oil until shimmering. Use a ¼-cup measure or a spring-loaded ice cream scoop to scoop the crab cake mixture into the hot oil, spacing the crab cakes about 1 inch apart. Work in batches to avoid crowding the pan. Gently flatten each portion with a spatula and fry until golden brown, 2 to 4 minutes per side. Transfer the finished cakes to the wire rack to drain. Serve the latkes with the Garlic-Caper aioli, lemon wedges, and fresh parsley.

TIPS & TRICKS

While the aioli can be made several days in advance, the latke mixture is best assembled when ready to cook, as the potatoes can oxidize, turning the mixture gray.

For an even easier aioli, dress up 1 cup of mayo with the garlic, capers and brine, lemon zest, and parsley.

Smoked Almond *and* Sharp Cheddar Wafers

Winter always calls to mind cocktail parties with lots of nibbly bits. These cheesy wafers are one of those perfect crunchy, salty accompaniments that people are always asking to get the recipe for. The smoked almonds add just a hint of savory complexity that belies how easy it is to make these. I also love making cheddar wafer gift bags—though they should be paired with a warning: You Will Inhale This Entire Package.

MAKES ABOUT 50 CRACKERS

¾ cup (90g) smoked almonds

1¼ cups (150g) all-purpose flour, plus more for dusting

8 ounces (227g) sharp cheddar cheese, shredded

2 teaspoons cornstarch

¼ teaspoon kosher salt

¼ teaspoon cayenne pepper

½ cup (1 stick/113g) cold unsalted butter, cubed

2 tablespoons whole milk

¼ cup (32g) poppy seeds (optional)

TIPS & TRICKS

Use your favorite brand of sharp yellow or white cheddar. Or you can add even more flavor by using a smoked cheddar. A mild cheddar could be substituted if needed, but sharp cheddar will give a better cheesy flavor once baked.

Try using other savory-flavored almonds like wasabi or salt-and-vinegar for a twist on these cheesy crackers.

In a food processor, add the almonds and pulse until finely chopped. Add the flour, cheese, cornstarch, salt, and pepper and process until the mixture is crumbly and well combined. Add the cold butter and process until the mixture resembles large bread crumbs. With the processor running, slowly add the milk. Continue mixing until a dough ball starts to form.

Turn the dough out onto a lightly floured surface and knead a few times to form a ball. Divide the dough in half and shape each piece into a 2-inch round log.

Place the poppy seeds, if using, in an even layer on a rimmed baking sheet or a dinner plate. Roll the outside of the dough logs in the poppy seeds. Tightly wrap each log in plastic wrap and chill for at least 2 hours or overnight.

Preheat the oven to 350°F. Line a baking sheet with parchment paper and set aside.

Slice one of the dough logs into ⅛-inch rounds and place them on the baking sheet 1 inch apart. Pierce the center of each round with a fork. Bake for 14 to 17 minutes, until golden brown on the bottom. Let the wafers cool for a couple of minutes on the baking sheet, then transfer to a wire rack to cool completely.

Repeat the process with the remaining dough log. The wafers can be stored in an airtight container for up to 4 days.

Garlicky White Beans *and* Rainbow Chard

1 pound (450g) dried white beans, rinsed and sorted

Warm water, for soaking

2 whole garlic heads

2 tablespoons extra-virgin olive oil, plus more for serving

Pinch of crushed red pepper (optional)

6 cups (1,420ml) unsalted or low-sodium vegetable or chicken broth, plus more if needed

1 sprig fresh sage

1 sprig fresh rosemary

1 bay leaf

Kosher salt

1 large bunch Swiss or rainbow chard, leaves and stems chopped separately and reserved

2 tablespoons unsalted butter

4 (1-inch-thick) slices Browned Butter and Sage Cornbread (page 109)

Freshly grated Parmesan cheese, for serving

TIPS & TRICKS

If you don't have time to soak the beans, you can start cooking them from dry, but the cook time will likely be two to three times longer and require a cup or two more broth. You can also use canned beans that you've drained and rinsed. Start by browning the garlic in the pot, and add the drained beans when directed and reduce the broth to 2 cups. Simmer for 15 minutes, then continue as directed.

As I've mentioned earlier, I have an emotional connection with rainbow chard because it was what my mom would always bring us from her garden when we were living in LA. So even though she's not tossing a few bunches into her carry-on to get to Connecticut (although, Mom, if you're reading this—it's not a bad idea . . .), I can still capture those memories of her and the panoply of color that comes with these gorgeous greens every time I work chard into a recipe. In this case, it's a pot of creamy garlic-infused beans served with crusty bread or, my favorite, Browned Butter and Sage Cornbread (page 109). It's like the best parts of a soup, without the soup.   SERVES 6 TO 8

In a large bowl, cover the beans with warm water by 3 inches and soak for at least 6 hours, ideally overnight. Drain and set aside.

Cut off about 1 inch from the top of each garlic head to expose the cloves and remove any loose peel. Heat the olive oil in a large Dutch oven over medium heat. Add the garlic heads cut side down and cook without disturbing until browned, about 3 minutes. Add the red pepper, if using, and let it fry for about 1 minute. Add the soaked beans, broth, sage, rosemary, and bay leaf and bring to a simmer. Partially cover and cook until the beans are almost tender, 45 to 55 minutes, adjusting the heat as needed to keep the beans at a low simmer. Add additional broth if needed to keep the beans just barely covered.

Remove the garlic heads, sage, rosemary, and bay leaf. Add salt to taste. Stir in the chard stems and continue cooking, partially covered, for 10 minutes, stirring occasionally. Squeeze the garlic heads to remove the cloves and gently mash the cloves. Stir in the mashed garlic and chard leaves and cook for another 5 minutes. Taste again and add additional salt, if needed. Cover the pot and remove from the heat.

Melt the butter in a large skillet over medium heat, swirling to coat the pan. Add the cornbread slices and cook until browned and toasted, about 3 minutes per side.

Place a slice of the toasted cornbread in the bottom of a shallow bowl. Ladle the brothy white beans and chard over the toast and serve with a generous grating of Parmesan and lashings of olive oil.

Mini Seafood Gratins *with* Garlic Bread Crumbs

3 thick slices artisan sourdough bread

5 tablespoons (70g) unsalted butter

2 tablespoons minced garlic (from about 6 cloves)

1½ teaspoons kosher salt

3 shallots, peeled and minced

3 tablespoons plus 2 teaspoons all-purpose flour

1¼ cups (300ml) heavy whipping cream

½ cup (120ml) dry vermouth

1 cup (100g) shredded Gruyère cheese

2 tablespoons minced fresh tarragon, plus more for garnish

Zest of 1 lemon, plus more for garnish

1 teaspoon freshly ground black pepper, plus more for garnish

1 pound (450g) small (51 to 60 count) shrimp, peeled and deveined

1 pound (450g) bay scallops

TIPS & TRICKS

Don't be tempted to take a shortcut with store-bought bread crumbs—fresh is best here.

When shopping for seafood, don't be discouraged if you can't find bay scallops. Regular scallops will work in the recipe, but I would recommend cutting the scallops into quarters before adding them to the sauce to ensure a similar bake time and even cooking.

Normally when you think of seafood you think of light, bright dishes that are perfectly suited for warm weather, like ceviche or mussels in white wine. Luckily, those meals have delicious cold-weather counterparts, particularly dishes like this gratin, which embraces the warm, creamy, and cheesy. It still delivers on perfectly cooked seafood—because nothing's worse than rubbery bits—but hits those decadent notes that winter begs for. And to ensure that it does just that, I call for a crust of my signature bread crumbs, which get tossed in browned butter. I encourage you to make extra and keep them on hand for the next time you make mac 'n' cheese or scrambled eggs.   SERVES 6

Preheat the oven to 375°F. Place six (8-ounce) oven-safe ramekins or gratin dishes on a rimmed baking sheet and set aside.

Cut any hard crust off the sourdough slices. Finely chop the bread with a chef's knife or pulse in a food processor until coarsely ground. Place the bread crumbs in a large bowl and set aside.

In a large skillet, melt 3 tablespoons of the butter over medium-high heat until foaming and starting to brown. Add 1 tablespoon of the minced garlic and cook, stirring constantly, until very fragrant, about 1 minute. Add the garlic to the bread crumbs, plus ½ teaspoon of the salt, and toss to combine.

In the same skillet over medium heat, melt the remaining 2 tablespoons of butter. Add the shallot and cook, stirring frequently, until softened and beginning to brown, 3 to 5 minutes. Stir in the remaining tablespoon of garlic and cook for 1 minute more. Add the flour and cook, stirring constantly, for 1 minute. Slowly stir in the cream and vermouth, bring to a simmer, and cook for another minute.

Stir in the cheese a few tablespoons at a time until incorporated. Remove the pan from the heat and stir in the tarragon, lemon zest, pepper, and the remaining teaspoon of salt. Fold in the shrimp and scallops and turn to coat thoroughly. Divide the seafood mixture among the ramekins and top with the bread crumbs.

Bake the gratins until the seafood is just cooked through, 15 to 20 minutes. If the bread crumbs are not browned, broil for 1 to 2 minutes. Let cool slightly before serving and garnish with additional tarragon, lemon zest, and pepper, if desired.

Wild Mushroom Bolognese *with* Hand-Cut Pappardelle

Bolognese, or Italian meat sauce, is a fixture on the hearty winter dish list, but it can also suffer from lasagna syndrome—one-note and heavy. You need something to add a little depth, which is why I make this version with earthy, meaty portobellos.

You could certainly use a dried pasta off the shelf here, but a rustic, handmade version is such a luxury, and it doesn't take much more time. You could use it as an excuse to dust off your KitchenAid pasta roller attachment, if you have one, but doing this by hand is also a very viable—and pleasurable—option.

SERVES 6 TO 8

FOR THE HOMEMADE PAPPARDELLE

1 cup (120g) all-purpose flour, plus more for dusting

1 cup (167g) semolina flour (can substitute with all-purpose; see Tips & Tricks)

½ teaspoon kosher salt, plus more for cooking the pasta

3 large eggs

1 tablespoon extra-virgin olive oil

FOR THE MUSHROOM BOLOGNESE

4 slices thick-cut bacon, diced (optional)

2 tablespoons extra-virgin olive oil, plus more if needed

2 cups (110g) diced yellow onion

2 cups (250g) peeled and diced carrot

2 teaspoons kosher salt

1½ teaspoons freshly ground black pepper

12 ounces (338g) portobello mushrooms, gills removed and diced (see Tips & Tricks)

8 ounces (225g) cremini or oyster mushrooms, diced

2 tablespoons minced fresh garlic (from about 6 cloves)

2 (4.5-ounce/128g) cans tomato paste

1 cup (240ml) dry red wine, such as Chianti

1 cup (240ml) chicken or vegetable broth

⅓ cup (80ml) heavy cream

Grated Parmesan cheese, for serving

Chopped fresh parsley, for serving

MAKE THE HOMEMADE PAPPARDELLE: In a medium bowl, whisk together the all-purpose flour, semolina flour, and salt. Make a deep well in the center. Crack the eggs and add the olive oil into the well. Using a fork, start in the center and beat just the eggs and olive oil together. Slowly work your way to the edges of the well and begin incorporating the flour. Once most of the flour is incorporated and becomes too heavy to work with the fork, begin kneading by hand until a cohesive dough forms.

Transfer the dough to a lightly floured counter. Continue kneading by hand, adding more flour as needed to keep it from sticking to you or the counter, until the dough is smooth and elastic, 5 to 10 minutes. (The dough should bounce back when poked with your finger.) Wrap the dough tightly with plastic wrap and let stand at room temperature for at least 30 minutes or up to 4 hours.

MAKE THE MUSHROOM BOLOGNESE: In a large Dutch oven over medium heat, add the bacon, if using, and olive oil and cook, stirring occasionally, until the bacon is browned and crisp. Add the onions, carrots, 1 teaspoon of the salt, and ½ teaspoon of the pepper and cook, stirring occasionally, until the vegetables have softened, 8 to 10 minutes. (You may add another tablespoon or two of oil if not using the bacon.)

Add the mushrooms, garlic, 1 teaspoon of the salt, and 1 teaspoon of the pepper. Cook, stirring often, until the mushrooms release their liquid and start to brown, about 5 minutes. Add the tomato paste and stir to coat the mushrooms. Cook, stirring constantly, until the tomato paste is fragrant

continued

Mushroom Matters: While this recipe calls for portobello and cremini mushrooms, you can use any mix of mushrooms of equal weight, such as oyster, shiitake, or even plain old white button mushrooms. I prefer buying whole mushrooms over sliced, because they are typically fresher. Before dicing, wipe any debris from the whole mushrooms using damp paper towels; remove and discard any large woody stems.

Removing the gills from the portobello mushrooms keeps the sauce brighter in color but can be skipped to save time, if desired. To remove the gills, flip the mushrooms stem side up and cut off the stem. Use a spoon to scrape the dark gills off the mushroom and discard.

Pasta Flour Power: I've used a mix of all-purpose flour and semolina flour in this recipe, because semolina flour has a high gluten content that gives the finished pasta a lovely texture and sturdiness. You can find it in some grocery stores or online. If all you can find is all-purpose, don't worry—your pasta will taste just fine. If using store-bought pasta for this recipe, I would cook about 1½ pounds of dried pasta, such as linguini, pappardelle, or even bucatini.

The homemade pappardelle can be made well in advance and frozen for a homemade pasta dinner in a fraction of the time. Roll and cut the pasta dough as directed in steps 6 through 8. Arrange the cut pasta into six small mounds on a sheet tray and freeze until hard. Transfer the frozen pasta to resealable freezer-safe bags and freeze up to 2 months.

and starts to caramelize, about 1 minute. Add the wine and broth, scraping to release any browned bits from the bottom of the pan.

Bring the mixture to a simmer and reduce the heat to low. Cook uncovered, stirring occasionally, until thickened and reduced, about 1 hour.

Bring a large pot of well-salted water to a boil.

Unwrap the dough and cut it into 4 equal portions. Work with one piece of dough at a time and keep the remaining dough covered. Slightly flatten the dough piece into an oval shape about ¼- to ½-inch thick. Using the pasta attachment for a stand mixer or a hand-cranked pasta roller, roll the dough through the thickest setting twice, lightly flouring the dough between rolls as needed. Bring the long ends of the dough together to fold in half. Lightly flour the outside of the folded dough and roll through at the thickest setting one more time.

Adjust the pasta roller to the second-thickest setting. Repeat the rolling, flouring, and folding process, adjusting the pasta roller one setting at a time, until the dough is thin enough to see your hand through.

Place this long pasta sheet (it will be 2 to 3 feet long) on a lightly floured surface. Lightly dust the pasta sheet with flour, bring the long ends together to fold in half, then fold in half again two or three more times. Cut the dough into ribbons ¼- to ½-inch wide. Transfer the pasta ribbons to a baking sheet and toss with flour to prevent sticking. Repeat with the remaining dough pieces.

Stir the pasta into the boiling salt water and cook until just tender, 4 to 6 minutes.

Just before the pasta is done, stir the cream into the Mushroom Bolognese. Use tongs or a slotted spoon to add the cooked pasta directly to the Bolognese. Gently stir the pasta into the sauce to coat. If needed, add ¼ cup pasta water to loosen the sauce. Serve with the Parmesan and parsley.

Cacio e Pepe *with* Cavatelli Pasta

1 tablespoon whole black peppercorns

½ lemon

3 tablespoons kosher salt

1 pound (450g) dried cavatelli (see Tips & Tricks)

2 tablespoons unsalted butter

1 tablespoon extra-virgin olive oil

2 ounces (57g) cream cheese, cubed

¼ cup (60ml) heavy whipping cream

1¾ cups (140g) grated Parmesan cheese, for serving

½ teaspoon freshly ground black pepper, plus more for serving

Chopped fresh herbs, such as basil or thyme, for serving

Even though there's not much that needs to go into making a great Cacio e Pepe, a simple, quintessentially Italian dish of creamy, black pepper–flecked pasta, there are a few ways to do it. My favorite is to make a black pepper "broth" by infusing the pepper into the water first before adding the other ingredients. The result is a deeply flavored sauce with gentle pepper flavor, rather than the more brash spice you'd get if you added all the pepper at the end. SERVES 6 TO 8

Place the peppercorns in a square of cheesecloth and tie with cooking twine, or seal in a tea ball infuser.

Fill a large pot with 6 quarts of water and add the peppercorn sachet. Juice the lemon into the water, catching any seeds, then add the rind. Bring to a boil over high heat and cook, partially covered, for 20 minutes. Add the salt, stir briefly to dissolve, and add the pasta. Cook, stirring occasionally, until the pasta is nearly tender, about 10 minutes or 2 minutes less than the package instructions. Use a heatproof measuring cup or glass to reserve 1 cup of pasta water. Drain the pasta and discard the peppercorn sachet and lemon rind.

In the same pot over medium heat, add the butter and olive oil and heat until the butter is melted and foamy. Add the cream cheese, cream, and reserved pasta water and whisk until fully combined. Add the pasta, Parmesan, and ground black pepper, and continue stirring until the sauce is thickened and very creamy, about 3 minutes. Serve immediately topped with additional Parmesan, black pepper, and chopped herbs.

TIPS & TRICKS

In general, whenever I cook pasta I reserve a cup of the cooking water. This starch-rich broth has the ability to make pasta dishes even creamier, loosen up sauces, and help everything cling to the pasta.

Feel free to use any shape of small pasta. I chose cavatelli because it holds the cheese sauce well.

Avgolemono
(Greek Chicken Soup)

FOR THE CHICKEN BROTH

1 (3- to 5-pound/1.3 to 2.2kg) whole chicken

1 white onion, peeled and quartered

3 carrots, peeled and chopped

2 celery stalks, chopped

8 garlic cloves, peeled and smashed

10 whole black peppercorns

A few sprigs of fresh oregano

2 teaspoons kosher salt

1 bay leaf

FOR THE SOUP

1 cup (180g) long grain white rice

4 large eggs

⅔ cup (160ml) lemon juice (from about 4 large lemons)

¾ teaspoon kosher salt

¾ teaspoon freshly ground black pepper, plus more for serving

Thin lemon slices, for serving

Fresh oregano leaves, for serving

TIPS & TRICKS

Whipped egg whites might seem like an unorthodox addition to chicken soup, but they create a luxuriously creamy broth. The eggs will foam and puff as they are stirred into the hot broth—don't worry, that's normal and it will subside as they cook.

The broth for this soup can be made and used anywhere broth is called for in this book. To make a batch of broth to freeze, cook as directed in steps 1 and 2. Save the chopped meat for chicken salad or meals throughout the week. To deepen the broth's flavor, add the chicken bones back to the strained broth, cover the pot, and simmer covered on low for another hour. Strain again and discard the bones. The broth can then be transferred to freezer containers and frozen for up to 6 months.

Thanks to my dad's Greek heritage, my mom learned how to make a number of traditional Greek dishes. This one was what was offered whenever my brother and I got sick. And let me tell you, it blows regular chicken soup out of the water. Thickened with egg, this soup somehow manages to be both rich and light, made that much more so with traditionally Mediterranean herbs like oregano and plenty of lemon, which adds a much-needed acidic lift to the broth, juicy pieces of chicken, and rice.

SERVES 8 TO 10

MAKE THE CHICKEN BROTH: In a large stockpot, add the chicken, onion, carrots, celery, garlic, peppercorns, oregano sprigs, salt, and bay leaf. Cover with 4 quarts of water and set the pot over medium-high heat. Bring to a boil and reduce the heat to medium-low. Simmer for 45 minutes, or until the chicken is cooked through, skimming the top of the broth occasionally to remove any foam.

Set a large fine mesh sieve or a colander lined with cheesecloth over a large bowl. Use tongs to transfer the chicken to a rimmed sheet pan to cool. Strain the broth through the sieve and discard the vegetables and herbs. Return the broth back to the pot.

When the chicken is cool enough to handle, separate the meat from the bones. Cut the meat into small pieces and discard the skin and bones.

MAKE THE SOUP: Return the stockpot of broth to medium heat and bring to a simmer. Stir in the rice and cook for 20 minutes or until tender, stirring occasionally. Add the chicken.

Separate the eggs over a large bowl to catch the whites and add the yolks to a separate bowl. With an electric hand mixer on medium speed, beat the egg whites until soft peaks form, about 4 minutes. Add the egg yolks and beat just until combined.

Reduce the heat to low. Stirring constantly, very slowly add the beaten eggs to the broth. The eggs will get puffy as they are added to the broth—just keep stirring! Once all the eggs are added to the pot, slowly stir in the lemon juice, salt, and pepper. Continue simmering, stirring frequently, until the soup is very creamy and the foam has subsided, about 15 minutes. Serve bowls of the soup topped with a thin slice of lemon, fresh oregano leaves, and more black pepper.

Maple *and* Balsamic–Roasted Salmon *with* Oranges *and* Fennel

¼ cup plus 1 tablespoon (75ml) balsamic vinegar

¼ cup (60ml) maple syrup

2 tablespoons whole grain Dijon mustard

2 tablespoons extra-virgin olive oil

1 (2- to 2½-pound/900g) salmon fillet

1 tablespoon flaky sea salt

2 teaspoons freshly ground black pepper

1 fennel bulb, halved, cored, and thinly sliced, fronds reserved for garnish

1 cup (180g) mixed pitted olives, such as Castelvetrano and kalamata, drained

1 tablespoon fresh orange juice

2 navel oranges, peeled and sliced into ¼-inch rounds

TIPS & TRICKS

To prepare the fennel bulb, start by pinching off a handful of the fronds for garnish. Then cut off the stalks where they branch out from the bulb and discard the stalks. With the base of the fennel bulb on your cutting board, slice downward to cut the fennel in half lengthwise. Cut out the core of both halves of the fennel bulb (the thick, dense portion near the base). Once the core is removed, thinly slice each half crosswise into ¼-inch-thick slices.

This is one of those crucial, keep-it-in-your-back-pocket recipes that you could just as easily reach for in the name of a quick weeknight meal as for impromptu entertaining. It takes about 30 minutes to pull everything together, cooks in under 10 minutes, and the result is a dish that looks as impressive as it tastes. The maple and balsamic create a deeply flavored, salty-sweet glaze, which gets balanced freshness from the oranges and fennel—a classic flavor combination made in Italian heaven.

SERVES 4 TO 6

In a medium bowl, whisk together ¼ cup of the balsamic vinegar, the maple syrup, and Dijon mustard.

Brush a large rimmed baking sheet with 1 tablespoon of the olive oil. Place the salmon on one side of the pan, skin side down. Season the salmon with 2 teaspoons of the salt and 1 teaspoon of the pepper. Spoon half of the balsamic mixture over the salmon and reserve the remaining mixture. Let the salmon marinate at room temperature for 15 to 30 minutes.

In a medium bowl, toss together the sliced fennel and the olives with the remaining tablespoon of balsamic vinegar, the orange juice, the remaining tablespoon of olive oil, and the remaining 1 teaspoon each of salt and pepper. Arrange the fennel mixture next to the salmon on the other half of the pan.

Position an oven rack in the top third of the oven and set to high broil.

Broil the salmon for 6 minutes. Toss the fennel mixture and continue broiling until the salmon flakes easily with a fork, 6 to 12 minutes more, depending on the thickness of the fillet.

Transfer the salmon to a serving platter and arrange the fennel mixture and orange slices around the salmon. Drizzle with the remaining balsamic mixture and garnish with the fennel fronds just before serving.

Roasted Garlic *and* Olive–Stuffed Chicken Breasts

My childhood family dinners were oftentimes the product of new dishes and techniques that my mom had learned from her books. One of her favorites was Chicken à la Archduke, or stuffed chicken breast. It made me realize that the perfect antidote to Plain Jane chicken was butterflying, stuffing, and baking it. Here I call for roasted garlic and olives, but you could experiment with any of your favorite herbs and aromatics.   SERVES 4

FOR THE ROASTED GARLIC

4 garlic heads
Extra-virgin olive oil, as needed

FOR THE STUFFED CHICKEN BREASTS

2 tablespoons unsalted butter
3 tablespoons extra-virgin olive oil
5 ounces (140g) shiitake mushrooms, cleaned, trimmed, and finely chopped
¼ red onion, thinly sliced
½ teaspoon freshly ground black pepper
1 (6-ounce/170g) jar pitted green olives, drained and chopped
1 cup (113g) crumbled feta cheese
1 teaspoon ground fennel seeds
½ teaspoon kosher salt
4 boneless, skinless chicken breasts
1 lemon
Chopped fresh parsley, for serving

MAKE THE ROASTED GARLIC: Preheat the oven to 400°F.

Cut the tops off each head of garlic to expose the cloves and remove any loose skin on the outside. Place the heads in the center of a piece of foil and drizzle lightly with olive oil. Scrunch up the foil over the garlic and seal to create a packet.

Place the garlic packet on a baking sheet and roast for 40 minutes, until the cloves are very tender. Carefully open the foil and let the garlic cool completely. The roasted garlic heads can be stored whole in an airtight container for up to 2 weeks. You can also squeeze out the cloves, place in a jar, cover with olive oil, and store in the refrigerator for up to 1 month.

MAKE THE STUFFED CHICKEN BREASTS: In a 12- or 14-inch nonstick skillet over medium-high heat, melt the butter with 1 tablespoon of the olive oil. Add the mushrooms and cook, stirring occasionally, until they start to release their moisture and reduce in size by about half, 5 to 8 minutes. Add the red onion and ¼ teaspoon of the pepper and cook for 5 more minutes, until the onions are softened and the mushrooms start to brown.

Transfer the mushroom mixture to a bowl and add the chopped olives. Squeeze the cloves from one head of the roasted garlic into the bowl and add ¾ cup of the feta. Stir to combine.

In a small bowl, combine the ground fennel seeds, salt, and the remaining ¼ teaspoon of black pepper. Set aside.

Place the chicken pieces on a cutting board. Starting on the thickest side, use a paring knife to carefully cut a pocket into the side of each piece, cutting about three-quarters of the way through the chicken. Sprinkle the outside and the pocket of the chicken with the fennel seed mixture.

continued

Stuff each of the pockets with about ¼ cup of the mushroom mixture, securing the opening with a toothpick if needed. (You will have some filling left.)

In the same skillet, add the remaining 2 tablespoons of olive oil and swirl to coat the bottom of the pan. Place the chicken breasts in the pan.

Cook over medium heat without disturbing until well browned, about 14 minutes. Carefully flip each piece and sprinkle the remaining stuffing mixture around the chicken breasts in the pan. Continue cooking until the chicken is browned and an instant-read thermometer registers 165°F when inserted into the thickest portion of the chicken, about 14 minutes more. After flipping, you can partially cover the pan if it appears the center of the chicken isn't cooking through. Remove the pan from the heat.

Sprinkle the remaining ¼ cup of the feta around the pan. Zest the lemon over the chicken, cut it in half, and squeeze the juice over the pan. Garnish with chopped parsley.

TIPS & TRICKS

Cutting pockets into the chicken breast fillets versus butterflying the fillets holds the filling best. Place a fillet on a cutting board. Running a small knife into the thickest side, make a 3- to 4-inch slit down the length of the fillet. Continue making shallow cuts into the fillet following the shape of the chicken piece. This should leave the fillet intact on three sides and create a cavity in the middle.

To reinvent leftovers, chop the chilled, stuffed chicken into small pieces and combine with mayonnaise, sour cream, red onion, and celery, then season with salt and pepper for an incredibly tasty chicken salad.

Sweet-Sour Roast Pork *with* Chicories

1 (4- to 5-pound/1.8 to 2.25kg) bone-in Boston butt or pork shoulder

1 tablespoon plus 2½ teaspoons kosher salt

1 tablespoon freshly ground black pepper, plus more for the sauce

2 teaspoons granulated sugar

1 teaspoon ground fennel seed

½ teaspoon crushed red pepper

¼ cup plus 2 tablespoons (90ml) extra-virgin olive oil

1 orange, zested and cut into wedges

5 large shallots, peeled and halved lengthwise

½ cup (120ml) balsamic vinegar

½ cup (120ml) vegetable or beef stock

12 ounces (340g) frozen pitted cherries

¼ cup (86g/60ml) honey

2 radicchio heads, trimmed and halved

Fresh parsley leaves, for garnish

There's something about a pork roast that feels like a winter must, but one worries that the meat will almost always be bland . . . because pork. I've found that a sweet, sticky shellac of marinade does wonders for this dish, particularly when home-made. Jarred sweet and sour sauce is not what we're talking about here. When you compare it to a homemade version, it's almost like it's speaking a different language—way too sweet and not nearly as nuanced. And the perfect finishing touch is a bed of chicories, like radicchio, or bitter greens, which add even more dimension to the sweet-sour affair.   SERVES 8 TO 10

Preheat the oven to 300°F.

Set the pork on a rimmed baking dish or a large plate. In a small bowl, stir together 5 teaspoons of the salt, the pepper, sugar, fennel, and red pepper. Season the pork on all sides with the spice mixture.

Heat 3 tablespoons of the olive oil in a large Dutch oven over medium-high heat. Sear the pork until lightly browned on all sides, 3 to 5 minutes per side. Remove the pot from the heat and add the orange zest and 2 cups of water. Cover and place in the oven, baking until the pork is tender, about 4 hours.

Remove the pot from the oven and add all but one of the shallot halves. (You'll use the last half for the sauce.) Nudge the shallot halves around the pork to ensure they have contact with the braising liquid. Return the pot to the oven, uncovered, and cook until the shallots are tender, about 30 minutes more. Set the pot aside and increase the oven temperature to 425°F.

In a small saucepan over medium heat, heat 1 tablespoon of the olive oil. Dice the remaining shallot half and add it to the pan. Cook until soft-ened, stirring occasionally, about 4 minutes. Add the vinegar, stock, and cherries and bring to a simmer. Cook, stirring occasionally, until mixture has reduced by about half and reaches a syrupy consistency, 15 to 20 minutes. Stir in the honey and pepper to taste and simmer for 5 min-utes more. Remove the pan from the heat.

continued

This dish has three delicious components, but it's easy to tackle in stages. Once you get the pork seared and into the oven, it's almost completely hands-off for hours. During that time, tackle the sauce and simply reheat it before serving. I like to roast the radicchio just before serving so it retains a nice crunch.

Since it's bone-in and super tender, this roast isn't best for slicing. I like to arrange it whole on a platter so guests can feast their eyes on it, then I whisk it away to the kitchen to shred the meat into large pieces, discarding the bone and any remaining non-meaty bits. Mound the crispy, tender pork in the middle of a platter, spoon over some of the pan juices, and serve with the remaining cherry-balsamic sauce.

On a rimmed baking sheet, toss the radicchio with the remaining 2 tablespoons of olive oil and the remaining $\frac{1}{2}$ teaspoon of salt. Roast until slightly tender, 8 to 10 minutes.

To serve, set the whole pork roast in the center of a serving platter. Alternatively, you can shred the meat and mound it in the center of a platter.

Halve the roasted radicchio into wedges and surround the pork with the radicchio and braised shallots. Squeeze one orange wedge over the radicchio and drizzle with the cherry-balsamic sauce. Garnish with the remaining orange wedges and parsley and serve the remaining sauce on the side.

Italian Sausage Meatballs *and* Polenta

The trick I've found when making meatballs is to use ground sausage instead of just ground beef. It's like instead of starting at zero in terms of flavor, you're starting at fifty miles per hour thanks to all the spices already included in the sausage. You can put the meatballs on just about anything—pasta being one obvious choice—but rich, creamy polenta has the cozy vibes that you need in your winter rotation. And it's not much more effort than making a quick hot breakfast cereal. You get a lot for just a little effort. SERVES 4 TO 6

FOR THE MEATBALLS

1 pound (450g) Italian chicken or pork sausage, casings removed if using links

¾ cup (70g) homemade bread crumbs (see Tips & Tricks)

⅓ cup (83g) whole-milk ricotta

1 large egg

¼ cup finely chopped fresh basil leaves or 2 tablespoons dried basil

½ teaspoon kosher salt

½ teaspoon garlic powder

¼ teaspoon freshly ground black pepper

2 tablespoons extra-virgin olive oil, plus more as needed

FOR THE SAUCE

1 (28-ounce/788g) can crushed San Marzano tomatoes

½ cup (120ml) red wine, any non-sweet variety

2 garlic cloves, minced

½ teaspoon kosher salt

¼ teaspoon freshly ground black pepper

¼ teaspoon crushed red pepper

2 to 3 sprigs fresh basil

FOR THE CREAMY POLENTA

1 cup (240ml) vegetable or chicken broth

1 cup (180g) polenta or yellow grits

½ teaspoon kosher salt

¼ teaspoon garlic powder

¼ cup (120ml) heavy whipping cream

4 ounces (113g) mascarpone cheese

1 tablespoon finely chopped fresh chives

MAKE THE MEATBALLS: In a large bowl, combine the sausage, bread crumbs, ricotta, egg, basil, salt, garlic powder, and pepper. Mix by hand until the ingredients are well incorporated. Scoop 1 to 2 tablespoons of the mixture and loosely shape into meatballs. Set the rolled meatballs on a plate or baking sheet as you work.

Heat the olive oil in a large, high-sided pan over medium heat. Working in batches to avoid crowding the pan, add the meatballs and cook until browned on two sides, about 4 minutes per side. Transfer the browned meatballs to a plate or baking sheet and repeat, adding more olive oil to the pan as needed.

MAKE THE SAUCE: In the same pan over medium heat, add the tomatoes and scrape the bottom of the pan with a wooden spoon to loosen any brown bits. Stir in the wine, garlic, salt, pepper, and crushed red pepper. Bring the sauce to a simmer and cook for about 3 minutes. Gently return the browned meatballs to the pan, along with any resting juices. Nestle in the basil sprigs, partially cover, and reduce the heat to low. Simmer for 25 minutes, stirring occasionally.

MAKE THE CREAMY POLENTA: In a medium saucepan over medium-high heat, combine the broth with 2 cups of water and bring to a boil. Whisk in the polenta, salt, and garlic powder. Reduce the heat to medium-low and continue cooking, whisking frequently, until the polenta is thick and the grains are soft, 15 to 20 minutes. (Depending on the brand of polenta, you may need up to an additional ½ cup of water or broth.) Whisk in the cream, mascarpone, and chives. Taste and add more salt if needed. Remove the polenta from the heat and let stand, covered, for at least 5 minutes.

Chopped fresh basil

Freshly grated Parmesan cheese

Freshly ground black pepper

TIPS & TRICKS

Make your own bread crumbs by processing a couple of slices of leftover sourdough or other crusty bread. Follow the instructions in the recipe for Chicken Milanese with Roasted Grapes and Rosemary (page 217).

For a quick weeknight meal, use precooked frozen meatballs. You can add them straight to the sauce in step 3 and heat through as the sauce cooks.

SERVE: Check on the meatballs—they'll be done around the same time the sauce has reduced and thickened. (If you like, you can use an instant-read thermometer to check that the meatballs' internal temperature is 165°F.) Remove and discard the basil stems from the sauce. Serve the polenta in bowls and top with the meatballs and tomato sauce. Finish with chopped basil, black pepper, and freshly grated Parmesan.

Beef Tenderloin *with* Miso-Honey Caramel

¾ cup (150g) granulated sugar

¾ cup (180ml) beef stock

5 tablespoons (70g) unsalted butter, softened

3 tablespoons red miso paste

2 tablespoons honey

1 tablespoon aged balsamic vinegar

1 tablespoon plus ¼ teaspoon freshly ground black pepper

1 (5-pound/2.27kg) beef tenderloin, trimmed

1 tablespoon plus 2 teaspoons kosher salt

Blood oranges, halved and quartered, for serving

Fresh rosemary sprigs, for serving

TIPS & TRICKS

Make friends with your butcher to get your hands on the right tenderloin to suit your needs. Most butchers will trim the tenderloin for you, which is essential to help it cook evenly. For further insurance, I recommend tying it with butcher's twine in 2-inch intervals; it helps hold the tenderloin in a compact shape. For extra flavor, season the tenderloin one day ahead and refrigerate it uncovered. Let it stand at room temperature for 30 minutes before roasting.

If you're new to making caramel without stirring, don't be nervous; just pay attention. Err on the side of cooking it a little lower and slower if that makes you more comfortable. Whatever you do, don't walk away; distraction is the archnemesis of caramel. This Miso-Honey Caramel holds wonderfully in the fridge, so feel free to make it the night before and reheat gently just before serving.

Miso and honey are an expected pair when it comes to salmon, but you don't often see them complementing beef. And yet, that sweet-savory-salty combination is perfect for bringing the tenderloin to a whole new level of richness and flavor.

SERVES 10 TO 12

In a small saucepan, swirl together the sugar and ¼ cup of the beef stock until the sugar is just moistened. Cook over medium-high heat, without stirring, until the mixture is dark amber in color, about 15 minutes. Carefully add the remaining ½ cup of the stock, 3 tablespoons of the butter, the miso paste, and honey. (The mixture may clump or bubble up temporarily.) Cook, stirring constantly, until the caramel is redissolved and the miso and butter are combined. Stir in the balsamic and ¼ teaspoon of the pepper. Simmer until the mixture is thick and glossy and registers between 230°F to 235°F on a candy or instant-read thermometer, 8 to 12 minutes more. Remove the pan from the heat and set aside.

Preheat the oven to 450°F.

Tie the beef tenderloin tightly with butcher's twine in 2-inch intervals. Pat the beef dry with paper towels and rub it with the remaining 2 tablespoons softened butter. Season on all sides with the salt and the remaining tablespoon of pepper. Place the seasoned tenderloin on a rimmed baking sheet or in a roasting pan.

Roast the tenderloin until a meat thermometer inserted near the center registers 120°F, about 25 minutes. Remove the pan from the oven and brush the top and sides of the tenderloin with ¼ cup of the Miso-Honey Caramel. Return the pan to the oven and roast to your desired degree of doneness, about 5 minutes more for medium. Let the beef rest for 10 minutes.

Carve the tenderloin as desired. Arrange the pieces on a platter with the oranges slices and rosemary and serve with remaining Miso-Honey Caramel.

Greek Leg of Lamb

FOR THE ROASTED LAMB

2 teaspoons sea salt

1 teaspoon freshly ground black pepper

12 garlic cloves, thinly sliced

1 (4- to 5-pound/1.8 to 2.25kg) semi-boneless leg of lamb, tied

¼ cup (60ml) extra-virgin olive oil

4 lemons, halved

12 small to medium Yukon Gold potatoes

5 fresh rosemary sprigs

FOR THE RED WINE GRAVY

1 tablespoon unsalted butter or extra-virgin olive oil

1 to 2 tablespoons all-purpose flour

1 cup (240ml) red wine, such as Cabernet Sauvignon

This was pretty much always on our table on Sunday nights when we'd have dinner with our grandparents. The lamb would get riddled with knife holes, into which garlic cloves were stuck before the meat got cooked for what felt like hours. The house would fill with an increasingly provocative smell, which teased the appearance of a perfectly cooked piece of meat with a slightly crisp, caramelized outside and a buttery, tender inside. It's what we cooking professionals call "heaven on a stick."

SERVES 6 TO 8

MAKE THE ROASTED LAMB: In a small bowl, stir together 1½ teaspoons of the salt and the pepper. Add the sliced garlic and toss gently to coat.

Set the leg of lamb in a roasting pan or large rimmed baking sheet. Using a paring knife, make small cuts, about 1 inch deep, all over the lamb. Rub 3 tablespoons of the olive oil all over the meat and insert the seasoned garlic slivers into the slits. Squeeze the lemons all over the lamb, catching the seeds through your fingers or a sieve. Add the lemon rinds to the pan and season the lamb with any remaining salt and pepper mixture. Cover the pan tightly with plastic wrap and refrigerate for a few hours or overnight.

Preheat the oven to 375°F. Remove the lamb from the fridge to take off a bit of the chill.

In a large bowl, toss the potatoes with the remaining tablespoon of olive oil and the remaining ½ teaspoon of salt. Scatter the potatoes in the pan around the lamb and nestle the rosemary sprigs among the potatoes. Transfer the pan to the oven and slowly pour 1¼ cups of water into the pan.

Roast for 1 hour, turning the lamb every 20 minutes. Reduce the oven temperature to 350°F and cook for 20 to 40 minutes more, until an instant-read thermometer reads 145°F when inserted in the thickest portion of the lamb. If the pan becomes dry at any point during roasting, add another cup of water as needed.

Transfer the roasted lamb and potatoes to a serving platter and discard the lemon rinds and rosemary sprigs. Loosely cover the platter with foil to keep warm. Carefully pour any pan drippings into a liquid measuring cup.

MAKE THE RED WINE GRAVY: In a small skillet or saucepan over medium heat, melt the butter. Whisk 1 tablespoon of flour per cup of pan drippings into the butter. Cook, stirring constantly, for 1 minute. Slowly whisk in the pan drippings and the red wine and bring the mixture to a strong simmer. Cook, stirring frequently, until the mixture thickens and reduces slightly, 5 to 10 minutes. Serve the gravy with the carved lamb and potatoes.

TIPS & TRICKS

Sometimes the grocery store butcher may only have a boneless leg of lamb, and you can absolutely use that here. The cook time will be a bit shorter, so start checking the internal temperature 15 to 20 minutes sooner.

Orange Linzer Cookie Wreaths

These traditional holiday cookies make a festively decorative addition to cookie tins and platters. You can use any kind of jam sandwiched inside, but I prefer orange marmalade because it's sweet but not too sweet, with just a little bit of bitter to keep you coming back for more.   MAKES ABOUT 20 COOKIE SANDWICHES

3¼ cups (390g) all-purpose flour, plus more for kneading

½ teaspoon kosher salt

¼ teaspoon baking powder

1 cup (2 sticks/226g) unsalted butter, softened

1 cup (225g) granulated sugar

1 large egg

1 teaspoon vanilla extract

¾ cup Citrus Confetti Marmalade (page 106), or store-bought, plus more for gluing decorations

Thinly sliced fresh cranberries, for decoration (optional)

Gold sprinkles, for decoration (optional)

Fresh rosemary sprigs, for decoration

Powdered sugar, for topping

TIPS & TRICKS

You can decorate the wreath cookies with sprinkles instead of fruit and rosemary. Or go the more traditional route and leave them plain, dusting with a heavy coat of powdered sugar before assembling.

If you're using a store-bought marmalade that has large, thick strips of zest, pulse it in a food processor to break them up or strain them out before assembling the cookies.

In a large bowl, sift together the flour, salt, and baking powder. In the bowl of a stand mixer fitted with the paddle attachment, beat the butter and sugar on medium speed until creamy, about 3 minutes. Add the egg and vanilla and continue beating until fluffy, about 2 minutes, stopping to scrape the sides of the bowl as needed.

Reduce the mixer speed to low and slowly add the flour mixture. Beat just until a dough starts to form, 1 to 2 minutes. Turn out the dough onto a lightly floured surface, knead gently into a ball, and divide in half. Shape each half into a disk and wrap tightly with plastic wrap. Chill the dough disks for at least 45 minutes or up to 3 days.

Preheat the oven to 350°F. Line two baking sheets with parchment paper and set aside.

On a lightly floured surface, roll out each disk of dough to about an ⅛-inch thickness. Cut the dough into rounds using a 2¼-inch round cutter, rerolling to use the scraps if needed. Place half of the rounds 1 inch apart on the prepared baking sheet.

Using a ¾-inch round cutter, cut out the center of the remaining rounds. Place them 1 inch apart on the other prepared baking sheet and decorate with the cranberries and sprinkles, if desired.

Bake the cookies one sheet at a time for 12 to 15 minutes, or until the edges just start to brown. Let the cookies cool completely on the baking sheets.

To garnish the cutout cookies, use your fingertip or a small brush to spread a small spot of orange marmalade on a cutout cookie and press a slice of cranberry (if using), gold sprinkles (if using), and a piece of rosemary on top. Let the marmalade dry for a few minutes and lightly dust the cookie all over with powdered sugar.

On the flat side (most likely the underside) of each solid cookie, spread about ½ teaspoon of orange marmalade and place a cutout cookie on top. Gently press to adhere; repeat with the remaining cookies. These cookies are best if they are assembled several hours or the day before they are served. Store in an airtight container at room temperature for up to 4 days.

Brûléed Blood Orange Cheesecake

FOR THE CRUST

8 ounces (230g/about 36 cookies) gingersnap cookies

2 tablespoons granulated sugar

¼ cup (60ml) unsalted butter, melted

FOR THE FILLING

3 (8-ounce/227g) blocks cream cheese, room temperature

1 cup (200g) granulated sugar

¼ teaspoon kosher salt

⅓ cup (80g) sour cream, room temperature

2 teaspoons orange zest (from about 2 blood oranges)

2 teaspoons vanilla extract

2 large eggs, room temperature

2 large egg yolks, room temperature

2 tablespoons Grand Marnier

3 tablespoons all-purpose flour

FOR THE TOPPING

2 to 3 blood oranges, peeled and cut into ¼-inch rounds

2 tablespoons granulated sugar

Cheesecake is the ultimate blank slate of a dessert, offering the ideal opportunity to play with more interesting seasonal flavors. Blood oranges—like all citrus—offer such a welcome brightness in the winter, so they were a natural fit for me. I love the unexpected twist of brûléeing them to add caramelly sweetness. I also add a splash of Grand Marnier—the orange liqueur that made an appearance in many of my mom's desserts, citrus syrups, and infused whipped creams—which rounds out a complex citrus flavor. And while many cheesecake crusts are a soggy, drab letdown, this gingersnap version adds the warm spice that makes this cake truly special.   MAKES 1 (9-INCH) CAKE

MAKE THE CRUST: Preheat the oven to 350°F.

In the bowl of a food processor, add the gingersnaps and process until finely ground. Add the sugar and pulse until fully incorporated. Continue pulsing and stream in the melted butter until fully incorporated. If some of the butter gets trapped in the corners of the processor bowl, you can remove the blade and finish incorporating the butter by hand using a spatula.

Transfer the mixture to a 9-inch springform pan. Using a tall glass, press the crumbs into the bottom and 1 inch up the sides of the pan. Set the pan on a rimmed baking sheet and bake for 10 to 15 minutes, until fragrant and dark golden in color. Set aside to cool.

MAKE THE FILLING: In the bowl of a stand mixer fitted with the whisk attachment, add the cream cheese and beat at medium speed until smooth and fluffy, about 1 minute. Add the sugar and salt and continue beating until incorporated, another minute or so, stopping to scrape the sides of the bowl as needed. Add the sour cream, orange zest, and vanilla extract, beating just until combined. Add the eggs one at a time, beating until fully incorporated before adding the next. In a small bowl, whisk together the egg yolks and Grand Marnier until well incorporated. (Don't be tempted to mix this ahead of time or skip this step and add the alcohol directly to the batter. Mixing the eggs with the alcohol too early can cause the eggs to curdle, and adding the alcohol directly to the cream cheese batter can separate the dairy, both resulting in an unpleasant or broken

continued

Room temperature cream cheese is key to a smooth cheesecake batter. I usually leave the blocks of cream cheese out at room temperature overnight or for at least 5 hours so they are very soft. Otherwise, you can remove cold blocks from the wrapper and microwave at 50 percent power for about 20 seconds.

For extra decadence, drizzle a small bit of Grand Marnier over each cheesecake slice when serving.

The cheesecake can also be topped with plain blood or navel oranges if you don't have a kitchen torch. While you can some-times use a broiler for toasting in place of a kitchen torch, that method doesn't work well with a juicy fruit like oranges.

Unlike many cheesecake recipes, this one does not require a water bath. A water bath is typically used to keep the cake (which is technically a custard) from cracking or over-baking and causing a more curdled texture. My recipe includes the addition of egg yolks and flour to help stabilize the filling. Keeping the oven door closed after turning it off also allows the cake to cool very slowly to reduce the risk of cracking.

cheesecake texture.) Add this mixture to the batter and beat just until combined. Sprinkle in the flour and beat until combined. Scrape the sides of the bowl and beat again just until the mixture is fully combined and smooth, barely a minute.

Pour the batter into the cooled crust (it should come up over the edge of the crust) and bake for 15 minutes. Reduce the oven temperature to 300°F and continue baking for another 30 to 35 minutes, or until the filling is slightly puffed and the edges are set but the center is still wobbly. Turn the oven off and allow the cake to rest for an additional hour in the oven without opening the door. Remove from the oven and cool to room temperature. Cover with a tea towel or paper towel and chill overnight.

MAKE THE TOPPING: When ready to serve, place the orange slices in a single layer on a baking sheet and sprinkle generously with the sugar. Using a kitchen torch, brûlée the tops of the oranges. Let cool for a few minutes.

Run a thin knife around the edge of the springform pan and release the sides. Carefully transfer the cheesecake from the base of the pan to a serving plate. Arrange some of the brûléed orange slices over the chilled cheesecake and serve with any extra slices.

Chocolate-Cardamom Pot de Crème

FOR THE BOOZY CHERRIES

15 Luxardo cherries

2 teaspoons Luxardo cherry syrup

2 teaspoons Grand Marnier or other orange liqueur

FOR THE POT DE CRÈME

4 large egg yolks

3 tablespoons granulated sugar

⅛ teaspoon kosher salt

2 cups (480ml) heavy whipping cream

½ cup (120ml) whole milk

1 teaspoon instant espresso powder

½ plus ⅛ teaspoon ground cardamom

4 ounces (116g) semisweet chocolate bars, chopped

This classic French dessert is essentially the perfect adult chocolate pudding. These smooth-as-silk baked custards are rich and well balanced with a deep chocolate flavor that is complemented by earthy cardamom. Topped with a cloud of sweet cardamom whipped cream and boozy maraschino cherries, these individual indulgences could easily be the final course in an elegant dinner or just a sweet treat after family supper. They'll also keep in the fridge for a few days, so it's a great dessert to make ahead or have on hand for those late-night cravings.   SERVES 5

MAKE THE BOOZY CHERRIES: In a glass jar, combine the cherries, syrup, and orange liqueur. Cover and let stand for at least 3 hours or store at room temperature for up to 1 month.

MAKE THE POT DE CRÈME: Preheat the oven to 300°F. Place five (6- to 8-ounce) ramekins in a large casserole dish.

In a large heatproof bowl, whisk together the egg yolks, 2 tablespoons of the sugar, and salt until combined. Set aside.

Place a fine mesh sieve over a large glass measuring cup or other heatproof pouring vessel and set aside.

In a small saucepan over medium heat, combine 1½ cups of the cream, the milk, espresso powder, and ½ teaspoon of the cardamom. Whisk occasionally, just until the milk starts to simmer. Remove the pan from the heat and whisk in the chocolate until smooth.

While whisking, slowly pour the chocolate mixture into the egg yolks. Strain the mixture through the sieve and divide the strained batter among the ramekins.

Carefully pour hot tap water into the pan until the water comes halfway up the sides of the ramekins. Cover the pan tightly with foil and poke several holes in the top with a fork. Place the pan on the center rack of the oven.

continued

Don't have or can't find Luxardo cherries? Try Tillen Farms Bada Bing cherries. Remove the stems from the cherries before using. Since Bada Bing cherries are larger than Luxardo, increase the syrup and liqueur to 1 tablespoon each.

Use a good quality chocolate. Since these custards are low on sugar, the flavor of the chocolate is front and center, and a lower-quality chocolate may be too bitter. If you prefer a sweeter custard, use a chocolate with a lower percentage of cocoa or even milk chocolate.

You can use baking bars or your favorite specialty chocolate bar. Do *not* use chocolate chips or morsels as they usually contain an anti-melting agent to help them keep their shape. These can result in a mixture that isn't smooth or is gooey.

Bake until the edges look set but the centers jiggle when shaken, about 35 minutes. Carefully remove the pan from the oven and remove the foil. Transfer the ramekins to a wire cooling rack and let cool until slightly warm, about an hour. Or cool completely, cover, and chill until ready to serve, up to 3 days.

When ready to serve, make the whipped cream. In a medium bowl with a whisk, beat together the remaining $1/2$ cup of cream, remaining tablespoon of sugar, and remaining $1/8$ teaspoon of cardamom until soft peaks form. Dollop over the custard and top with the Boozy Cherries.

Black Bottom Cranberry Tart

Most people's only introduction to cranberries is from a can or a juice carton, but the juice from the fruit itself—when not watered down or loaded with sugar—is intensely concentrated and tart. So if you're going to pair something with it, it needs to be a *flavor*—much like the bold dark chocolate in this tart. The combination screams holiday but in a deliciously unexpected way. And if you have any cranberry juice left over—the good stuff—I highly recommend it splashed over soda water for a refreshing palate cleanser between slices of this tart.

MAKES 1 (9-INCH) TART

FOR THE TART CRUST

1¾ cups (210g) all-purpose flour, plus more for rolling

¾ cup (90g) powdered sugar

¼ teaspoon kosher salt

6 tablespoons (85g) unsalted butter, cubed

3 large egg yolks, lightly beaten

1 teaspoon vanilla extract

FOR THE FILLING

¼ cup (60ml) heavy whipping cream

4 ounces (113g) dark chocolate, chopped bars or baking chips

¼ teaspoon ground allspice

2 cups (210g) fresh or thawed frozen cranberries

1¼ cups (250g) granulated sugar

Zest and juice of 1 orange

2 large eggs

2 large egg yolks

½ cup (1 stick/113g) cold unsalted butter, cubed

FOR THE SUGARED CRANBERRIES

¾ cup (150g) granulated sugar, plus more for coating

½ cup (52g) fresh or frozen cranberries

MAKE THE TART CRUST: Preheat the oven to 350°F.

In the bowl of a food processor, add the flour, sugar, and salt and pulse to combine. Add the butter and pulse until very crumbled. Add the egg yolks and vanilla and pulse until a dough ball starts to form.

Turn the dough out onto a lightly floured surface and knead a few times until it comes together. Shape the dough into a disk and roll it between two pieces of parchment paper into an 11-inch (⅛-inch-thick) circle. Remove the top piece of parchment. Flip the dough into a 9-inch fluted tart pan with a removable bottom and peel off the remaining piece of parchment. Press the dough into the bottom and sides of the tart pan. Trim the excess dough by running a sharp knife along the top edge of the pan. Place the pan on a rimmed baking sheet and pierce the bottom of the dough all over with a fork. Line the pan with parchment paper and fill it with pie weights or dried beans.

Bake for 20 minutes and carefully remove the parchment and weights. Continue baking until golden brown and dry in appearance, about 8 more minutes. Let the tart crust cool completely.

MAKE THE FILLING: In a small saucepan over medium heat, heat the cream until it is very steamy, about 3 minutes. Remove the pan from the heat and add the chocolate and allspice, stirring until the chocolate is completely melted and smooth. Pour the ganache into the tart shell and spread it to evenly cover the bottom. Chill until firm to the touch, about 30 minutes.

continued

Set a fine mesh sieve over a large bowl and set aside.

In a large saucepan over medium heat, combine the cranberries, sugar, and orange zest and juice. Cook, stirring occasionally, until the berries burst and have softened, about 12 minutes. Pour the mixture into the sieve and press on the solids with the back of a spoon. Discard any remaining solids.

Return the strained cranberry mixture to the saucepan and whisk in the eggs and egg yolks. Cook over medium heat, whisking gently and constantly, until the mixture is thickened and the whisk leaves a trail as it goes through, about 5 minutes. Remove the pan from the heat and whisk in the cold butter until fully combined. Pour the cranberry curd into the chilled tart shell. Gently tap the pan on the counter to level the curd and remove any air bubbles. Chill for at least 4 hours or overnight.

MAKE THE SUGARED CRANBERRIES: In a small saucepan over medium heat, whisk the sugar with $1/2$ cup of water and bring to a simmer. Turn off the heat and add the cranberries. Let stand, stirring occasionally, for 1 hour. Remove the cranberries and toss in more granulated sugar to coat. Spread the coated cranberries on a parchment paper–lined baking sheet and let sit for a few minutes to dry.

To serve, place the tart pan on top of an elevated flat container (like a large coffee can or soup bowl). Gently press the outer rim of the tart pan down until it slips off the crust. Set the tart, still on the bottom of the pan, on a plate or platter. Slip the blade of a large offset spatula or long thin knife between the bottom of the crust and the bottom of the tart pan. Run the blade all the way around the tart to release it and carefully remove the tart pan bottom. Top the tart with the sugared cranberries when you're ready to serve.

TIPS & TRICKS

The sugared cranberries are best if made the day you are planning to decorate and serve the tart. After about 24 hours, the sugar will absorb moisture and they can start to turn sticky and not look crystallized. They'll still taste delicious!

Candied Kumquat Flan

FOR THE CANDIED KUMQUATS

2¼ cups (450g) granulated sugar

1 pound (450g) kumquats, sliced and seeds removed

½ vanilla bean, split lengthwise

FOR THE FLAN

⅔ cup (133g) granulated sugar

¼ cup (60ml) candied kumquats syrup

5 large eggs

1 (14-ounce) can (396g) sweetened condensed milk

1 (12-ounce) can (354ml) evaporated milk

2 teaspoons vanilla extract

½ teaspoon almond extract

⅛ teaspoon kosher salt

Hot water, for the pan

Growing up surrounded by Greeks, I learned early how to appreciate bitter as one of the five primary flavors. Greek food often embraces bitter as a way to balance a dish: think dandelion greens or bitter herbs like chicory or black bryony with feta, or olive oil and lemon. And because my grandparents had a kumquat tree at their house here in the States, I also came to love this sour, slightly bitter fruit that delivered such intense, concentrated flavor from a cute little package. I especially enjoy baking with kumquats because of the way they add an explosion of bright citrus flavor that cuts the sweetness of whatever they're paired with. Yet you can still taste the nuance of each ingredient of this simple custard—the milk, the eggs—which to me is the gold standard. **SERVES 6**

MAKE THE CANDIED KUMQUATS: In a large saucepan over medium heat, combine the sugar and 2 cups of water and bring to a boil. When the sugar has dissolved, add the kumquats and vanilla bean and cook for 15 minutes, or until the slices start to soften and turn translucent. Use a slotted spoon to transfer the kumquats to a quart-size heatproof glass jar and set aside.

Continue simmering the syrup for 15 minutes or until it thickens to the consistency of maple syrup. Remove the pot from the heat.

Pour the hot syrup over the kumquats in the jar and let cool to room temperature. Cover the jar and chill overnight or up to 3 months.

MAKE THE FLAN: Preheat the oven to 325°F. Place an 8-inch round cake pan inside a roasting pan or large baking dish and set aside.

In a small saucepan over medium-high heat, add the sugar, kumquat syrup, and 2 tablespoons of water. Stir lightly to moisten sugar, if needed. Bring to a boil and cook, without stirring, for 8 to 12 minutes, until the sugar turns amber in color. Immediately pour the mixture into the cake pan. Carefully tilt and rotate the pan to spread the caramel out to the edge. Return the cake pan to the roasting pan to cool and harden.

In a large bowl, add the eggs, condensed milk, evaporated milk, vanilla extract, almond extract, and salt. Whisk until well combined, being

continued

Popping the kumquats in the freezer for 20 minutes can firm them up a bit and make them easier to slice. A small, sharp knife is also key.

To easily seed your kumquat slices, use a toothpick to poke the seeds through the slices. Any small or very thin seeds can stay. Just focus on the big ones.

For a dairy-free version, use evaporated and sweetened condensed coconut milk in place of the classic dairy versions.

If your custard doesn't want to release from the pan when flipped, soak the pan in hot water for a few more seconds and rerun your knife around the edges, making sure the blade goes all the way to the bottom of the pan. You can also tilt the pan and let some caramel run up over the sides of the custard to help it release.

The baked custard can be made up to 2 days in advance and refrigerated in the cake pan. Some caramel may remain on the bottom of your pan once inverted; continue to soak the pan in hot water to melt the caramel and pour over the custard.

careful to not whisk too vigorously to limit air bubbles forming. Pour the custard over the set caramel in the cake pan. Place the roasting pan in the oven and fill the pan with 1 inch of hot water.

Bake for 50 to 55 minutes, until the edges are set and the center is jiggly when gently shaken. Let the custard cool to room temperature in the water bath, then chill for at least 2 hours.

When ready to serve, dip the bottom of the pan in hot water for several seconds. Run a knife around the edge of the custard to loosen it and place a large, rimmed plate on top of the cake pan. Quickly flip the plate and pan to invert the custard. Top the flan with $\frac{1}{4}$ cup candied kumquats before serving. (The remainder can be stored in the refrigerator for up to 3 months.) Store the flan covered and refrigerated for up to 3 days.

Strawberry-Lavender Victoria Sponge

1 cup (2 sticks/226g) unsalted butter, room temperature, plus more for the pans

2 cups (240g) all-purpose flour, plus more for the pans

1 tablespoon baking powder

½ teaspoon kosher salt

1¼ cups (250g) granulated sugar

Zest of ½ lemon

4 large eggs, room temperature

¼ teaspoon crushed lavender flowers

¼ cup (120ml) whole milk, room temperature

1 cup (240ml) heavy whipping cream

2 tablespoons powdered sugar, plus more for dusting

2 teaspoons cornstarch

⅓ cup Strawberry-Lavender Jam (page 191)

I like the idea of preserving simplicity when it counts, so I didn't want to do much to this classic dessert that isn't much more than a layer of jam sandwiched between sponge cakes. However, I'm not above adding my own twist, which in this case is infusing the cake layers and strawberry jam with a hint of lavender, giving you a gentle perfume that rounds out the sweetness of the berries but doesn't taste like potpourri.

MAKES 1 (8-INCH) CAKE

Preheat the oven to 350°F. Butter and lightly flour two (8-inch) round cake pans and set aside.

In a large bowl, whisk together the flour, baking powder, and salt.

In the bowl of a stand mixer fitted with the paddle attachment, add the butter and sugar and beat on medium speed until very light and fluffy, about 5 minutes. Add the lemon zest and mix until combined. Reduce the mixer speed to medium-low, add 2 eggs, one at a time, waiting until fully incorporated before adding the next. Scrape down the sides of the bowl. Add ¼ cup of the flour mixture and beat just until combined. Add the remaining 2 eggs, one at a time. Once the eggs are incorporated, increase the speed to medium and beat for 2 minutes. Beat in the lavender flowers.

Reduce the mixer speed to low. Add half of the remaining flour mixture and mix until incorporated. Add the milk, followed by the rest of the flour. Scrape down the sides of the bowl and beat again just until combined. Divide the batter between the cake pans and use a spatula to spread it to the edges and smooth the tops.

Bake for 30 minutes or until the tops are golden brown, the edges are slightly pulling away from the sides of the pan, and the cake feels springy when gently pressed. (Do not test with a toothpick. It can cause the cakes to sink in the middle if they aren't fully done.) Let the cakes cool in the pan for 10 minutes. Carefully remove and let them cool completely on a wire rack.

In the bowl of a stand mixer fitted with the whisk attachment, add the cream, powdered sugar, and cornstarch. Beat on medium speed until stiff peaks form.

Set one cake layer on a cake plate and spread the top with the Strawberry-Lavender Jam. Spread the whipped cream over the top and gently place the remaining cake layer on top. Dust lightly with powdered sugar and serve immediately.

TIPS & TRICKS

A store-bought jam of your favorite flavor can be used in place of the homemade Strawberry-Lavender Jam. I recommend a whole-fruit jam, not a jelly.

I recommend setting a timer when beating the egg mixture. This aerates the mixture, producing a light and springy sponge cake.

A Victoria sponge has a signature dome that gives an elegant look to this simple treat. While I advocate for the use of cake strips for most cake layers, using them here will create flat layers, eliminating that dome. If you're looking for an elegant sponge cake to turn into a frosted layer cake, bake up this recipe as directed with cake strips around the pans for perfectly even and soft layers. Frost with a buttercream of your choice from this book.

Chocolate Peppermint Bark Cake

I'm not what you'd call a peppermint lover, but when combined with chocolate, that's another story. I'm particularly fond of this easy bark that can be a snack, a party favor, or an adornment to this perfectly moist, tender, melt-in-your-mouth cake that has just a kiss of mint. It's amazing what a subtle—and I mean subtle—addition can do to deepen the chocolate flavor.

MAKES 1 (8-INCH, 3-LAYER) CAKE

FOR THE PEPPERMINT BARK

4 (3.5-ounce) bars (400g) dark chocolate, chopped

4 (4.4-ounce) bars (500g) white chocolate, chopped

½ cup crushed soft peppermint candies or buttermints

FOR THE CHOCOLATE CAKE

Nonstick baking spray

1 cup (240ml) strong coffee, hot

¾ cup (60g) Dutch-process cocoa powder

2½ cups (300g) all-purpose flour

1½ cups (300g) granulated sugar

2½ teaspoons baking powder

½ teaspoon baking soda

1 teaspoon kosher salt

4 large eggs

¾ cup (180ml) vegetable oil

½ cup (120ml) whole milk

½ cup (110g) sour cream

½ cup (110g) firmly packed light brown sugar

1 tablespoon vanilla extract

MAKE THE PEPPERMINT BARK: Line a baking sheet with parchment paper and set aside.

Fill a small pot with 2 inches of water and bring to a simmer over high heat. Reduce the heat to medium. Place the dark chocolate in a medium heatproof bowl and set the bowl over the top of the pot. Stir frequently until the chocolate is melted and smooth, about 5 minutes. Pour the chocolate onto the parchment paper and spread it into a thin ⅛- to ¼-inch-thick layer. Set aside until just slightly set, about 10 minutes.

Repeat the same melting process in a clean bowl with the white chocolate. Pour the white chocolate over the cooled dark chocolate and carefully spread to cover. Sprinkle with the crushed peppermints and let the chocolate cool until firm, about 2 hours.

Break apart the bark with your hands or cut it with a hot knife, wiping the knife clean between cuts for sharp edges. The bark can be stored in an airtight container at room temperature for up to 2 weeks.

MAKE THE CHOCOLATE CAKE: Preheat the oven to 350°F. Spray three (8-inch) round cake pans with baking spray. Wrap each cake pan with water-soaked cloth baking strips, if desired.

In a large bowl, whisk together the hot coffee and cocoa powder until well combined and let stand for a few minutes. (This blooms the cocoa, intensifying the flavor.)

In a large bowl, sift together the flour, granulated sugar, baking powder, and baking soda. Whisk in the salt and set aside.

To the coffee mixture, whisk in the eggs, oil, milk, sour cream, brown sugar, and vanilla until smooth. Add the coffee mixture to the flour

continued

1½ cups (3 sticks/340g) unsalted butter, room temperature

¾ teaspoon kosher salt

3 teaspoons vanilla extract

2¼ pounds (1,013g) powdered sugar

⅓ cup plus 2 tablespoons (110ml) heavy whipping cream, room temperature

1¼ teaspoons peppermint extract

¼ cup crushed soft peppermint candies or buttermints, plus more for garnish

2 (3.5-ounce) bars (200g) dark chocolate, chopped

½ cup plus 2 tablespoons (150ml) heavy whipping cream

mixture and whisk until just combined. Divide the batter between the cake pans.

Bake for 30 to 35 minutes, until a wooden pick inserted into the center comes out clean. Let the cakes cool in the pans for 10 minutes. Invert the cakes onto a wire rack and let cool completely.

MAKE THE PEPPERMINT BUTTERCREAM: In the bowl of a stand mixer fitted with the paddle attachment, beat the butter and salt on medium-low speed until smooth, about 1 minute. Add the vanilla and beat until combined. Reduce the mixer speed to low and slowly add the powdered sugar. Continue beating on low and slowly add the cream. When the cream is fully incorporated, increase the mixer speed to medium. Continue beating until light and fluffy, about 3 minutes. Beat in the peppermint extract.

Set a cake layer on a cake plate or stand. Spread with ¾ cup of the peppermint buttercream and sprinkle with half of the crushed peppermint candies. Top with another cake layer and repeat with buttercream and the remaining candies. Top with the remaining cake layer and frost the outside of the cake with the remaining buttercream. Press more crushed peppermints around the bottom edge of the cake, if desired. Chill the cake for at least 30 minutes or up to 1 day before serving.

MAKE THE TOPPING: Place the chocolate in a medium heatproof bowl. Heat the cream in a small saucepan over medium heat until very steamy and just starting to simmer. Let stand for 5 minutes. Stir until the chocolate is fully melted and combined with the cream.

Pour the chocolate mixture over the top of the chilled cake, letting the excess drip off the sides. Chill until the chocolate is set, about 30 minutes, or until ready to serve. Garnish with peppermint bark.

TIPS & TRICKS

The type of chocolate used for the Peppermint Bark is key. I like melting down chocolate bars since the chocolate has been nicely tempered and will melt down smoothly. My go-to brands are Lindt or Ghirardelli.

The Peppermint Bark recipe makes extra. Serve leftover shards alongside the cake or knock out a few Christmas gifts by packing them up in a pretty tin.

Chocolate Ginger Tart

FOR THE GINGERSNAP CRUST

¼ cup (57g) unsalted butter

1 ounce (30g) semisweet chocolate, baking chips or chopped bars

8 ounces (230g/about 36 cookies) gingersnap cookies

¾ cup (105g) toasted hazelnuts

¼ cup (45g) chopped crystallized ginger

FOR THE GANACHE FILLING

11 ounces (310g) semisweet chocolate, baking chips or chopped bars

1 cup (240ml) heavy whipping cream

¼ teaspoon kosher salt

5 tablespoons (70g) unsalted butter, softened

½ teaspoon vanilla extract

FOR THE GINGER SUGAR

1 tablespoon minced crystallized ginger

2 teaspoons sparkling sugar

Whipped cream, for serving (optional)

I often find that ganache tarts can be a little too heavy on the chocolate. I know, I know, like there is such a thing. But if we're being honest, they can be a bit like soft chocolate bricks. Lightening up the tart with extra cream is one excellent solution. As is adding ginger, which lends a punch of spice to the chocolate flavor without taking over the whole situation.

MAKES 1 (9-INCH) TART

MAKE THE GINGERSNAP CRUST: Place a 9-inch fluted tart pan with a removable bottom on a plate or tray and set aside.

In a microwave-safe measuring cup, add the butter and chocolate. Microwave on high in 15-second intervals until the butter is melted, 45 to 60 seconds. Stir to finish melting the chocolate. (It's okay if the chocolate and butter still look slightly separated.)

In the bowl of a food processor, add the gingersnaps and pulse a few times to break them into small pieces. Add the hazelnuts and process until finely ground, about 30 seconds. Add the crystallized ginger and pulse a few more times to combine. Stream in the butter and chocolate mixture, continuing to pulse until the mixture is well combined. Stop and scrape down the sides of the bowl as necessary.

Transfer the crumb mixture to the tart pan. Use the bottom of a glass to press the mixture into the bottom and sides of the pan. Freeze the crust while you work on the filling.

MAKE THE GANACHE FILLING: Set a small saucepan with 2 inches of water over medium heat and bring to a simmer.

In a large heatproof bowl, combine the chocolate, cream, and salt. Set the bowl over the saucepan and stir until the chocolate is melted and combined with the cream, about 10 minutes. Remove from the saucepan. Add the butter and vanilla and stir until the mixture is completely smooth and combined. Pour the ganache mixture into the chilled crust and refrigerate at least 4 hours or overnight.

MAKE THE GINGER SUGAR: In a small bowl, rub together the minced ginger and sparkling sugar with your fingertips until well combined. Sprinkle the ginger sugar around the edge of the tart.

continued

Since this tart is all about the chocolate, this is definitely a time to use a high-quality brand. You can use bars or baking chips, but do not use any product labeled "morsels" for this recipe. They typically contain setting agents that make them great for holding their shape in baking but difficult to melt and may give the ganache a grainy texture when chilled.

If you don't have or can't find crystallized ginger (sometimes called candied ginger), substitute ¼ teaspoon ground ginger in the crust and decorate the top of the tart with sparkling sugar only or chocolate shavings.

To serve, place the tart pan on top of an elevated flat container (like a large coffee can or soup bowl). Gently press the outer rim of the tart pan down until it slips off the crust. Set the tart, still on the bottom of the pan, on a plate or platter. With a large offset spatula or long thin knife, slip the blade between the bottom of the crust and the bottom of the tart pan. Run it all the way around the tart to release and carefully remove the tart pan bottom. Make sure to keep the tart chilled until ready to serve. Slice and serve the tart with the whipped cream, if desired. The tart will keep refrigerated for up to 5 days.

Rummy Chocolate Crinkle Cookies

Everyone needs a great cookie to bring to a party or fill out a dessert platter, and this is one of them. These are basically fudge that has somehow turned into a cookie. They have a crisp sugared shell on the outside, but the inside is pure melt-in-your-mouth chocolate heaven. Then a dash of rum adds a little spirit of the holidays. **MAKES ABOUT 24 COOKIES**

1½ cups (180g) all-purpose flour

¾ cup (50g) unsweetened cocoa powder

1 teaspoon espresso powder

¾ teaspoon baking soda

½ teaspoon kosher salt

¾ cup (150g) granulated sugar

½ cup (110g) firmly packed light brown sugar

½ cup (1 stick/113g) unsalted butter, melted

1 large egg, room temperature

¼ cup (60ml) aged or spiced rum

2 teaspoons vanilla extract

½ cup (60g) powdered sugar, plus more for dusting

TIPS & TRICKS

Mix up the flavor by swapping out the type of alcohol you use. Cointreau, bourbon, Kahlua, or Irish cream would all be delicious in these cookies! Or go alcohol-free and use milk or water instead of spirits.

The dough can be chilled overnight, but the cookies can also be rolled into balls, covered, and refrigerated for up to 2 days before sugaring and baking. They may not spread quite as much when baked, but they will be just as delicious.

In a medium bowl, sift together the flour, cocoa powder, espresso powder, and baking soda. Whisk in the salt. In a large bowl, combine ½ cup of the granulated sugar, the brown sugar, melted butter, egg, rum, and vanilla. Whisk together until well combined. Using a silicone spatula, fold the flour mixture into the sugar mixture until the dough is uniform. Cover and refrigerate for at least 2 hours or overnight.

Preheat the oven to 350°F. Line two rimmed baking sheets with parchment paper and set aside.

Sift the powdered sugar into a small bowl. In another small bowl, place the remaining ¼ cup granulated sugar.

Scoop the dough with a spoon and roll into 1-inch balls. Roll each dough ball in the granulated sugar followed by the powdered sugar. Place the coated dough balls 2 inches apart on the prepared baking sheet and lightly sift additional powdered sugar over the top. Chill the remaining dough balls (probably about half of the dough) and coat in the sugars right before baking.

Bake one sheet at a time until the cookie edges are set and cracks have formed, about 10 minutes for gooey-center cookies and up to 12 minutes for fully baked but soft cookies. Let cool completely on the pans. The cookies can be stored in an airtight container for up to 4 days.

Orange Tiramisu

FOR THE MASCARPONE FILLING

16 ounces (450g) mascarpone cheese, room temperature

3 tablespoons aged or spiced rum

3 tablespoons orange liqueur, such as Grand Marnier or Cointreau

Zest of 2 oranges (about 4 teaspoons)

8 large egg yolks

¾ cup (150g) granulated sugar

2½ cups (600ml) cold heavy whipping cream

1 tablespoon vanilla extract

FOR THE TIRAMISU

1 cup (240ml) very strong coffee, cooled

Juice of 2 oranges (about ⅔ cup/160ml)

½ cup (120ml) aged or spiced rum

⅓ cup (80ml) orange liqueur, such as Grand Marnier or Cointreau

About 45 ladyfinger cookies

¼ cup unsweetened cocoa powder

FOR SERVING

2½ cups (600ml) cold heavy whipping cream

¼ cup powdered sugar

1 teaspoon cornstarch

2 tablespoons unsweetened cocoa powder

When I was in high school, one of the first dishes I made as part of my discovery of baking (or what I sometimes refer to as my "nerding process") was an extra-boozy tiramisu—with crystallized pansies on top. I remember having to drag my mom to an Italian import store just to find the mascarpone. . . . Luckily, it's no longer a schlep to find mascarpone, and my tiramisu game has leveled up since then, though I'm still partial to a rich, spirit-forward cake. This time, it's with a touch of orange juice, orange zest, and Grand Marnier or Cointreau to brighten up the traditional rum and coffee.   SERVES 12

MAKE THE MASCARPONE FILLING: In the bowl of a stand mixer fitted with the paddle attachment, add the mascarpone, rum, orange liqueur, and orange zest and beat on low speed just until combined.

In a small saucepan over medium heat, add 2 inches of water and bring to a simmer. In a large heatproof bowl, whisk together the egg yolks and sugar until combined. Set the bowl on top of the pot, making sure no water touches the bowl. Continue whisking until the egg yolks are light in color and very thick and fluffy in texture, about 10 to 12 minutes. (You can also do this with a handheld electric mixer on medium-low speed.) Be patient during this process. If there is any runny liquid in the bottom of the bowl, keep beating until it's gone.

Add the egg yolk mixture into the mascarpone and beat on low speed until just combined, 1 or 2 minutes. Refrigerate the mixture, uncovered, until cooled, about 20 minutes.

In the bowl of a stand mixer fitted with the whisk attachment, add the cream and vanilla and mix on low speed for about 30 seconds. Slowly increase the speed to high and beat until stiff peaks have formed, about 5 minutes. Fold the whipped cream into the chilled mascarpone mixture until just combined.

ASSEMBLE THE TIRAMISU: In a wide, shallow bowl, whisk together the coffee, orange juice, rum, and orange liqueur. Quickly dip each ladyfinger one at a time in the coffee mixture, not even a second per side, and place snugly in a single layer covering the bottom of a 13x9-inch dish. You'll use roughly 20 ladyfingers for this first layer, depending on the shape of your dish and size of the cookies. Lightly dust the layer with

2 tablespoons of the cocoa powder and pour half of the chilled mascarpone filling over the top. Smooth with an offset spatula and repeat the layers with the remaining coffee mixture, ladyfingers, cocoa powder, and mascarpone filling. Chill for at least 2 hours or until ready to serve. For the best flavor, make 1 day in advance of serving.

SERVE: In the bowl of a stand mixer fitted with the whisk attachment, add the cream, powdered sugar, and cornstarch and beat on medium speed until stiff peaks form. Spread the whipped cream on top of the tiramisu, or transfer to a piping bag fitted with a decorative star tip and pipe it on top. Dust the top with the cocoa powder. Leftovers can be refrigerated for up to 4 days.

TIPS & TRICKS

This classic Italian dessert is filled with boozy flavor. To lessen the alcohol, substitute equal parts orange juice or more coffee for the liquor.

Ladyfinger cookies are often referred to as biscotti savoiardi on packaging and can be found with the specialty cookies in most grocery stores.

Tiramisu holds well for a few days after assembly. Adding the cornstarch to the whipped cream topping helps the cream hold its shape and not water out in the fridge, keeping the dessert as pretty and tasty as it was on day one.

Eggnog

6 large eggs

2 cups (480ml) heavy whipping cream

½ vanilla bean, scraped or 1 teaspoon vanilla bean paste

½ cup (100g) granulated sugar

1 tablespoon firmly packed light brown sugar

¾ cup (180ml) spiced rum

½ cup (120ml) bourbon

4 cups (960ml) half-and-half or whole milk

Freshly grated nutmeg, for serving (optional)

Orange zest, for serving

TIPS & TRICKS

Since eggnog is essentially just mixing together fresh ingredients, it's important to use high-quality, fresh-tasting eggs, dairy, and alcohol to make the best batch of 'nog. On the farm, we use our eggs, but when purchasing from the store, buy quality pasture-raised eggs for richly colored yolks and good flavor.

You can spice up your batch by adding a bit of ground cinnamon or even a sprinkling of ground cardamom.

If your largest bowl is a punch bowl for serving the eggnog, you can beat the egg yolks with sugar in a smaller bowl and add it to the punch bowl, then whisk in your rum, bourbon, and half-and-half.

I would hazard to say that if you've only had eggnog from a carton, then you have not really had eggnog. The stuff you buy at the store is a mere impersonation of the real thing, essentially half-and-half with cinnamon, nutmeg, and a whole lot of sugar. Where's the meringue folded in to make it somehow creamy and rich yet logic-defyingly light as air? Where's the festive nip of bourbon and spiced rum? No, I daresay that the only way to do eggnog true justice is to make it at home. It's easy to make, and if you happen to have leftovers, you can use it to replace milk in basically any baked good for almost instant holiday magic.

MAKES ABOUT 5 QUARTS

Separate the eggs between two large bowls, putting the yolks in the largest bowl you have, and set aside.

In another large bowl, add the cream and vanilla and use an electric hand mixer to beat on medium speed until stiff peaks form, 5 to 7 minutes.

With clean beaters, beat the egg whites on high speed until stiff, about 3 minutes.

Add the sugars to the egg yolks and beat, again with clean beaters, on medium-high speed until very pale and fluffy, about 4 minutes. Add the rum and bourbon and whisk until well combined. Add the half-and-half and whisk once more to combine.

Add half of the egg whites to the bourbon mixture and whisk until combined. Repeat with the remaining half of the egg whites. Add the whipped cream and whisk until the mixture is foamy but homogenous.

Grate fresh nutmeg to taste into the eggnog, if desired, and chill until ready to serve. Serve each glass of eggnog with a strip of orange zest and more grated nutmeg.

Spiked Eggnog Crème Brûlées

1½ cups (360ml) heavy whipping cream

1 cup (240ml) whole milk

Freshly grated nutmeg, to taste

1 teaspoon vanilla extract

6 large egg yolks

⅔ cup (133g) granulated sugar

¼ teaspoon ground cinnamon

2 tablespoons bourbon

1 tablespoon spiced rum

2 tablespoons superfine sugar

Orange zest, for serving

Crème brûlée is one of those multisensory desserts—the crack of the caramelized sugars, the ooze of the silky contents—that adds up to a pure holiday bliss moment. To really drive the point home, I flavor these custards with the same ingredients I use to make eggnog: a hint of spice and a splash of bourbon and spiced rum. SERVES 5

Preheat the oven to 325°F. Place five (6-ounce) shallow ramekins in a large roasting pan or in two (13x9-inch) baking dishes.

In a medium saucepan, combine the cream and milk. Heat the mixture until the milk steams heavily but isn't boiling, 8 to 10 minutes. Remove the pot from the heat, add a few grates of fresh nutmeg, and stir in the vanilla.

In a medium heatproof bowl, whisk together the egg yolks, sugar, and cinnamon. Very slowly whisk the hot milk mixture into the egg yolks. Whisk in the bourbon and rum and divide the mixture among the ramekins.

Place the roasting pan in the oven and pour very hot water into the pan until the water comes about halfway up the sides of the ramekins.

Bake for 25 to 30 minutes, until the custard is set but the center still jiggles slightly. Carefully remove the pans from the oven and let cool completely. Remove the ramekins from the water bath and refrigerate for at least 3 hours or up to 2 days.

When you're ready to serve, sprinkle the tops of the chilled custard with about a teaspoon of sugar and caramelize the sugar with a kitchen torch. You can also set the ramekins on a baking sheet and broil on the top rack in the oven until the tops are golden and caramelized, about 3 minutes. Garnish with orange zest and serve immediately.

TIPS & TRICKS

You can use smaller ramekins (4-ounce), but the cook time may vary by 5 or 10 minutes depending on the depth of the custard.

You can leave the alcohol out of the custard if desired. I would recommend increasing the vanilla by 1 teaspoon if so.

SPECIAL PROJECTS

Winter Wreaths

MAKES 1 MEDIUM WREATH

Roughly 60 evergreen branches, 12 inches or shorter in length

Green floral wire

Secateur and scissors

Wreath form, either wire or grapevine

Wire-edged 2.5-inch ribbon

Pine cones, red winter berries, and other decorative items from nature (optional)

TIPS & TRICKS

You can use various varieties of evergreen boughs—like a mix of Juniper, Cedar, Pine, and Douglas Fir—for more interest, or stick with just one type for a clean, classic look.

I find red winter berries on our farm, but you can get them from the flower market in the winter or buy faux ones online.

A wreath using live branches will last longest in a cold environment, so if you live somewhere warm, a wreath of pine cones or other long-lasting elements such as faux boughs will be a better fit.

We really got a lesson in the holidays when we moved out here. In New York and LA, we could basically pick up a wreath or a tree anytime we wanted to from one of the tree lots that sprouted up on pretty much every corner around the city. They'd never run out, and most important, they'd deliver, set it up, done. In rural Connecticut, on the other hand, not so much. First of all, there's no wishy-washy decorating-as-you-think-of-it approach—after Thanksgiving the holiday decorations go up, and by January 1, they're back down again, like clockwork. We also realized we were no longer living in the world of delivery or on-demand decorations. Around here, people put in their orders for freshly foraged wreaths no later than Halloween. Any later and you're out of luck! If you wait too long to get your tree—which comes from an actual farm versus a parking lot and needs to be tied to the top of your car and schlepped all the way up to your house—they go yellow in the cold, dry wind. Needless to say, we were caught unprepared. Now, though, we know the drill—and have Lisa, the "wreath lady," programmed in my phone.

For us, decorating isn't important because of its relationship with any particular holiday. More than that, it's bringing light and festivity to a time of year when those things can be scarce. When it gets dark at 4 p.m. and you're no longer running into friends and neighbors at the market or the shops because it's so darn cold, having a little something special to light the way feels in order, no matter which holidays you celebrate.

These simple wreaths are inspired in part by our New England tradition of decorating all the windows and doors. They are sort of like the mini version of cutting down your own Christmas tree, but all you need are clippings. Making my own winter wreaths is also an homage to my aunt, who taught my mom how to make handsomely elaborate wreaths using not much more than craft supplies and treasures found outside. I like taking a walk through the farm and snipping a variety of low-hanging evergreen branches and red winter berries. You can do your own creative foraging, or buy branches at a tree lot, flower market, or craft store.

First, create small bundles by layering 3 to 4 branches on top of one another and securing their ends with the floral wire. If you're combining different varieties, layer them on top of one another so you get a nice play of textures. Repeat this process until you have enough bunches to complete your wreath, usually about 15 for a medium-size wreath.

Tie the end of the floral wire to your form, then place the first evergreen bunch on the form and loop the wire tightly over the base so it's secure. Layer the second bunch over the first, but about 4 inches below so there's enough overlap to look full. Loop the wire over, securing it as you did the first. Repeat until the wreath form is completely covered.

Create a large bow with the wire-trimmed ribbon (I love a deep-red velvet) to complete the top of the wreath. Affix it on top of the boughs using floral wire. At this point you can tuck in and attach any other adornments you like, such as winter berries, pine cones, or small ornaments.

Lastly, attach a small loop of ribbon on the back of the form to hang your wreath; you don't want any sharp bits of wire poking out, which would scrape your windows and doors.

PLANNING A KITCHEN GARDEN

When I was living on my own, I fell in love with planting a garden. I had a small one full of different specimens and varieties of succulents, which were right at home in the dry, hot LA climate. After I met Brian and we moved to a house with a larger yard, I started growing all different types of plants, which were basically evergreen because of the year-round growing season. So you can imagine the learning curve when we moved to Connecticut, where that season is cut in half. And throughout that window there's a wave of sprouting, flowering, and dormancy that ripples through the garden, from the first shoots of tender greens in the spring to the beans and peppers at the height of summer to hearty greens and root vegetables in the first frosts of the fall. I realized that if I were going to plan a kitchen garden—something I'd always wanted to do as a way to always have fresh versions of my favorite ingredients on hand—I was going to have to plan with intention. But with just a little forethought and planning—which is best done before spring and planting season arrive—I've been able to bring that dream to life.

A kitchen garden can be anything—a row of pots on a sunny windowsill or fire escape, a small raised bed, or several irrigated rows edged with flowers or boxwoods (which we've done to bring a whiff of English gardens to the farm). So when planning your garden, consider:

- Where will my plants get the most sun exposure? Pretty obvious—plants need sun to grow.
- How much space do I have to devote to this garden? Don't plan on an acreage of plants if you live in a city apartment. Even a pot of fresh thyme and basil goes a long way on your eggs and pizza.
- How much do I want to be gardening? The idea of gardening and actual gardening are very different things. I find it to be a meditative pleasure and don't mind the tending and weeding. If that doesn't sound like you, maybe just stick with a row of herbs outside your door that you use occasionally and keep clean.
- What do I like to eat? This is the most important piece. The whole point of a kitchen garden is that you are giving yourself the gift of the best, freshest ingredients. I knew that I wanted all manner of heirloom lettuce, tomato, and cucumber varieties because those are things that spark so much joy when assembled as a salad next to just about any meal. If you love making mussels with white wine and herbs—as I most certainly do—grow the chervil to sprinkle on top. Conversely, if you hate zucchini, don't grow them. You can have a lot of fun researching heirloom breeds and different varieties of plants that look nothing like what you'd find at a grocery store. If you find something you like at the farmers' market, grow that. Or do what my mom does and save the seeds from your favorite melons and tomatoes to plant.

Flavored Goat Cheeses

BLUEBERRY-HONEY:

8 ounces (227g) fresh goat cheese

Zest of 1 lemon

1 tablespoon honey

¾ cup (120g) finely chopped dried blueberries

BLACK PEPPER-HERB:

8 ounces (227g) fresh goat cheese

½ teaspoon freshly ground black pepper

½ teaspoon chopped fresh dill
(or ¼ teaspoon dried)

¼ teaspoon kosher salt

⅛ teaspoon garlic powder

1 cup (25g) finely chopped fresh parsley

¼ cup edible flower petals (weight will vary depending on the petals)

SPICY PISTACHIO-WALNUT:

8 ounces (227g) fresh goat cheese

¼ teaspoon crushed red pepper

¼ teaspoon kosher salt

⅛ teaspoon smoked paprika

¼ cup (30g) roasted pistachios, finely chopped

¼ cup (30g) roasted walnuts, finely chopped

I'm not only partial to goat cheese because we have our own sweet little herd who give us the most beautiful milk. I'm crazy about how creamy and rich it is, and yet it's brightened by tangy sourness. And no matter whether you're making it yourself or buying it at the market, plain goat cheese is the perfect canvas for an infinite number of flavorings that can elevate this humble cheese into the perfect solution for pressure-free yet very impressive entertaining. I like to think of blending flavors into goat cheese as arranging a symphony or combining different notes, such as floral, sweet, spicy, and savory. You're really limited only by your own imagination and preferences.

There are two basic approaches: coating the outside of a goat cheese log with things such as cracked black pepper, herbes de Provence, fresh dill, or sesame seeds; or mixing your ingredients in. The latter is a little more of a workout, but worthwhile. This approach is great for honey, preserves, and dried fruit—and could be shaped back into a log and rolled in additional flavorings on the outside. Just taste as you go until it's right. Both end results work equally well on a cheese plate with plenty of crackers. And by the by, if you're thinking of getting a new pet, goats just so happen to be among our favorite animals on the farm.

Here are a few recipes to get you started.   SERVES 6 TO 8

For each flavor, let the goat cheese stand at room temperature for 30 minutes to soften slightly.

For the Blueberry-Honey: In a medium bowl, combine the softened goat cheese, half the lemon zest, and honey. Mix with a spatula until well combined. Transfer the mixture to a sheet of wax paper, roll it up, and twist the ends to create a 2-inch round log.

Freeze for 20 minutes or until firm to the touch, or refrigerate for at least 2 hours. Unwrap the log and roll in the blueberries and the remaining lemon zest. Chill until ready to serve.

For the Black Pepper–Herb: In a medium bowl, combine the softened goat cheese, black pepper, dill, salt, and garlic powder. Mix with a spatula until well combined. Transfer the mixture to a sheet of wax paper, roll it up, and twist the ends to create a 2-inch round log.

The blueberry goat cheese is prettiest if made at least 24 hours in advance, giving the outside of the log a pretty purple hue.

Your favorite dried fruit, herbs, and nuts can be used in these recipes—think of them as a starting point for inspiration and have fun!

Freeze for 20 minutes or refrigerate for at least 2 hours. Unwrap the log and roll in the parsley and flower petals. Chill until ready to serve.

For the Spicy Pistachio-Walnut: In a medium bowl, combine the softened goat cheese, red pepper, salt, and paprika. Mix with a spatula until well combined. Transfer the mixture to a sheet of wax paper, roll it up, and twist the ends to create a 2-inch round log.

Freeze for 20 minutes or refrigerate for at least 2 hours. Unwrap the log and roll in the pistachios and walnuts. Chill until ready to serve.

Each goat cheese log can be shaped, covered, and chilled for up to 2 days before serving. The Blueberry-Honey and Black Pepper–Herb goat cheeses can be coated in advance, but the Spicy Pistachio-Walnut is best if coated with nuts the day it's served.

SPRING

Every time we had visited Connecticut from New York or LA, it was in the fall or over the winter holidays. So to say that we were completely and utterly bowled over by our first spring is a major understatement. As enchanting as changing leaves and snow-topped steeples had been, they paled in comparison to those first few weeks after the frost when the grass, trees, flowers, and even the animals took a big collective breath and burst forth in all their green, lush, post-cold glory. Our fields were speckled with crocuses, hyacinth, and daffodils; the magnolias were heavy with their giant Dr. Seuss–like blooms; and even the chickens got in the spirit by giving us more eggs than ever before.

We're still humbled by the transformation that happens here in the spring, with each day bringing something new to look at. It also brings a flurry of activity as we get to work repairing damage to our trees and picking up fallen branches, making sense of our gravel driveway that gets trounced by the snowplows, unwrapping the burlap from the hedges, and making sure our rescued mini horses aren't spending too much time at pasture because all that fresh, nutrient-dense grass doesn't agree with their sensitive digestive systems. We also start getting excited about what we want to grow in the garden, always picking something new to add and experiment with. And of course, there's the anticipation of finally cooking with all those fresh flavors that we've missed during the colder months.

The recipes in this section are meant to deliver just that—a much-needed dose of light and bright. Tender greens, herbs, and baby vegetables; asparagus, radishes, and lettuces adorn these dishes intended to usher in the sunshine.

RECIVES

SPECIAL PROJECTS

RECIPES

Shirred Eggs *with* Leeks, Spring Herbs, *and* Gruyère

¼ cup (57g) unsalted butter

5 baby leeks, roots trimmed and thinly sliced (about 1¼ cups)

2 garlic cloves, minced

¼ teaspoon kosher salt

2 tablespoons finely chopped fresh tarragon, plus more for serving

1 tablespoon finely chopped fresh thyme, plus more for serving

¾ cup (75g) shredded Gruyère cheese

6 large eggs

¼ cup plus 2 tablespoons (90ml) heavy whipping cream

Flaky sea salt, for serving

Freshly ground black pepper, for serving

Toast points, for serving

Not only does this dish embrace the gentle green-ness of early spring produce, it's also an ideal way to serve eggs to a number of people. I like to bake these off in individual ramekins, which is much easier than scrambling or coddling eggs like a mad person. The presentation says, "I'm effortlessly elegant." SERVES 6

Preheat the oven to 350°F. Rub 1 tablespoon of the butter inside six (8-ounce) ramekins and place them on a rimmed baking sheet.

In a large skillet over medium-high heat, melt the remaining 3 tablespoons of butter. Add the leeks, garlic, and salt and cook, stirring frequently, until the leeks have softened and are just starting to brown, about 8 minutes. Stir in the tarragon and thyme and remove the pan from the heat.

Divide the leek mixture between the ramekins and top with the cheese, about 2 tablespoons per ramekin. Crack an egg into each ramekin and pour 1 tablespoon of cream over each egg. Season each egg lightly with flaky salt and pepper.

Bake until the eggs are set, 15 to 20 minutes, depending on how you like yours cooked. The eggs will continue to set for a few minutes after they come out of the oven, so if you want a runny yolk, pull them when there's still a very faint translucent ring of egg white around the yolk. Top with more flaky salt and fresh herbs and serve with toast points.

TIPS & TRICKS

Parmesan-Herb Variation: Before baking, sprinkle each with 1 tablespoon grated Parmesan and ½ teaspoon fresh thyme or parsley leaves.

Mushroom-Kale Variation: Add ½ cup diced mushrooms and 1 cup chopped kale to the leeks when cooking.

Avocado-Cilantro Variation: After baking, top each with 2 tablespoons diced avocado, cilantro leaves, and a dash of hot sauce.

If you can't find baby leeks, use two regular leeks, and cut just the white and light-green parts. Save the darker, firmer tops for flavoring homemade broth.

Asparagus Spears *with* Poached Eggs *and* Butter-Fried Bread Crumbs

4 slices sourdough bread, torn into 1-inch pieces

5 tablespoons (70g) unsalted butter

1 garlic clove, smashed

¾ teaspoon kosher salt

1 pound (450g) fresh asparagus, woody ends trimmed

1 tablespoon extra-virgin olive oil

¼ teaspoon freshly ground black pepper

½ teaspoon lemon zest plus 1 tablespoon fresh lemon juice

1 tablespoon white vinegar

4 large eggs

Flaky sea salt, for serving

Crushed red pepper, for serving

I've mentioned it before, but butter-fried bread crumbs have the power to completely elevate any dish. Because the beauty of this particular recipe is its simplicity—perfectly runny egg, lightly blanched asparagus—these bread crumbs are that essential finishing touch that brings everything together and makes this the ideal spring meal any time of day.   SERVES 4

In a food processor, add the bread and pulse to create coarse crumbs with some larger pieces remaining.

In a high-sided 12-inch nonstick skillet over medium heat, melt the butter. Add the garlic and cook, stirring occasionally, until the garlic is toasted, about 3 minutes. Add the bread crumbs and ¼ teaspoon of the salt and cook, stirring occasionally, until the bread crumbs are crispy and lightly browned, 6 to 8 minutes. Transfer the mixture to a medium bowl and discard the garlic clove. Wipe out the skillet and set aside.

Preheat the oven to high broil (500°F).

On a rimmed baking sheet, toss the asparagus with the olive oil, the remaining ½ teaspoon of the salt, and the pepper and arrange it in an even layer. Broil, watching carefully and rotating the pan halfway through, until the asparagus is tender and lightly charred, 6 to 8 minutes. Drizzle the lemon juice over the asparagus and loosely cover the pan with foil to keep warm.

In the same skillet over medium-high heat, add 1½ inches of water and bring to a gentle simmer. Stir in the vinegar. Crack the eggs into a small bowl and drop each egg just over the surface of the water into one "corner" of the skillet (think North, South, East, West). Cover and remove the skillet from the heat. Leave covered until the eggs reach the desired degree of doneness, about 5 minutes for a soft and runny yolk. Use a slotted spoon to transfer the eggs, one at a time, to a paper towel–lined baking sheet. Gently pat the eggs dry and trim any ragged edges.

Arrange the asparagus on a serving platter and top with the lemon zest and half of the bread crumbs. Place the eggs on top of the asparagus and top with the remaining bread crumbs, flaky salt, and red pepper. Serve immediately.

TIPS & TRICKS

Poached eggs seem fussy because they're usually accompanied by a laundry list of "essential" practices. I opt for this easy method, where you simply simmer the water with a little bit of vinegar, crack the eggs in, cover, and cook. The vinegar will help keep the egg white as tight as possible, but the real secret is to not get hung up on "perfect" poached eggs. They don't need to come out looking like pristine globes to be delicious!

Using fresh eggs is also a good way to ensure a tidy poached egg. The egg whites get more watery and thin the older the eggs get, so look for eggs with an expiration date that is far out, or buy fresh from your local farmers' market.

Asparagus Size Matters: It never fails; if I'm looking for thin asparagus spears at the market, I find big, fat, kindergarten-pencil size; if I need thicker ones, all I find are No. 2 pencils. This recipe was tested with No. 2 pencil size; if you can only find thicker asparagus, broil on low for 4 to 6 minutes to get them tender, then crank it up to high broil to get the color and char you want. Just watch carefully, and no matter what size you use, trim about an inch off the ends.

Strawberry-Lavender Jam

4 pounds (1,800g) fresh or frozen strawberries

4 cups (800g) granulated sugar

½ cup (120ml) fresh lemon juice (from about 3 lemons)

¼ teaspoon crushed lavender flowers

2 to 4 teaspoons pectin (optional)

TIPS & TRICKS

This jam recipe can easily be adapted to use any juicy berries or stone fruit with your favorite flavoring. I like to swap the strawberries and lavender for these combinations depending on what's in season: peaches with a split vanilla bean and grated zest of 1 orange, blackberries with 2 teaspoons ground ginger, or plums with 1 teaspoon ground cardamom. Just be sure to pit and chop or slice any stone fruit before cooking.

For a quick and easy thickness test, place a small plate in the freezer when you start cooking your jam. When the jam reaches temperature, place a small spoonful on the frozen plate and return to the freezer for 1 minute. Check the consistency of the jam and add the pectin, if desired.

While we love going berry picking with the boys in the summer, I personally am more about grabbing some of the pre-picked berries from the farm stands to save myself the work. The only problem is that these sweet, juicy gems are at their peak, peak ripeness when they're picked, meaning it's just a matter of days—if not hours—before they've gone from sweet snacks to compost. I've since figured out that I can buy as many berries as I want without guilt because I can preserve any overage with this simple jam recipe. I can also easily change things up by steeping a traditional berry base with flavors like lavender, rosewater, orange zest, and rosemary.

MAKES ABOUT 7 CUPS/8 (8-OUNCE) JARS

If you're using fresh strawberries, rinse them well under cold water and cut off the stem ends.

In a large pot or Dutch oven, combine the strawberries, sugar, lemon juice, and lavender flowers. Stir together and let the mixture stand for 10 to 15 minutes, just until the strawberries start to release their juices.

Set the pot over medium heat and cook, stirring occasionally, until the mixture comes to a boil. Continue boiling, stirring frequently, until the mixture is thick and jammy, or reaches 215°F to 220°F, about 1½ hours for fresh berries and 2 hours for frozen berries. For a smoother jam, you can mash the strawberries with a potato masher occasionally during cooking, or pulse with a stick blender when the jam has reached temperature. Test the jam for thickness (see Tips & Tricks). If you like a more set jam, lightly sprinkle the pectin over the surface of the jam and stir it in. Cook for 2 more minutes to activate the pectin.

From here, the hot jam can be transferred to jars and kept refrigerated for up to 3 months. Or, it can be placed in eight sterilized 8-ounce canning jars and processed in a water bath for 12 minutes (see Pickling, page 308, for sterilizing and canning instructions).

Crudité Platter *with* Arugula-Avocado Ranch

1 to 2 ripe Hass avocados (8 ounces/225g), peeled and pits removed

¾ cup (180ml) whole buttermilk

½ cup (110g) sour cream

½ cup (12g) packed baby arugula

½ small shallot, finely chopped

¼ cup (3g) fresh dill leaves

Zest and juice of 1 lemon

1 garlic clove, smashed

½ teaspoon kosher salt

½ teaspoon freshly ground black pepper

Crunchy, fresh vegetables, such as carrots, radishes, and sugar snap peas

TIPS & TRICKS

If you want a thinner dressing to use on salads, add more buttermilk, 1 tablespoon at a time, until you reach the desired consistency.

Whole plain Greek yogurt or skyr can be used in place of sour cream.

My grandparents used to take me to a restaurant called Taix, which has been open for more than ninety years. Instead of putting bread on the table, they'd bring a crudité platter, which always struck me as elegantly European. Since then, I've liked the idea of starting a meal with a vibrant spread of fresh, perfectly crisp vegetables served alongside a chilled dip. It's refreshing and light, almost like a palate cleanser. You could also use this dressing on pretty much anything—salads, casseroles, baked potatoes. Ranch tends to get a bad rap, but it's a prime example of just how delicious and dimensional something can be when you make it yourself. SERVES 8 TO 10

In a blender, add the avocado, buttermilk, sour cream, arugula, shallot, 2 tablespoons of the dill, lemon zest and juice, garlic, salt, and pepper and blend until completely smooth.

Finely chop the remaining 2 tablespoons of the dill. Transfer the avocado mixture to a container and stir in the chopped fresh dill. Cover and refrigerate for 30 minutes or up to 3 days in advance. Taste and stir in additional salt, if needed.

Pour the chilled ranch into a serving bowl and set it on a large platter or board. Arrange the vegetables around the bowl and serve.

Crispy Flatbread *with* Spring Herbs, Radishes, *and* Whipped Feta

1 pound (450g) chicken tenders

3 tablespoons extra-virgin olive oil

1 teaspoon kosher salt

½ teaspoon ground cumin

½ teaspoon dried thyme

1 garlic clove, minced

Zest and juice of 1 lemon

4 ounces (113g) crumbled Bulgarian feta cheese, at room temperature

1½ cups (428g) whole-milk Greek yogurt, at room temperature

2 teaspoons fresh mint leaves, minced (or 1 teaspoon dried mint)

¼ teaspoon freshly ground black pepper

2 store-bought lavash flatbreads

2 cups (120g) fresh parsley leaves, roughly chopped

1 cup (25g) fresh mint leaves, roughly chopped

1 cup (120g) sliced fresh radishes

Aleppo pepper, for garnish

Flaky sea salt, for garnish

TIPS & TRICKS

Look for lavash flatbreads near the premade pizza crusts and wraps in your grocer's deli section. They're super thin and grill up nice and crispy, like a hard taco shell.

I particularly love dishes that are meant to be grazed over communally with good conversation and lots of wine. So when I first had this Persian dish—called *panir sabzi*—it was a standout moment. Essentially, it's a Middle Eastern charcuterie board featuring salty chunks of feta cheese, delicate slivers of peppery radishes, mountains of fresh herbs, and soft lavash flatbread for tearing and scooping up the perfect bite. It's that sweet spot of a dish that's light and refreshing enough for summer but still plenty filling. Here I've put my own spin on the traditional spread, including adding spiced chicken to the mix to make it a more well-rounded meal, which would be perfect for a hearty lunch or light supper. SERVES 4

In a medium bowl, combine the chicken with 1 tablespoon of the olive oil, plus the salt, cumin, thyme, garlic, and lemon zest and juice. Let the chicken marinate in the refrigerator for 30 minutes.

In another medium bowl, whisk together the softened feta, yogurt, minced or dried mint, and pepper until combined. Set aside or cover and refrigerate until ready to use.

Preheat the grill to medium heat (about 350°F) or a grill pan on the stove over medium heat.

Grill the chicken over direct heat, covered, until cooked through, about 5 minutes per side. Let the chicken cool for 5 minutes and chop into bite-size pieces.

Meanwhile, brush the lavash with the remaining 2 tablespoons of olive oil. Grill the flatbreads until they are crispy and toasted, 1 to 2 minutes per side.

Spread about 1 cup of the feta mixture over each flatbread and top each evenly with the chicken, herbs, and radish slices. Garnish with Aleppo pepper and flaky salt, if desired.

Silky Spring Greens Soup *with* Parmesan-Kale Crisps

There's no better way to drink in the bounty of spring than with a velvety soup. It's a great way to use up all those greens you're finding at the market, while also giving your salad rotation a break. Then add the cheese crisps to take your greens to an indulgent place you didn't think was possible.   SERVES 4

FOR THE PARMESAN -KALE CRISPS

4 ounces (113g) Parmesan cheese, cut into cubes

¼ cup (17g) finely chopped kale

¼ teaspoon extra-virgin olive oil

⅛ teaspoon kosher salt

⅛ teaspoon crushed red pepper

FOR THE SOUP

1 tablespoon extra-virgin olive oil

1 cup (150g) diced white onion

¾ teaspoon kosher salt

¼ teaspoon freshly ground black pepper

4 cups (960ml) low-sodium chicken stock

1 cup (170g) fresh or frozen English peas

2 cups (60g) firmly packed baby spinach leaves

2 cups (70g) firmly packed baby arugula

½ cup (30g) fresh parsley leaves, plus more for serving

2 avocados, peeled and pits removed

1 cup (227g) whole-milk Greek yogurt

Zest and juice of 1 lemon

2 teaspoons champagne or white wine vinegar

Crème fraiche or sour cream, for serving

Chopped fresh mint and chives, for serving

Lemon wedges, for serving

MAKE THE PARMESAN-KALE CRISPS: Preheat the oven to 350°F. Line a baking sheet with parchment paper and set aside.

In the bowl of a food processor, add the Parmesan and pulse until coarsely ground. Measure ½ cup into a bowl and set aside. Chill or freeze any remaining cheese for another use.

In a medium bowl, toss together the kale, oil, salt, and red pepper until combined. Stir in the reserved Parmesan. Use a tablespoon to spoon the mixture into mounds on the prepared baking sheet. Lightly press each mound into 2-inch disks, spacing 1 to 2 inches apart. Bake until the cheese is lightly browned and the kale is crisp, 10 to 12 minutes. Let the crisps cool completely on the pan. Store in an airtight container at room temperature for up to 5 days.

MAKE THE SOUP: In a medium saucepan over medium heat, heat the olive oil. Add the onion, ¼ teaspoon of the salt, and the pepper. Cook, stirring occasionally, until the onion is translucent and softened, about 5 minutes. Add the chicken stock, cover, and bring to a boil. Add the peas, cover, and cook for 3 minutes. Stir in the spinach, arugula, and parsley, cover, and cook until the greens are wilted, about 3 minutes more.

Transfer the greens mixture to a blender. Remove the plug in the blender lid, place the lid on the blender, and cover the hole with a clean kitchen towel. Puree the greens until smooth. Add the avocado, yogurt, lemon zest and juice, and vinegar. Blend until smooth. Add salt if needed.

Serve immediately or cover and refrigerate until cold, about 5 hours. Top with the crème fraiche or sour cream and sprinkle with the herbs. Serve with the lemon wedges and the Parmesan-Kale Crisps.

> **TIPS & TRICKS**
>
> The idea of cold soup can be quite polarizing, but don't fret! This recipe is equally delicious hot or cold, so serve as desired.

Mustard-Roasted Salmon Niçoise Salad

Traditionally you'd find Niçoise salad made with fresh tuna (or, in some really unfortunate cases, canned tuna). While I like the original version, salmon achieves a melt-in-your-mouth buttery softness that far surpasses anything tuna could ever do. It's the perfect counterpart to the crunch of the fresh peas and haricots verts, brought together by the bright tang of the mustard vinaigrette. SERVES 6 TO 8

FOR THE DRESSING

⅓ cup (80ml) extra-virgin olive oil

⅓ cup (80ml) champagne or sherry vinegar

1 tablespoon coarse-ground Dijon mustard

1 tablespoon honey

½ teaspoon kosher salt

¼ teaspoon freshly ground black pepper

FOR THE SALAD

1½ pounds (675g) fingerling potatoes, halved lengthwise

¼ cup (60ml) extra-virgin olive oil

2¾ teaspoons kosher salt

1 teaspoon freshly ground black pepper, plus more for serving

1 tablespoon champagne or sherry vinegar

1 tablespoon coarse-ground Dijon mustard

1 tablespoon honey

1 (2-pound/900g) salmon fillet (skinless, if available)

½ pound (225g) haricots verts (French-style green beans)

3 cups (108g) torn lettuce, such as romaine or green leaf

2 cups (300g) cherry tomatoes, halved

6 soft-boiled eggs, halved

1 cup (180g) mixed pitted olives, such as Niçoise, Kalamata, and/or Castelvetrano, drained

Flaky sea salt, for serving

Torn baguette, for serving

MAKE THE DRESSING: In a medium bowl or medium lidded jar, add the olive oil, vinegar, mustard, honey, salt, and pepper and whisk or shake until well combined. Set aside.

MAKE THE SALAD: Preheat the oven to 400°F.

On a rimmed baking sheet, combine the potatoes, 2 tablespoons of the olive oil, 1 teaspoon of the salt, and ½ teaspoon of the pepper and toss to coat. Arrange the potatoes cut side down in an even layer and bake until lightly browned and tender when pierced with a fork, about 15 minutes.

In a small bowl, whisk together 1 tablespoon each of the oil, vinegar, mustard, and honey until smooth.

Remove the potatoes from the oven and increase the oven temperature to 450°F. Flip the potatoes cut side up and push them to the perimeter of the pan. Set the salmon in the center of the pan (skin side down if the skin is on) and spoon the mustard mixture evenly over the fish. Season the salmon with 1½ teaspoons of the salt and ¼ teaspoon of the pepper. Scatter the haricots verts around the salmon, drizzle them with the remaining tablespoon of oil, and season with the remaining ¼ teaspoon each of salt and pepper. Return the pan to the oven and roast until the thickest portion of the salmon flakes easily with a fork, about 10 minutes for a thin fillet and up to 20 minutes for a thicker fillet.

Let the salmon cool for about 5 minutes and transfer to a large serving platter. Surround the salmon with the roasted potatoes and haricots verts, plus the torn lettuce, tomatoes, halved eggs, and olives. Shake or whisk the dressing to recombine and drizzle about ½ cup over the salad and salmon. Sprinkle flaky salt and pepper over the eggs and tomatoes, if desired. Serve with the torn baguette and remaining dressing.

Shrimp *and* Tomato Salad *with* Ricotta-Stuffed Squash Blossoms

I love cooking with squash blossoms when they're in season because they have a surprisingly peppery flavor that punctuates a creamy ricotta stuffing, not to mention the fact that you get a giant edible flower on your plate to adorn the pretty pinks, oranges, and reds of this salad. But I should make one thing clear: you do not need squash blossoms to make this a great dish. But if you do come across them at the market during the short window that they're available, don't hesitate. If squash blossoms aren't in the cards for you, you can serve the ricotta filling on the side, and consider tossing some arugula in the salad to bring a similar peppery quality. SERVES 6

FOR THE CHAMPAGNE-SHALLOT VINAIGRETTE

½ cup (120ml) champagne vinegar

1 shallot, halved and thinly sliced

1 tablespoon fresh lemon juice

Leaves from 1 sprig fresh thyme

⅛ teaspoon kosher salt

¼ cup (60ml) extra-virgin olive oil

FOR THE RICOTTA-STUFFED SQUASH BLOSSOMS

1 cup (220g) whole-milk ricotta cheese

3 tablespoons grated Parmesan cheese

1 tablespoon chopped fresh tarragon

Zest of ½ lemon

¼ teaspoon freshly ground black pepper

⅛ teaspoon kosher salt

18 squash blossoms

MAKE THE CHAMPAGNE-SHALLOT VINAIGRETTE: In a pint-size Mason jar, combine the champagne vinegar, shallot, lemon juice, thyme, and salt. Seal the lid and shake vigorously, then set aside to let the shallots pickle for 10 minutes. Add the olive oil and shake well once more to combine. Set aside until ready to use.

MAKE THE STUFFED SQUASH BLOSSOMS: In a medium bowl, mix together the ricotta, Parmesan, tarragon, lemon zest, pepper, and salt. Transfer the mixture to a piping bag fitted with a round tip (or you can use a zip-top bag and snip about ¼ inch off the tip).

Carefully open the squash blossom petals, insert the tip of the piping bag, and fill the blossom about halfway with the ricotta mixture (1 to 2 tablespoons). Gently close the petals and give them a light twist at the top to keep them closed. Set the stuffed blossoms on a plate or baking sheet and keep chilled until ready to serve.

MAKE THE SHRIMP AND TOMATO SALAD: Use a paring knife to trim off the top and bottom of each orange to make a flat surface. Set the oranges on a cutting board and cut along the sides of the fruit to remove the peel and pith completely. Hold the orange over a large bowl and carefully cut out the segments by running the knife along each membrane. Discard the membrane and add the orange segments to the bowl. Repeat with the remaining orange. Add the cherry tomatoes, toss to combine, and set aside.

In a large skillet over medium-high heat, heat the butter and olive oil until the butter is melted and foamy. Add the garlic and thyme and cook,

FOR THE SHRIMP AND TOMATO SALAD

2 navel oranges

1 pound (450g) mixed heirloom cherry tomatoes, halved

2 tablespoons unsalted butter

1 tablespoon extra-virgin olive oil

7 garlic cloves, minced

3 sprigs fresh thyme

1 pound (450g) large (16 to 20 count) shrimp, peeled and deveined

¼ teaspoon kosher salt

¼ teaspoon freshly ground black pepper

Chopped fresh herbs, such as basil, tarragon, or thyme, for serving

TIPS & TRICKS

Depending on the size of your squash blossoms, you could have a little bit of ricotta filling leftover. Dollop it around the salad after plating, if desired.

Not all ricotta brands are the same. For this filling, a firmer, less watery ricotta is ideal. My preferred brand is Galbani.

If you're picking squash blossoms from your own garden, try to cut a little bit of stem with them. This will give you a good way to hold them while filling. They can also wilt quickly, so pick them a short time before using.

stirring constantly, for about 1 minute. Add the shrimp and season with the salt and pepper. Cook the shrimp, flipping once, until pink and almost firm, about 2 minutes. Remove the pan from the heat.

Add about half of the vinaigrette to the orange-tomato mixture and toss to coat. Divide the mixture among 6 serving plates and top with the shrimp. Drizzle with additional vinaigrette if desired. Arrange the stuffed squash blossoms alongside the salad and finish with the fresh herbs.

Beet *and* Grapefruit Salad

8 ounces (225g) feta cheese, broken up into chunks

¾ cup (200g) whole-milk Greek yogurt

½ teaspoon kosher salt

1 tablespoon whole milk, plus more if needed

¼ cup (60ml) extra-virgin olive oil

2 tablespoons red wine vinegar

1 tablespoon Dijon mustard

¼ teaspoon freshly ground black pepper, plus more for finishing

6 fresh mint leaves, chopped, plus more for finishing

2 small Chioggia or golden beets, peeled, trimmed, and thinly sliced (use a mandoline if you have one)

2 ruby red grapefruits

4 cups (80g) baby arugula

½ cup (50g) toasted walnuts (see Tips & Tricks)

TIPS & TRICKS

If you prefer cooked beets, place ½ pound of unpeeled beets, greens removed, in a pot and fill with enough water to cover. Bring to a boil over medium-high heat and cook, partially covered, until fork tender, 45 to 90 minutes. Drain and let cool. Use a paper towel to rub the skins of the beets off and discard. Chop or slice the cooked beets and use in place of the fresh Chioggia beets.

You can use blood oranges, Cara Cara, or navel oranges in place of grapefruit, if desired.

To toast your own walnuts, arrange the walnuts in a single layer on a baking sheet. Bake at 350ºF for 12 to 15 minutes, or until lightly browned, stirring every 5 minutes.

This salad could easily be a year-round staple because you have the most delicious, tender beets coming out of the ground in the spring and continuing to pop up at the market until they're part of the cold storage root vegetable array through the winter. No matter what, beets bring their natural sweetness to this salad, which gets rounded out here by the sweet-bitter grapefruit, salty feta, and peppery arugula. It's the kind of combination that just works. A word to the wise: don't let your kids catch you supreming the grapefruit or it will be the only way they'll agree to eat citrus. SERVES 4 TO 6

In a food processor, add the feta, yogurt, and ¼ teaspoon of the salt. Process until very smooth, about 3 minutes, adding the milk if needed to thin it out slightly. Transfer the mixture to an airtight container and chill until ready to serve.

In a large bowl, whisk together the olive oil, vinegar, mustard, the remaining ¼ teaspoon of salt, and the pepper. Stir in the chopped mint. Add the sliced beets and toss to coat. Set aside or cover the bowl and chill for up to 2 hours for even more flavor.

Cut the peel and pith off the grapefruit. Working over a bowl and using a small knife, cut the grapefruit into wedges by slicing on either side of each membrane. Discard the membrane. Add the grapefruit segments and arugula to the dressed beets and toss thoroughly.

On a large serving plate, or dividing among smaller ones, spread the whipped feta. Arrange the beet and grapefruit mixture on top and sprinkle with the toasted walnuts and additional fresh mint and black pepper.

Gingery Apple *and* Cucumber Slaw

1 (3-inch) piece fresh ginger root

½ cup (54g) raw slivered almonds

3 tablespoons vegetable oil or avocado oil

¼ cup plus 1 tablespoon fresh lime juice

1½ teaspoons granulated sugar

¼ teaspoon kosher salt

¼ teaspoon ground ginger

2 cups (100g) thinly sliced Napa or green cabbage

2 medium carrots, peeled and shaved into ribbons

2 Persian cucumbers or ½ seedless English cucumber, sliced into thin half-moons

1 Honeycrisp apple, cored and cut into matchsticks

3 scallions, light green and green parts only, thinly sliced

TIPS & TRICKS

If you can't find Napa cabbage, green or savoy cabbage can be substituted. Red cabbage can also be used, but it will turn the slaw pink.

Take this slaw from a side dish to a meal by topping it with a piece of roasted chicken or fish or pan-seared scallops.

Coleslaw makes a frequent appearance in my kitchen during the spring and summer because it holds up nicely in the fridge and makes a great light lunch or side for several days. But we're not talking mayo-heavy, overly creamy slaws. When I was growing up, coleslaw wasn't much more than sliced cabbage and lemon or lime tufted over a bowl of pozole. It was the perfect balance of sweet, sharp, and bright—which I still believe is the key to a successful slaw. SERVES 6

Peel the ginger using the side of a spoon to scrape off the skin. Grate 1 inch of the ginger into a large heatproof bowl and set a small sieve over the top. Set aside.

Very thinly slice the remaining 2 inches of ginger and cut the slices into matchsticks. Set aside.

Add the almonds to a small skillet and set the skillet over medium heat. Toast the almonds until fragrant, 4 or 5 minutes, shaking the pan frequently to avoid burning. Transfer the almonds to a small plate to cool.

Return the skillet to medium-high heat and heat the oil until shimmering. Carefully add the ginger matchsticks and fry until very lightly golden and crisp, barely 1 minute, tilting the pan if needed to keep the ginger in the oil. Pour the fried ginger and oil into the sieve so the hot oil drains into the bowl with the grated ginger. Transfer the fried ginger to a plate and set aside.

In the bowl with the hot oil and grated ginger, whisk in the lime juice, sugar, salt, and ground ginger. Set the dressing aside for about 10 minutes to cool completely. Add the cabbage, carrots, cucumber, apple, scallions, and toasted almonds to the cooled dressing and toss to coat.

Transfer to a serving bowl. The slaw is best served immediately, but can be refrigerated for up to 2 hours before serving. Sprinkle with the crispy ginger just before serving.

Stuffed Grape Leaves *with* Lemon-Yogurt Sauce

Greek stuffed grape leaves, or *dolmathes*, are a light starter that hit the sweet spot for my mom. She loved a 1970s- and '80s-style dinner party and its requisite hors d'oeuvres, and also made a point of mastering traditional Greek dishes. These practically beg to be made in the spring, between their ultra-herby rice and tart lemony sauce, plus the fact that they're parceled up in leaves. Rolling them is a little bit of a labor of love, but it became one of my favorite memories of spending time in the kitchen with my mom, and it's a process that's well worth it.

MAKES ABOUT 70 PIECES

FOR THE FILLING

2 tablespoons extra-virgin olive oil

1 large sweet onion, finely chopped

1 pound (450g) lean ground beef or lamb

3 garlic cloves, grated

½ cup (120ml) plain tomato sauce

½ cup (120ml) deep red wine, such as Shiraz or Cabernet Sauvignon

2 tablespoons minced fresh mint leaves

2 tablespoons minced fresh oregano, plus more for serving

¾ teaspoon kosher salt

½ teaspoon freshly ground black pepper, plus more for serving

1 cup (200g) long grain white rice

FOR THE DOLMATHES

1 (16-ounce) jar grape leaves (or about 80 leaves)

Juice of 1 lemon

2 bay leaves

FOR THE CREAMY LEMON SAUCE

1 cup (240ml) low-sodium chicken broth

3 large eggs

Zest and juice of 2 lemons

¼ teaspoon kosher salt

MAKE THE FILLING: In a deep 12- to 14-inch skillet or braiser over medium-high heat, heat the olive oil. Add the onion and cook, stirring frequently, until just starting to brown, about 10 minutes. Add the beef or lamb and garlic and cook, stirring occasionally, until the meat is browned and only slightly pink, 5 to 8 minutes. Add the tomato sauce, wine, mint, oregano, salt, pepper, and 1½ cups of water and stir until combined. Stir in the rice and reduce the heat to medium-low. Simmer, stirring once or twice, until the liquid is mostly absorbed, about 12 minutes.

Transfer the mixture to a bowl and let cool for about 20 minutes, until it's cool enough to handle. Clean the skillet and set aside.

MAKE THE DOLMATHES: In a large bowl or baking dish, lay the grape leaves flat and cover with cold water. Soak for 10 minutes and drain.

Line the bottom of the same skillet with several grape leaves, overlapping the edges slightly so the bottom of the skillet isn't visible. Reserve 4 more grape leaves for the top of the batch.

Place a grape leaf flat on a clean surface with the stem end facing you. Spoon about 1 tablespoon of the filling near the stem end. Fold the right side of the leaf toward the center, over the filling. Repeat with the left side. Fold the end closest to you just up over the filling and roll away from you into a log. Place the roll seam side down in the prepared skillet. Repeat with the remaining filling, arranging the rolls snugly and layering the rolls as needed. (You may not use all the grape leaves.)

Drizzle the rolls with the lemon juice and place the bay leaves on top. Pour 2 cups of water down the side of the skillet and cover the rolls with the remaining 4 grape leaves. Place a large dinner plate upside down on top of the rolls (this should fit snugly just inside the skillet). Cover partially with a lid.

Set the skillet over medium heat and bring to a boil, about 10 minutes. Reduce the heat to medium-low and simmer for about 1 hour, until a little more than half of the liquid is evaporated. Remove the pan from the heat.

MAKE THE CREAMY LEMON SAUCE: In a small saucepan over medium heat, bring the broth to a simmer. Cover to keep warm.

In a large mixing bowl, whisk the eggs, lemon zest and juice, and salt until well combined. While whisking, slowly stream in half of the hot broth. Slowly whisk the egg mixture into the broth remaining in the saucepan.

Continue cooking over medium-low heat until the sauce is thickened and coats the back of a spoon, about 7 minutes. Remove from the heat and immediately pour into a serving bowl or gravy boat. (Keeping the sauce in the hot pan could cause it to curdle as it sits.)

SERVE: Carefully remove the dinner plate, the top grape leaves, and the bay leaves from the skillet. Serve immediately with the Creamy Lemon Sauce, oregano, and black pepper.

TIPS & TRICKS

Jarred grape leaves can be found in the international foods section of some grocery stores, and if you have a specialty Mediterranean foods market in your area, they should have them. If you can't find them, you can blanch small collard or Swiss chard leaves to use as the wrappers.

This recipe is easy to assemble but does take some time. It's a great dish to get family or friends involved and make the rolls together. (A little wine helps make it fun, too!)

Creamy Spring Vegetable Linguini *with* Goat Cheese *and* Prosciutto

Kosher salt

¾ pound (338g) asparagus, woody ends trimmed, spears chopped into 1-inch pieces

2 cups (340g) fresh or frozen English peas

3 tablespoons extra-virgin olive oil

6 thin slices prosciutto

2 tablespoons unsalted butter

6 rainbow carrots, peeled and very thinly sliced on the diagonal

4 garlic cloves, minced

½ teaspoon freshly ground black pepper

½ cup (120ml) dry white wine, such as Sauvignon Blanc

1 pound (450g) linguini

¼ cup (60ml) heavy whipping cream

8 ounces (225g) goat cheese, room temperature

Zest and juice of 1 lemon

1 or 2 pinches crushed red pepper (optional)

Finely chopped fresh herbs, such as basil, parsley, or chives, for serving

No one said that just because it's not winter anymore, we can't continue to indulge. We're still featuring our vegetables here, but now we're just dressing them up in a shortcut cream sauce with goat cheese and a splash of cream or milk, crispy prosciutto, and plenty of fresh green herbs. They're similar flavors to those you'd enjoy in the fall or winter, but with a slightly lighter vibe for spring. SERVES 4 TO 6

Bring a large pot of salted water to a boil over high heat. Add the asparagus and peas and cook until bright green, about 2 minutes. Use a slotted spoon or fine mesh sieve to transfer to a bowl. Cover the vegetables with cold water and let sit for 3 minutes to cool slightly. Drain the vegetables and set aside. Remove the pot from the heat and cover to keep warm.

In a large skillet over medium-high heat, heat 1 tablespoon of the oil. Add a few slices of prosciutto and cook until it shrivels and crisps slightly, 1 to 2 minutes per side. Transfer the crisped prosciutto to a plate to cool and repeat with the remaining slices.

Return the skillet to medium heat. Add the butter and the remaining 2 tablespoons of olive oil and swirl until the butter is melted and foamy, about 2 minutes. Add the carrots, garlic, and pepper and cook, stirring occasionally, 1 or 2 minutes, just until the garlic is very fragrant. Add the wine and cook until the carrots are crisp-tender, about 5 minutes. Remove the pan from the heat and stir in the asparagus and peas. Set aside.

Return the pot of water to a boil over medium-high heat. Add the linguini and cook according to the package instructions. Reserve 1½ cups of the pasta water and drain the pasta.

Add the pasta water and cream back into the pot and return the pot to medium heat. Add the goat cheese and whisk until smooth. Stir in the lemon zest and juice, plus the red pepper, if using. Add the drained pasta and vegetable mixture and toss until the pasta is well coated. Garnish with the fresh herbs and crumble the crisped prosciutto on top.

TIPS & TRICKS

When seasoning the water for cooking the vegetables and pasta, be generous with the salt. You want the water to taste as salty as ocean water. Generally, a ratio of 1 tablespoon of salt to 2 quarts of water is ideal.

Breakfast-for-Dinner Tart *with* Farm Eggs, Asparagus, *and* Radishes

If you can't tell, I have a thing for eggs—which comes in handy when you have a whole bunch of chickens. They're the ideal way to add richness to any dish, are infinitely versatile, and couldn't be easier to dress up. So it stands to reason that, to me, breakfast for dinner is a completely acceptable and normal proposition. This tart isn't much more than baked eggs atop a flaky crust, adorned with asparagus (or another vegetable of your choice) and sliced radishes for crunch and a peppery heat—a signature of my Mexican heritage. SERVES 6

All-purpose flour, for dusting

1 recipe Rough Puff Pastry (page 71) or thawed frozen puff pastry

1 large egg, beaten

4 slices thick-cut bacon, cut into 1-inch pieces

1 pound (450g) asparagus, woody ends trimmed, spears sliced on the bias into 1-inch pieces

½ cup (110g) thinly sliced radishes

½ teaspoon kosher salt, plus more to taste

¼ teaspoon freshly ground black pepper, plus more to taste

6 small to medium eggs

1 cup (108g) shredded Fontina cheese

½ cup (45g) grated Parmesan cheese

1 tablespoon chopped fresh chives, for garnish

TIPS & TRICKS

The secret to a crispy, flaky tart is to treat your puff pastry with respect. Keeping the puff pastry cold until you're ready to bake is essential; the cold butter in the dough evaporates in the oven, lifting the layers of dough like an inflating hot-air balloon.

Nearly every part of this tart is customizable, based on how much time you have and what's hanging out in your refrigerator and freezer. Trade the Fontina for mozzarella or Gruyère; skip the asparagus and sprinkle the tart with a lightly dressed arugula salad.

On a piece of lightly floured parchment paper, roll the Rough Puff Pastry into a 10x14-inch rectangle. Use a paring knife to lightly score the inside perimeter of the pastry about ½ inch from the edge. Use a fork to dock the pastry about forty times all over inside the scored perimeter. Transfer the prepared pastry to a baking sheet and brush lightly with the beaten egg. Freeze for 20 minutes.

Preheat the oven to 425°F.

In a large nonstick or cast iron skillet over medium heat, cook the bacon until crisp, 5 to 7 minutes. Transfer the cooked bacon to a paper towel–lined plate and reserve the drippings in the pan. Add the asparagus, radishes, salt, and pepper and cook, stirring occasionally, until just tender, about 5 minutes. Remove from the heat. Transfer the vegetable mixture to a bowl, leaving any remaining drippings in the skillet, and set aside.

Remove the crust from the freezer and bake on the middle rack until puffed and lightly browned, about 15 minutes. Remove the pastry from the oven and reduce the temperature to 350°F.

Gently press down the center of the pastry with a large spoon to remove any major puffing. Sprinkle half of the Fontina and half of the Parmesan over the pastry and set aside.

Return the same skillet to medium heat and fry the eggs in batches, seasoning with salt and pepper if desired. Cook until they reach your desired degree of doneness, 3 to 4 minutes for sunny side up. Transfer the eggs to the crust and scatter the vegetable mixture, cooked bacon, and remaining Fontina and Parmesan around and over the eggs.

Bake just until the cheese melts, about 5 minutes more. Garnish with the chives and serve immediately.

Champagne-Butter Clams *with* Herby Sourdough Toasts

Clams are often done the disservice of being overcooked and rubbery, to the point that most people wouldn't know a good clam if you threw one in their mouths. They should be soft and taste like the ocean, with their brine allowed to mingle with butter, champagne vinegar, and herbs for an indulgent sopping-up sauce. There's really nothing better to enjoy with a glass of wine.

SERVES 4 TO 6

1 whole garlic head

1 teaspoon extra-virgin olive oil

½ teaspoon sea salt, plus more as needed

¼ teaspoon freshly ground black pepper, plus more as needed

4 pounds (1.8kg) littleneck clams, scrubbed

1 cup (2 sticks/226g) unsalted butter, softened

¼ cup (15g) chopped fresh tender herb leaves, such as thyme, parsley, and chives, plus more for garnish

8 slices sourdough bread

1 cup (240ml) champagne or any dry sparkling white wine

Flaky sea salt, for serving

Lemon wedges, for serving

TIPS & TRICKS

When shopping for clams, opt for the smallest you can find; they'll be the most tender. To make sure they stay as fresh as possible, store them in an open bag set in a bowl of ice in the refrigerator. Tap any open clams before cooking; if they don't close, discard them.

Even after soaking, clams will purge a bit of sand during cooking, so be sure to carefully decant the cooking liquid to preserve every delicious drop and avoid the grit. Clams will also differ in saltiness, so add more salt to taste based on your preference and the flavor of your clams.

Preheat the oven to 350°F.

Trim about ¼ inch from the top of the head of garlic so all the cloves are exposed. Place the garlic on a small piece of aluminum foil, drizzle with the olive oil, and season with a pinch of salt and pepper. Wrap the garlic in the foil, set on a baking sheet, and bake until the garlic is tender, about 40 minutes. Set aside the foil packet until it's just cool enough to handle, then unwrap the garlic head and let it cool completely.

In a large bowl, add the clams and enough cold water to cover. Let them stand for 20 minutes, drain, and rinse again.

Squeeze the roasted garlic cloves into a medium bowl and mash them with a fork until mostly smooth. Add the butter, salt, pepper, and mixed fresh herbs and stir until smooth and combined.

Preheat the oven to high broil (500°F).

Lay the bread slices on a large baking sheet. Spread half of the garlic herb butter on the bread slices. Broil until golden brown, 2 to 3 minutes.

Place the remaining garlic herb butter in a large Dutch oven and melt over medium heat. Add the drained clams and champagne. Bring to a simmer, cover, and cook until all the clams are open, 6 to 9 minutes.

Use a slotted spoon to transfer the clams to a deep rimmed platter or individual serving bowls, discarding any unopened clams. Ladle the cooking liquid over the clams, being careful to leave any grit at the bottom of the pan. Finish with additional fresh herbs and flaky salt and serve with the sourdough toasts and lemon wedges. If you're not serving the clams immediately, cover the platter with foil to keep warm and garnish just before serving.

Steamed Mahi-Mahi *with* Macadamia Nuts *and* Spring Herbs

I'm officially demystifying simple fish cooking for weeknights, especially a light, flaky fish like mahi-mahi that pairs well with bright flavors. I remember the first time I had fish en papillote—fish steamed in parchment paper—at a restaurant. It seemed so fancy, and far beyond my skills at the time. But one day I decided to try it, and it was so shockingly easy. The parceled fish steams to perfection every time, basting itself in flavorful juices. No sticking to the pan or overcooking to worry about, plus you get a very impressive presentation. SERVES 2

2 lemons

1 cup (60g) fresh parsley leaves, lightly packed and roughly chopped

½ cup (56g) toasted macadamia nuts, roughly chopped

¼ cup (7g) fresh mint leaves, roughly chopped

1 garlic clove, roughly chopped

1 teaspoon flaky sea salt

¼ teaspoon crushed red pepper

2 (6-ounce/170g) mahi-mahi fillets

1 tablespoon plus 1 teaspoon extra-virgin olive oil

¼ teaspoon freshly ground black pepper

TIPS & TRICKS

Can't find mahi-mahi? No problem. This recipe works with any thin, flaky whitefish, such as snapper or orange roughy. Frozen fish is fine; simply defrost overnight in the refrigerator.

Parchment paper is essential for this recipe. Do not use wax paper and avoid using foil, as the acid in the lemon can interact with the aluminum and produce a metallic taste.

You can assemble these packets several hours ahead of time and keep them refrigerated until you're ready to bake. Let it come to room temperature for 30 minutes before cooking.

Preheat the oven to 375°F.

Thinly slice one of the lemons into eight slices. Zest the remaining lemon and set the zest aside. Cut the zested lemon into wedges for serving.

On a cutting board, pile up the parsley, macadamia nuts, mint, garlic, ¼ teaspoon of the flaky salt, the crushed red pepper, and the lemon zest. Chop the ingredients together until they form a crumbly, finely chopped mixture.

Place a (11x15-inch) piece of parchment on a clean work surface. Set 3 lemon slices on the center of the parchment and sprinkle with about ¼ cup of the macadamia mixture. Top with a piece of the mahi-mahi and drizzle both sides of the fish with 2 teaspoons of the oil. Season with about ¼ teaspoon of the salt and ⅛ teaspoon of the pepper, followed by one more lemon slice and 2 more tablespoons of the macadamia mixture. Place another piece of parchment directly on top of the fish, lining up the edges of the paper. Starting at one corner and working your way around the edges, roll up the edges of the paper to seal, rolling and pressing to create a closed packet. (Don't worry about it being completely airtight.) Repeat the process for the other packet with the remaining ingredients and place the packets on a baking sheet.

Bake for about 15 minutes, or until the fish is just cooked through. Remove the pan from the oven and let the fish continue steaming for about 5 more minutes. Carefully cut a slit in the top of each packet and transfer the fish to a serving plate. Top with the remaining macadamia mixture and the remaining ¼ teaspoon of the salt. Serve with the lemon wedges.

Chicken Milanese *with* Roasted Grapes *and* Rosemary

3 slices crusty sourdough bread, torn into small chunks

1 large egg

3 tablespoons whole milk

2 tablespoons Dijon mustard

Kosher salt

Freshly ground black pepper

6 boneless, skinless chicken thighs

¼ cup (57g) unsalted butter

2 tablespoons extra-virgin olive oil

8 garlic cloves, smashed

4 fresh rosemary sprigs

½ large red onion, thinly sliced

1 pound (450g) green grapes, halved

Juice of ½ lemon

TIPS & TRICKS

Chicken thighs are the perfect cut for this recipe because they stay juicy while being kept warm in the oven. Chicken breast cutlets could be used here, but they may dry out.

The tartness of green grapes is a good contrast to the savory chicken and herbs, but red grapes could certainly be used.

If you have any chicken left over, make the Chive and Parmesan Buttermilk Biscuits (page 52) and stuff them with pieces of the chicken Milanese for outrageously delicious chicken biscuits.

People are often surprised when they hear that grapes can be worked into savory dishes as well as sweet. I'm particularly fond of pan-roasting them with thinly sliced onions, which take on their own caramelized sweetness. Combined with bright lemon, it's the perfect counterbalance to the crispy breaded chicken cutlets. SERVES 4 TO 6

Preheat the oven to 200°F. Set a wire rack on a baking sheet and place in the oven.

In the bowl of a food processor, add the torn bread and pulse until the bread is very fine. Transfer the bread crumbs to a shallow dish.

In another shallow dish, whisk together the egg, milk, mustard, and ½ teaspoon of salt until well combined.

Using a meat mallet or rolling pin, pound each chicken thigh between two pieces of plastic wrap to ½-inch thickness. Coat the chicken in egg mixture on both sides. Let any excess drip off and dredge in the bread crumbs, coating both sides well. Transfer the coated chicken to a baking sheet or large platter.

In a large skillet over medium-high heat, heat 2 tablespoons of the butter and 1 tablespoon of the olive oil until the butter is melted and foamy. Add 3 of the chicken pieces and scatter 4 garlic cloves and 2 rosemary sprigs around the pan. Cook until the chicken is golden brown and a meat thermometer inserted in the center registers 165°F, about 6 minutes per side. Transfer the cooked chicken to the wire rack in the oven to keep warm. Remove the garlic and rosemary with a slotted spoon and set aside. If the butter appears to be smoking or burning, carefully wipe the skillet clean. Repeat with the remaining butter, oil, chicken, garlic, and rosemary.

In the same skillet over medium-high heat, add the onion and toss to coat in the oil. Cook for 1 minute. Add the grapes and lemon juice, stirring frequently until the grapes are slightly softened, about 3 minutes. Season to taste with salt and pepper and remove the pan from the heat.

Transfer the warm chicken to a serving platter, season with salt and pepper, and surround with the roasted grapes and onions and the fried garlic and rosemary.

Pan-Roasted Chicken *with* Mushrooms, Asparagus, *and* Champagne Beurre Blanc

½ cup champagne or sparkling white wine

¼ cup diced shallot

2 tablespoons fresh lemon juice

1 tablespoon sherry or white wine vinegar

4 bone-in, skin-on chicken thighs (about 2 pounds/900g)

2½ teaspoons kosher salt

1 teaspoon freshly ground black pepper

¼ teaspoon crushed red pepper, plus more for serving

8 ounces (225g) cremini mushrooms, cleaned, trimmed, and quartered

3 shallots, halved

2 tablespoons extra-virgin olive oil

1 pound (450g) asparagus, woody ends trimmed, spears chopped into 1-inch pieces (see Tips & Tricks)

½ cup plus 6 tablespoons (1¾ sticks/198g) unsalted butter

2 teaspoons honey

Fresh tarragon leaves, for serving

TIPS & TRICKS

This delicious French sauce is notorious for "breaking" or separating. But don't be intimidated. The only thing you need to master for beurre blanc is patience. Whisk each tablespoon of butter in and wait until it's completely melted before adding the next.

Beurre blanc is a staple sauce that everyone should be making. It's not much more than melted butter lightened with white wine and shallots, and it manages to have a lot of decadent substance, yet just enough zing to not weigh down a dish. Draped over chicken and earthy vegetables like asparagus and mushrooms, it's the key to making a refined—yet very simple—meal.

SERVES 4

Preheat the oven to 400°F.

In a small saucepan, combine the champagne, diced shallot, lemon juice, and vinegar. Bring to a boil over medium-high heat and cook until most of the liquid has evaporated, about 10 minutes. (The liquid will appear syrupy and coat the bottom of the pan when ready.) Remove from the heat.

Season the chicken evenly with 1 teaspoon of the salt, ½ teaspoon of the pepper, and the red pepper. Arrange the chicken skin side down in a 12-inch cast iron skillet and set over medium heat. Cook undisturbed until the skin is crispy, about 12 minutes.

In a medium bowl, add the mushrooms, halved shallots, 1 tablespoon of the oil, ½ teaspoon of the salt, and ¼ teaspoon of the pepper and toss to coat.

Turn the chicken and add the mushroom mixture to the pan. Cook, stirring just the vegetables occasionally, until they are slightly browned, 5 to 7 minutes.

In the same bowl, toss the asparagus with the remaining tablespoon of oil, ½ teaspoon of salt, and the remaining ¼ teaspoon of pepper. Scatter the asparagus evenly around the chicken and transfer the pan to the oven. Bake for 10 to 12 minutes, until an instant-read thermometer inserted into the thickest portion of the chicken registers 165°F.

While the skillet bakes, return the champagne mixture to medium-low heat and add the butter 1 tablespoon at a time, whisking until the butter is completely incorporated before adding more. Adjust the heat as needed to keep the sauce from simmering or bubbling. Once all the butter is added, immediately remove from the heat. Whisk in the honey and remaining ½ teaspoon salt. For a traditional smooth beurre blanc, place a fine mesh sieve over a medium bowl and strain the sauce, discarding the shallots.

Serve the chicken and vegetables with the sauce and garnish with the fresh tarragon and red pepper.

Pork Tenderloin *with* Parsnips *and* Broccoli

2½ teaspoons kosher salt

1¼ teaspoons freshly ground black pepper

1¼ teaspoons Chinese five spice

1 (1-pound/450g) pork tenderloin, trimmed

1 pound (450g) parsnips, peeled and cut into 1- to 2-inch batons (about ½-inch thick)

¼ cup plus 3 tablespoons (105ml) extra-virgin olive oil

1 head broccoli, cut into florets (florets halved if large)

3 tablespoons honey

2 teaspoons soy sauce

1 teaspoon sriracha

Toasted sesame seeds, for garnish

Hot cooked rice, for serving

TIPS & TRICKS

When shopping for parsnips, you'll often find a mixed bunch with lots of different sizes. The trick is to cut them into evenly sized pieces, so they all cook at the same rate. That way every piece of parsnip is perfectly caramelized and sweet.

A 12-inch cast iron skillet deserves a spot in your kitchen arsenal. It's a sturdy workhorse and comes in handy for delivering one-pan dinners like this one. To take the best care of your skillet, wipe it clean with water (no soap if you can help it), then dry it thoroughly before wiping it down with a tiny bit of oil, inside and out. I like to pop mine in the oven, hit preheat to 400ºF, and then turn off the oven when it's preheated. I let it cool overnight, and then the skillet goes back in the cupboard the following morning, clean, seasoned, and ready for the next adventure.

This is the ultimate one-skillet supper. It's simple and quick, yet full of layered, balanced flavor—which is not always the norm when it comes to pork. The meat is the perfect canvas for Asian-inspired flavors, such as Chinese five spice, soy sauce, and sriracha. I also love this dish because it gives you a great reason to introduce yourself to the sweet, creamy wonders that are parsnips. SERVES 4

In a small bowl, combine the salt, pepper, and Chinese five spice. Season the pork with 2 teaspoons of the spice mixture and let the pork sit for 30 minutes or cover loosely and refrigerate overnight.

Preheat the oven to 400°F.

In a medium bowl, toss the parsnips with 1 tablespoon of the olive oil and 2 teaspoons of the spice mixture. Set aside.

In a 12-inch cast iron or other oven-safe skillet over medium-high, heat ¼ cup of the olive oil. Add the pork and sear on all sides, about 2 minutes per side. Transfer the pork to a plate and reduce the heat to medium. Add the parsnips and 1 tablespoon of oil to the skillet and cook, stirring occasionally, until the parsnips are lightly browned, about 5 minutes. Remove the pan from the heat and set aside.

In the same medium bowl, toss the broccoli with the remaining tablespoon of olive oil and the remaining teaspoon of spice mixture.

Move the parsnips to the outer edges of the pan and place the pork in the center. Scatter the broccoli evenly over the parsnips.

Roast for about 15 minutes, or until a meat thermometer inserted in the thickest portion of the pork reads 140°F. Let cool for 10 minutes.

In a small bowl, whisk together the honey, soy sauce, and sriracha and brush over the warm pork. Garnish the broccoli and parsnips with the toasted sesame seeds and slice the pork as desired. Serve with the rice and the remaining honey mixture.

Lemon-Elderflower Tea Cake

FOR THE CAKE

Nonstick baking spray, for the pan

1½ cups (180g) all-purpose flour

¼ teaspoon kosher salt

¼ teaspoon baking powder

⅛ teaspoon baking soda

1 cup (2 sticks/226g) unsalted butter, softened

1 cup (200g) granulated sugar

Zest and juice of 1 lemon

2 large eggs

1 teaspoon vanilla extract

½ cup (120ml) whole milk

¼ cup (60ml) elderflower cordial

FOR THE GLAZE

2 cups (240g) powdered sugar, sifted

3 tablespoons elderflower cordial

2 tablespoons whole milk

Lemon zest strips, for garnish (optional)

Elderflowers, for garnish (optional)

TIPS & TRICKS

My favorite loaf pan is the Nordic Ware Anniversary Loaf Pan, but you could use any metal 8x4-inch loaf pan for this.

If you can't find elderflower cordial, you can use a flavored simple syrup or a sweet elderflower liqueur like St. Germain.

Elderflower—which had already been popular in Canada and would be used by my dad's side of the family in cordials from time to time—had a whole moment in the '90s when it showed up in cocktails on almost every bar menu, and it's been love for me ever since. I'm partial to its floral flavor, which, when used in moderation, creates the perfect perfumed undertone for the bright lemon top notes in a moist tea cake. If Brian and I are going to enjoy an afternoon tea—and we often are—this cake will most likely make an appearance.

MAKES 1 (8X4-INCH) LOAF CAKE

MAKE THE CAKE: Preheat the oven to 325°F. Spray a (8x4-inch) decorative loaf pan with baking spray.

In a large bowl, whisk together the flour, salt, baking powder, and baking soda. Set aside.

In the bowl of a stand mixer fitted with the paddle attachment, add the butter, sugar, and lemon zest. Beat on medium speed until light and fluffy, about 3 minutes. Add the eggs one at a time, beating well after each addition. Beat in the vanilla until fully combined, scraping down the sides of the bowl if needed. Reduce the mixer speed to low and gradually add the flour mixture, alternating with the milk, until fully combined, scraping the sides of the bowl as needed. Beat in the elderflower cordial and lemon juice just until combined.

Transfer the batter to the prepared pan, gently tapping on the counter to settle the batter, and bake for 60 to 75 minutes, until a wooden pick inserted in the center comes out with a few moist crumbs. Let the cake cool in the pan for 15 minutes. Invert the pan onto a wire rack set inside a rimmed baking sheet and let the cake cool completely.

MAKE THE GLAZE: In a medium bowl, whisk together the powdered sugar, elderflower cordial, and milk until smooth. Carefully pour the glaze over the cooled cake, using the back of a spoon to help fully coat the cake. (You may coat the cake two or three times for a more opaque glaze.) Let stand for 30 minutes to dry. Garnish with lemon zest strips and elderflowers, if desired.

Classic Cream Scones

Somewhere along the line, someone got the idea that scones were meant to be dry and dense. But on the contrary, they're supposed to be light and fluffy—like the best biscuit you've ever had, but *better*. After suffering through way too many disappointing non-scone scones, I've taken matters into my own hands. Behold: the perfect scones.   MAKES 8 TO 10 SCONES

2 cups (240g) all-purpose flour,
plus more for the counter

¼ cup (50g) granulated sugar

2 teaspoons baking powder

¼ teaspoon kosher salt

¼ cup (55g) cold unsalted butter, cubed

⅔ cup (160ml) heavy whipping cream,
plus more for brushing

1 large egg

½ cup (80g) chopped dried apricots or
dried blueberries (optional)

Coarse sugar, for sprinkling

Clotted cream or whipped cream,
for serving (see Tips & Tricks)

Fruit jam of your choice, for serving

Preheat the oven to 375°F. Line a baking sheet with parchment paper and set aside.

In a large mixing bowl, sift together the flour, sugar, and baking powder and whisk in the salt. Add the butter and toss to coat the pieces with flour. Using a pastry blender or squeezing the pieces between your fingers, cut the butter into the flour until the pieces are no bigger than peas.

In a medium bowl, whisk together the cream and egg. Make a well in the center of the flour mixture and pour in the cream mixture. Fold the mixture together with a fork or silicone spatula until a sticky dough starts to form. Add the dried fruit, if using, and mix just briefly to incorporate.

Turn out the dough on a floured surface. Lightly flour the dough and pat it into a 1-inch thickness. Using a 2½-inch round cutter dipped in flour, cut out the scones. Place them about an inch apart on the prepared baking sheet. Brush the tops lightly with the cream and sprinkle with coarse sugar, if desired.

Bake the scones for 14 to 16 minutes, until the tops are lightly golden brown. The scones can be served warm or fully cooled. Split in half and serve with clotted cream or whipped cream and jam.

TIPS & TRICKS

These classic English tea scones are delicious plain or baked with dried fruit. For a bit of a twist from the traditional dried currants, I suggest dried apricots or blueberries. You can also use chopped dried cranberries or figs.

Clotted cream can sometimes be found in the specialty dairy or cheese sections of a grocery store. To make your own, place 4 cups of good quality heavy whipping cream (not ultra-pasteurized) in a 9x13-inch baking dish. Place in a 180°F oven for 12 hours (do not stir). Remove and let cool. Carefully drain off any liquid left in the pan. Store the thickened cream refrigerated in an airtight container for up to a week.

Passion Fruit Mille-Feuille

Mille-feuille is a classic French patisserie that translates to "thousand sheets" for the layers of light-as-air puff pastry that get filled with pastry cream. For this version, I'm infusing the traditional vanilla pastry cream with bright, tart passion fruit. The effect is a surprisingly refreshing-yet-sumptuous dessert that's perfect for spring.   MAKES 6

FOR THE PASSION FRUIT PASTRY CREAM

⅔ cup (133g) granulated sugar

¼ cup plus 1 tablespoon (45g) cornstarch

6 large egg yolks

Pulp of 2 passion fruit

1 teaspoon vanilla extract

2 cups (480ml) whole milk

1 tablespoon cold unsalted butter, diced

FOR THE MILLE-FEUILLE

1 recipe Rough Puff Pastry (page 71) or store-bought puff pastry

1 cup (120g) powdered sugar

1 tablespoon plus 2 teaspoons whole milk

Pulp of 1 passion fruit, strained and juice reserved

MAKE THE PASSION FRUIT PASTRY CREAM: Place a fine mesh sieve over a large bowl and set aside.

In a medium heatproof bowl, whisk together the sugar and cornstarch. Add the egg yolks, passion fruit pulp, and vanilla and whisk until well combined.

Add the milk to a medium pot and set over medium-high heat and bring to a boil, whisking occasionally. Remove the pot from the heat immediately. Whisking the egg yolk mixture, carefully add about ½ cup of the hot milk and whisk until well incorporated. Slowly whisk in the remaining hot milk and pour the entire mixture back into the saucepan.

Return the pan to medium heat and whisk constantly until the custard is very thick and holds its shape, 5 to 7 minutes. (You should feel some resistance when whisking.) Immediately remove the custard from the heat and whisk in the butter until fully combined. Strain the custard through the sieve and discard the passion fruit seeds. Cover the custard with plastic wrap, lightly pressing the plastic against the surface to prevent a skin from forming. Refrigerate for at least 3 hours or overnight.

MAKE THE MILLE-FEUILLE: Preheat the oven to 400°F.

Roll out the Rough Puff Pastry to a ¹⁄₁₆-inch-thick rectangle. Transfer the dough to a sheet of parchment paper and use a knife or pizza cutter to trim the pastry into a 12x16-inch rectangle. Carefully transfer the dough and the paper to a baking sheet. Place another sheet of parchment on top, followed by another baking sheet.

Bake for 25 to 30 minutes, rotating the baking sheet halfway through, until the pastry is an even deep golden brown all over. Remove the top baking sheet and parchment paper and let the pastry cool completely.

Carefully transfer the cooled pastry to a cutting board. Using a sharp serrated knife, cut the pastry into six equal strips about 2⅔ inches wide.

continued

Mille-feuille is a labor of love, but it can be made more manageable by breaking up the prep. The custard can be made up to 2 days in advance, as well as the Rough Puff Pastry. Bake the pastry the day you want to serve it. You can also use store-bought puff pastry, but I do recommend the homemade version.

Be gentle and patient when cutting the pastry into rectangles. Because the pastry is so flaky, it's very delicate. A patient hand and sharp serrated knife are your best tools here.

If passion fruit is unavailable, substitute with lemon juice: 3 tablespoons in the custard and 4 teaspoons in the glaze.

Cut each of those strips into thirds, creating 2⅔x4-inch rectangles. You should have eighteen rectangles in total.

Add ½ cup of the powdered sugar to each of two medium bowls. Add the milk to one bowl and whisk until smooth. Add 4 teaspoons of the passion fruit juice (supplement with water if needed) to the other bowl and whisk until smooth. If desired, whisk in a drop of pink food coloring as well. Transfer the passion fruit glaze to a piping bag.

Place six of the pastry rectangles on a wire rack. Spread the plain white glaze over the top of the pastry just to the edges. Snip the tip off the passion fruit glaze pastry bag and pipe thin stripes over the plain glaze. Create a chevron pattern by dragging a toothpick across the pink lines in alternating directions. Set aside until set, about 1 hour.

In a stand mixer fitted with the paddle attachment, beat the chilled pastry cream on medium-low speed just until smooth, about 30 seconds. Transfer the cream to a piping bag fitted with a large decorative or open tip.

Pipe two rows of the pastry cream onto one plain pastry piece and top with another plain piece. Pipe with more pastry cream and top with a glazed pastry piece. Mille-feuille is best enjoyed the day it's made, but any leftovers can be refrigerated in an airtight container for up to 2 days.

Raspberry–White Chocolate Meringue Kisses

Eggs from our friendly little chickens are what make these light-as-air confections that much more special. Luckily, it's easy to find good quality eggs at any farmers' market or your local grocery store, which makes all the difference when you're only using a small handful of ingredients. I especially love parceling these up in small bags and giving them out as just-because gifts to friends. **MAKES ABOUT 54 KISSES**

1 (1.2-ounce/34g) bag freeze-dried raspberries

1 cup (200g) granulated sugar

4 large egg whites, room temperature

¼ teaspoon cream of tartar or fresh lemon juice

Pinch fine salt

6 ounces (170g/about 1 cup) white chocolate baking chips or chopped bars

Position two oven racks in the middle third of the oven. Preheat the oven to 200°F.

Reserve 6 of the freeze-dried raspberries. In the bowl of a food processor, add the remaining raspberries and the sugar. Process until the raspberries have broken down into a fine powder and the mixture is well combined, 1 to 2 minutes. Sift the mixture through a fine mesh sieve into a bowl and set aside, discarding any bits left in the sieve.

In the bowl of a stand mixer fitted with the whisk attachment, add the egg whites, cream of tartar or lemon juice, and salt. Beat at medium speed until the egg whites are frothy and have doubled in volume, 1 to 2 minutes. With the mixer running, slowly begin adding the raspberry sugar a small spoonful at a time. Increase the mixer speed to medium-high and continue beating until the meringue is stiff and glossy, about 6 minutes. (You know it's ready if you can flip the meringue bowl upside down without any of the meringue shifting.)

Transfer the meringue to a piping bag fitted with a large open star or plain round tip.

Pipe small dollops of meringue in the corners of two baking sheets and press a sheet of parchment paper on top of each. (This will hold the paper in place as you pipe.) Pipe the meringue into 2-inch kisses, spaced 1 inch apart on the parchment, or pipe a rope to make 2-inch-long meringue cookies.

Bake for about 2 hours, until dry to the touch and hollow sounding when tapped. Turn off the oven and keep the door closed for an additional 1 to 2 hours, until the meringues are completely cooled. Gently lift each meringue to release it from the parchment and place it back down. Place the baking sheet back in the cooled oven.

continued

Fill a small saucepan with 2 inches of water and bring to a simmer over medium heat. Reduce the heat to low. Add the white chocolate to a heatproof bowl and set the bowl over the simmering water. Stir occasionally until the chocolate is smooth and fully melted, about 5 minutes. Remove the bowl from the pot.

Transfer the melted white chocolate to a piping bag, if desired, and drizzle the white chocolate over the meringues or dip the meringues in the melted chocolate. Crush the reserved freeze-dried raspberries and sprinkle over the meringues. Let the chocolate set fully, about 1 hour, before removing the meringues from the parchment paper. Store the finished meringues in an airtight container for up to 1 week (see Tips & Tricks).

Vanilla Bean Panna Cotta *with* Rosé Rhubarb

FOR THE PANNA COTTA

¼ cup (60ml) cold water

1 (¼-ounce/7g) packet unflavored gelatin

1½ cups (360ml) whole milk

½ cup (100g) granulated sugar

½ vanilla bean, seeds scraped,
or 2 teaspoons vanilla bean paste

1 cup (240ml) heavy whipping cream

FOR THE ROASTED RHUBARB

12 ounces (338g) fresh rhubarb stems,
any leaves removed, cut into 1- to 2-inch
pieces

¾ cup (150g) granulated sugar

¼ teaspoon almond extract

1 cup (240ml) rosé wine

1 orange

TIPS & TRICKS

If using small molds, you can serve the panna cotta in the molds or unmold them by quickly dipping the outside in hot water for a few seconds. Place a small plate over the top and quickly flip. Carefully remove the mold at an angle to release the panna cotta. This is a great way for your grandmother's vintage mini jello molds to shine!

If you can't find fresh rhubarb, use frozen rhubarb. For best results, do not thaw it before tossing with sugar and roasting. The cook time may increase by a few minutes.

I've long believed that baked goods should taste like the ingredients they're made with—good butter and good milk. Especially now that we're surrounded by top-notch dairies, I love celebrating the flavor of the latter, and there's no better dish to do that with than panna cotta. Like a good *fior di latte* gelato, you're celebrating the flavor of milk while also providing a blank—but not bland—canvas for other ingredients to highlight, like perfect-for-spring rhubarb and rosé. This is also a lesson in the perfect panna cotta consistency: it *should* have just enough gelatin to hold together as a custard; it *should not* jiggle like Jell-O.

SERVES 6 TO 8

MAKE THE PANNA COTTA: In a small bowl, add the cold water and sprinkle the gelatin on top. Set aside to hydrate.

In a medium saucepan over medium-low heat, combine the milk, sugar, and vanilla. Cook, stirring frequently, until the mixture is hot to the touch, about 140°F. Skim off any skin that may have formed on the top and whisk in the hydrated gelatin until fully dissolved. (Do not let this mixture come to a simmer.) Remove the pan from the heat and stir in the cream.

Divide the mixture among six to eight small molds or cocktail glasses. Chill in the fridge for at least 6 hours or overnight. (If chilling overnight or for a couple of days, cover loosely with plastic wrap after an hour.)

MAKE THE ROASTED RHUBARB: Preheat the oven to 400°F.

In a 9x13-inch baking dish, toss together the rhubarb, sugar, almond extract, and ½ cup of the rosé. Using a vegetable peeler, cut the outer peel from the orange in large strips. Nestle the orange peel among the rhubarb, halve the orange, and squeeze the juice over the rhubarb, catching and discarding any seeds.

Roast for 15 to 20 minutes, stirring once about halfway through, until the liquid is very bubbly and thickened. Drizzle the remaining ½ cup of rosé all around the pan and carefully swirl it around. Let the rhubarb cool completely in the pan.

To serve, spoon the rhubarb and syrup over the panna cotta. The rhubarb can be refrigerated in an airtight container for up to 1 week. Keep the panna cotta covered in the refrigerator and enjoy within 4 days.

Chocolate Carrot Cake

Somewhere down the line, someone got the idea that carrot cakes needed to be made with a lot of oil to keep them moist. I beg to differ. By using applesauce and sour cream, you can introduce a lot of moisture and get a tender, light cake that's not at all greasy. I've also lightened up the traditional buttercream with vanilla and orange zest, which, when combined with baking spices and chocolate, makes this just about the best carrot cake you've ever had. Another little-known carrot cake fact: there was a time when people would use carrots to make mock apricot jam because it was a cheaper, more accessible alternative. So when I call for adorning your cake with candied carrots, don't be so quick to judge. MAKES 1 (3-LAYER) 8-INCH CAKE

FOR THE CAKE

Nonstick baking spray

2½ cups (300g) all-purpose flour

½ cup (40g) unsweetened Dutch-process cocoa powder

2 teaspoons baking powder

1½ teaspoons kosher salt

1 teaspoon baking soda

1 teaspoon espresso powder

1 tablespoon ground cinnamon

¾ teaspoon ground allspice

½ teaspoon ground cardamom

1 cup (115g) toasted pecans, finely chopped

1⅓ cups (266g) granulated sugar

½ cup (110g) firmly packed light brown sugar

4 large eggs, room temperature

½ cup (1 stick/113g) unsalted butter, melted

½ cup (120ml) vegetable oil

½ cup (140g) applesauce

¼ cup (55g) sour cream

2 teaspoons vanilla extract

1 pound (450g) carrots, peeled and grated

3½ ounces (100g) grated or finely chopped dark chocolate

FOR THE CANDIED CARROTS

1 cup (200g) granulated sugar

1 large carrot, peeled and shaved into thin strips (about 24)

MAKE THE CAKE: Preheat the oven to 350°F. Spray three (8-inch) round cake pans with baking spray. Add a round piece of parchment paper to the bottom of each pan and lightly spray again. Wrap the outside of the pans with water-soaked fabric baking strips, if desired. Set aside.

In a large bowl, whisk together the flour, cocoa powder, baking powder, salt, baking soda, espresso, cinnamon, allspice, and cardamom.

In a small bowl, add the chopped pecans and 1 tablespoon of the flour mixture and toss to coat. Set aside.

In a large bowl, whisk together the sugars, eggs, melted butter, oil, applesauce, sour cream, and vanilla. Add the flour mixture and whisk just until combined. Fold in the carrots, pecans, and chopped chocolate just until incorporated. Divide the batter evenly between the prepared cake pans.

Bake for 30 to 35 minutes, until a toothpick inserted in the center comes out clean. Transfer the pans to a wire rack to let the layers cool completely.

MAKE THE CANDIED CARROTS: Preheat the oven to 225°F. Set a wire rack inside a baking sheet and set aside.

In a small saucepan over medium heat, add the sugar and 1 cup of water. Stir until the sugar dissolves and add the carrots. Cook until the carrots are softened and start to appear translucent, about 15 minutes. Lay the carrot strips in a single layer on the wire rack.

continued

2 (8-ounce/226g) blocks cream cheese, room temperature

1 cup (2 sticks/226g) unsalted butter, room temperature

1 tablespoon orange zest (from about 1 large orange)

½ teaspoon vanilla extract

¼ teaspoon kosher salt

1½ pounds (5⅔ cups/675g) powdered sugar

Shaved chocolate curls, for garnish

Bake until the carrots are tacky but not firm or dry when touched, 15 to 20 minutes. While the carrots are still warm, quickly spiral them around the handle of a silicone spatula or wooden spoon and return them to the wire rack. Let the carrot spirals cool at room temperature until hard, at least 1 hour. (If they harden while you're working, place the tray back in the oven for a few minutes to warm them back up.)

MAKE THE FROSTING: In the bowl of a stand mixer fitted with the paddle attachment, add the cream cheese and butter and beat on medium-high speed until smooth and fluffy, about 3 minutes. Add the orange zest, vanilla, and salt and beat until combined. Reduce the mixer speed to low and slowly add the powdered sugar, stopping frequently to scrape down the bowl. Continue beating on medium speed for 1 minute, until very fluffy.

Set one of the cooled cake layers on a cake stand or serving plate. Spread 1½ cups of the frosting on top of the cake. Top with another layer and repeat with more frosting. Top with the remaining cake layer and chill for 30 minutes.

Frost the outside of the cake with the remaining frosting and decorate with the chocolate curls. Chill for at least 1 more hour before serving. Top with the candied carrots just before serving.

TIPS & TRICKS

Dutch-process cocoa powder and regular cocoa powder are not created equal. While you can certainly use regular cocoa powder in this recipe, the cake may "tunnel," or bake with large air pockets in the layers. The Dutch process alkalizes the cocoa powder, neutralizing the acid in the cocoa. Because baking soda reacts with acids, and since regular cocoa hasn't had its acid neutralized, the baking soda can react more strongly with regular cocoa powder in the batter, creating air pockets. If you only have regular unsweetened cocoa powder, still make this cake! The flavor will be delicious, air pockets or not.

Candied carrots can be made several days in advance. If making ahead, keep the curls on the wire rack and let them fully air-dry overnight. At that point, they can be stored in an airtight container at room temperature for several days. Use a Y-shaped vegetable peeler or a mandoline on a thin setting to create your carrot strips.

If you don't have a box grater or want to save time, cut the carrots into 1-inch chunks. Place them in a food processor and pulse until they're finely chopped. This will give the cake a slightly different texture, but it will still be fluffy and delicious.

Espresso powder enhances the cocoa flavor in the cake, but if you don't have any or would prefer not to use it, it can be omitted.

Shortcakes *with* Strawberry *and* Pink Peppercorn Ice Cream

We're surrounded by berry farms where we go to pick cartons upon cartons of all manner of berries come spring. Their flavor is incomparable to anything that's been sitting in a package at the grocery store and all but begs to be featured atop flaky pull-apart shortcakes and milky vanilla ice cream flecked with the gentle heat of pink peppercorns. But not to worry, if your fruit isn't the best of the season, that's nothing a little maceration can't help. MAKES 12 SHORTCAKES

FOR THE ROASTED STRAWBERRIES

2 pounds (900g) fresh strawberries, hulled and halved or quartered

½ vanilla bean, seeds scraped, or 2 teaspoons vanilla bean paste

½ cup (100g) granulated sugar

FOR THE STRAWBERRY AND PINK PEPPERCORN ICE CREAM

1 (14-ounce) can (397g) sweetened condensed milk

1 teaspoon ground pink peppercorns

⅛ teaspoon kosher salt

2 cups (480ml) heavy whipping cream

FOR THE BUTTERMILK SHORTCAKES

3 cups (360g) all-purpose flour, plus more for dusting

¼ cup (50g) granulated sugar, plus more for sprinkling

1 tablespoon baking powder

½ teaspoon baking soda

½ teaspoon kosher salt

¾ cup (170g) cold unsalted butter, cubed

1 cup (240ml) cold whole buttermilk, plus more for brushing

½ teaspoon vanilla extract

MAKE THE ROASTED STRAWBERRIES: Preheat the oven to 425°F.

In a 9x13-inch baking dish, toss together the strawberries and vanilla. Add the sugar and toss again until fully coated. Gently shimmy the baking dish to settle the berries into an even layer.

Roast for 25 to 30 minutes, until berries are soft, very syrupy, and bubbling all over. Let the berries cool completely. Set aside ¾ cup for the ice cream and refrigerate the remaining berries (you'll use a bit more for serving).

MAKE THE STRAWBERRY AND PINK PEPPERCORN ICE CREAM: In a large bowl, whisk together the condensed milk, ground peppercorns, and salt. Set aside.

In another large bowl, whip the cream with an electric hand mixer until stiff peaks form. Fold the whipped cream into the condensed milk mixture in two batches. Transfer the mixture to a 2-quart freezer-safe dish. Cover with plastic wrap and freeze for 2 hours, until partially frozen but still soft.

In a food processor, add the reserved roasted strawberries and pulse a few times, just until the berries are mostly broken up but not smooth. Add the blended strawberries to the ice cream mixture and use a knife to swirl them in. Cover and freeze the ice cream until firm, about 6 hours or overnight.

MAKE THE BUTTERMILK SHORTCAKES: Preheat the oven to 400°F. Line a baking sheet with parchment paper and set aside.

In a large bowl, whisk together the flour, sugar, baking powder, baking soda, and salt. Cut in the cold butter with a pastry blender or

continued

Roasted strawberries are best made with fresh, not thawed frozen, berries. The roasted strawberry mixture can be frozen when finished, though, if you're trying to use up a big batch of fresh berries or want that peak-season flavor later in the year.

Pink peppercorns can be found at specialty grocery or spice stores or online. You can also leave them out, or substitute ¼ teaspoon ground black pepper in their place. Black pepper is spicier than pink pepper, but it is a very nice complement to the strawberries and the ice cream.

Shortcakes can be made ahead to bake when you're ready for them. Just before you would bake them, freeze them until they're firm, about 1 hour. Transfer to a freezer bag and store for up to 3 months. Bake from frozen as directed, increasing the bake time by about 5 minutes.

by squeezing between your fingers until the butter pieces are the size of peas. Make a well in the center of the flour mixture and add the buttermilk and vanilla. Fold in using a fork or spatula, just until a shaggy dough forms.

Turn out the dough onto a well-floured surface. Using floured hands, squeeze and pat the dough into a 1½-inch-thick square. (The dough may still feel dry and crumbly.) Cut the square in half and stack the halves on top of each other. Pat or roll the dough stack back to a 1½-inch thickness. Repeat the process three times. On the final stacking, pat or roll to a 1-inch thickness. Use a 2½-inch round cutter dipped in flour to cut the dough into twelve rounds, rerolling scraps once if needed. Space the dough rounds on the prepared pan about 2 inches apart and freeze for 10 minutes.

Brush the tops of the dough rounds lightly with more buttermilk and sprinkle with sugar, if desired. Bake until the tops are golden brown and the sides are flaky, 20 to 23 minutes. Let the shortcakes cool completely on a wire rack.

To serve, split the shortcakes in half and fill with a scoop of ice cream and a spoonful of roasted strawberries.

Strawberry-Rhubarb Pie

FOR THE GRAHAM CRACKER DOUGH

3 cups (360g) all-purpose flour,
plus more for dusting

1½ cups (170g) graham cracker crumbs

2 tablespoons granulated sugar

1 teaspoon kosher salt

1½ cups (3 sticks/340g) cold unsalted
butter, cubed

¾ cup (180ml) ice water,
plus more if needed

FOR THE STRAWBERRY-RHUBARB FILLING

1¼ pounds (675g) fresh strawberries,
hulled and quartered

½ pound (225g) rhubarb, large stalks
halved, cut into ¼-inch cubes

1½ cups (300g) granulated sugar

¼ cup plus 2 tablespoons (45g)
tapioca flour

¼ teaspoon freshly ground black pepper

1 large egg

Sparkling sugar, for sprinkling

Whipped cream, for serving (optional)

Strawberry and rhubarb are coming out of the ground around the same time in spring, making them perfect bedfellows in a pie. The rhubarb's slight sourness mellows and sweetens in the oven, but it still manages to balance out the syrupy baked strawberries. And if you've played your cards right by making crust that gets an extra hit of flavor from graham cracker crumbs and a swipe of egg wash, then you'll end up with a perfectly flaky, not-a-bit-soggy crust, plus a strawberry-studded rhubarb filling, which only leaves adding a massive pile of whipped cream.

MAKES 1 (9X13-INCH) SLAB PIE

MAKE THE GRAHAM CRACKER DOUGH: In a large bowl, add the flour, graham cracker crumbs, sugar, and salt and whisk to combine. Add the butter and toss to coat it with the flour mixture. Cut in the butter using a pastry blender or by squeezing the pieces between your fingers until the biggest pieces are the size of almonds and the smallest ones are about the size of peas.

Add half of the water and fold in with a fork. Continue adding the water 1 tablespoon at a time until the mixture forms a shaggy dough. Gently knead it together in the bowl until the dough clumps together, sprinkling more water on any very dry and crumbly areas. (Since the cracker crumbs are dry, this may take longer than a typical pie dough.) Turn out the dough on a lightly floured surface and cut in half. Shape each half into a square and wrap tightly in plastic wrap. Chill for 2 hours or up to 3 days.

MAKE THE STRAWBERRY-RHUBARB FILLING: In a large bowl, toss together the strawberries, rhubarb, sugar, tapioca flour, and black pepper. Set aside.

ASSEMBLE THE PIE: Preheat the oven to 425°F.

On a lightly floured surface, roll one dough square into a 13x16-inch rectangle. Transfer to a quarter-sheet-size (9x13-inch) rimmed baking sheet. Spread the fruit filling evenly over the dough, gently pressing down on the top to create a mostly even surface.

continued

Roll the remaining dough square into a 13x16-inch rectangle and cut into 8 (2x13-inch) strips. Arrange the strips in a lattice pattern over the top of the filling. Trim the pie dough within 1 inch of the edge of the baking sheet. Tuck under the excess dough.

In a small bowl, beat the egg and 1 teaspoon of water. Lightly brush the dough with the egg wash and sprinkle with the sparkling sugar. Place the quarter sheet on a larger rimmed baking sheet to catch any drips.

Bake for 20 minutes. Reduce the oven temperature to 375ºF and continue baking for 30 to 35 minutes, or until the crust is a deep golden brown and the filling is bubbling. If you see the crust browning too quickly, you can cover the pie with foil halfway through baking. Let the pie cool completely before cutting. Serve with whipped cream, if desired.

Pavlova *with* Orange Curd, Strawberries, *and* Whipped Cream

It's always seemed like an injustice to me that pavlovas aren't more popular in the United States. They're pretty much oversize marshmallow clouds that are baked until they're glossy and crunchy on the outside and yet still perfectly creamy and light on the inside. To keep things from getting too one-note sweet, however, I call for topping the whole lot with orange curd and strawberries for depth and brightness, and no shortage of whipped cream. MAKES 1 (12-INCH) PAVLOVA/SERVES 10 TO 12

FOR THE MERINGUE

1 cup (200g) superfine sugar

1 tablespoon plus 1 teaspoon cornstarch

8 large egg whites

1 tablespoon fresh lemon juice

½ teaspoon kosher salt

FOR THE ORANGE CURD

1 cup (200g) granulated sugar

8 large egg yolks

½ cup (120ml) fresh orange juice

¼ cup (60ml) fresh lemon juice

2 tablespoons orange-flavored liqueur, such as Grand Marnier (optional)

10 tablespoons (142g) cold unsalted butter, cubed

FOR THE TOPPING

1 pound (450g) strawberries, hulled and quartered if large

2 tablespoons orange-flavored liqueur, such as Grand Mariner

1 tablespoon granulated sugar

1¼ cups (300ml) heavy whipping cream

½ vanilla bean, seeds scraped, or 1 teaspoon vanilla extract

Orange zest, for garnish

Fresh mint leaves, for garnish

MAKE THE MERINGUE: Preheat the oven to 250°F. Trace a 10-inch circle on the back of a piece of parchment paper with a pencil. Place the traced side down on a rimmed baking sheet and set aside.

In a small bowl, whisk together the sugar and cornstarch. Set aside.

In the bowl of a stand mixer fitted with the whisk attachment, add the egg whites, lemon juice, and salt and beat on medium speed until foamy, about 1 minute. Gradually add the sugar and cornstarch mixture, a tablespoon at a time, beating until very stiff glossy peaks form, 10 to 12 minutes. Rub a small amount of meringue between your fingers. If the meringue feels gritty at all, keep beating until it feels smooth.

Pile the meringue in the center of the traced circle. Use an offset spatula to gently shape the mound into a 10-inch circle with a slightly concave center and smooth the sides. Holding the spatula at a 45-degree angle, swoop from the bottom to the top of the meringue, making a ridged swoop. Clean up the top edge if desired.

Bake for 2 hours or until the outside is creamy in color and very crisp when tapped. (See Tips & Tricks about very humid days.) Turn off the oven and leave the pavlova inside to slowly cool for at least 1 hour without opening the oven door. At this point, the meringue can be left in the oven without opening the door for up to 12 hours.

MAKE THE ORANGE CURD: In a small saucepan, whisk together the sugar and egg yolks. Gradually whisk in the orange and lemon juices and the orange liqueur, if using. Set the pan over medium-low heat and cook, whisking constantly, until mixture is thickened and starts to bubble, about 15 minutes. Remove the pan from the heat.

continued

Be sure to use superfine or caster sugar in the meringue. Regular granulated sugar has larger crystals and is harder to dissolve in a meringue that is made with uncooked egg whites. Any undissolved sugar crystals can cause the meringue to weep during or after baking, so superfine sugar gives you a little extra insurance that the sugar will dissolve by the time your meringue is all whipped up.

It's important to use a clean bowl and beaters when beating egg whites. Any residual oil or water could lead to a less-than-fluffy meringue.

Any time that you're working with meringue, a nice, dry day is ideal. Humidity and moisture are the enemies of meringue, so if it's raining on the day you want to make this, you can still have success, but your bake time will be much longer. Because the sugar will absorb more moisture from the humid air while the meringue is whipping up, it takes longer to bake it out in the oven. On a rainy day, it can take up to 4 hours to fully bake. It may be slightly more toasted in appearance, but it will be just as delicious!

To make spreading the beaten egg whites onto the parchment paper-lined pan easier, place a dab of meringue under the four corners of the parchment so that it sticks to the pan.

The components of this dessert can be made in advance. If the weather is dry, the meringue can be made a day ahead. The curd can be made several days in advance and stored in the refrigerator. Wait to whip the cream until just before you serve the dessert. Top with berries just before serving,. Serve with extra berries and juice on the side.

Immediately add the cold butter and whisk until fully melted and combined. For a silky-smooth curd, strain the mixture through a fine mesh sieve into a large bowl. Press a piece of plastic wrap directly onto the surface of the curd and let it cool to room temperature. Store refrigerated in an airtight container for up to a week.

Carefully remove the meringue from the parchment by gently peeling the paper off the bottom. (If it was baked well and dried enough, it should release easily.) Place the meringue on a serving plate.

MAKE THE TOPPING: In a medium bowl, toss the strawberries with the liqueur and sugar and set aside.

In a medium bowl, add the cream and vanilla seeds and use a handheld electric mixer to beat on medium speed until soft peaks form, about 3 minutes.

Spread the whipped cream over the cooled pavlova and top with about ⅔ cup of the orange curd. Spoon the strawberries on top and garnish with the orange zest and mint. Serve immediately.

SPECIAL
PROJECTS

AFTERNOON TEA

To say that Brian and I had different formative experiences growing up is a vast understatement. While he was busy ditching class and working as a rave promoter in high school (and still managing to go on to have an uber-successful career and become a well-adjusted adult), I was—to put it one way—a total nerd. But one afternoon, feeling a little rebellious and wild, my friends and I decided to skip school . . . and go to afternoon tea at a fancy hotel in Westwood. Decked out in authentic seventeenth-century French court costumes from a rental house. Did I mention I was a nerd? Now the ritual of afternoon tea is something Brian and I share. To me, it always felt like going to the opera or the symphony— a sort of step out of time. The practice itself was originally intended as a time for ladies to share moments from their day (and a little bit of gossip) but evolved into a more universal moment for people to sit and talk about their day in an elegant, composed way. Not to mention eat finger sandwiches and delicious desserts.

Now afternoon tea is a fixture in our home. It's a singular time when we hit pause on everything we're busy with and distracted by and allow our senses to be taken over by our favorite teas and good conversation. Implementing your own afternoon tea practice doesn't have to be much more complex than brewing a pot of your favorite tea. In fact, the best place to begin is figuring out what that is. Get to know different varieties and discover what you love—vegetal green tea? Smoky oolong? Floral rose, jasmine, or lavender? Bright lemongrass? Mossy, fruity Darjeeling?

Or better yet, use afternoon tea as an opportunity to invite people over. Here are the basics:

A variety of teas. Canvass the room to see what people drink and brew accordingly. I like having a teapot for each person.

Tea sandwiches. Put out a selection with fillings like egg salad, smoked salmon, and chicken salad. The fillings themselves can all be made ahead, then spread on good crustless white or potato bread along with watercress, arugula, or fresh herbs to really pump up the flavor. Don't forget to cover the sandwiches until you're ready to serve; there is nothing worse than a stale sandwich.

Something sweet. Don't feel like you need to go overboard with the pastries—you're not a hotel. Just choose one. You can't go wrong with a Lemon-Elderflower Tea Cake (page 222) or Raspberry–White Chocolate Meringue Kisses (page 229).

Scones. An afternoon tea must. Please do yourself a favor and make the recipe for my Classic Cream Scones (page 225) to spare yourself from the triangular clods you find at the store.

Clotted cream and jams. Another requisite accessory to tea. You can buy clotted cream or easily make it yourself.

SPRING FORCED BRANCHES

Years ago, I learned from friends that you can buy branches at the very beginning of spring and they'll flower indoors. I was immediately smitten with the idea of bringing home these oversize twigs and then watching them explode into these incredible, dramatic floral arrangements. I still love doing this, and will go out and scout for the branches around our house, catching them right before they blossom and nurturing them with water until they can be convinced to bloom. Like many things I choose to decorate with, these arrangements bring a piece of the outside in and remind me to take some time to appreciate the beautiful moments before they fade.

There's not much more to forcing blooms than acquiring branches from flowering trees, such as cherry or apple blossom, forsythia, or quince; arranging them in a large vase of water; and leaving them in a sunny spot.

SUMMER

Living in LA, you don't think much about things like lawns. You maybe
have a little patch of green—or most likely brownish—grass, but usually not.
So when we found ourselves with acres upon acres of the stuff come our first
summer, we had no idea what it entailed. We thought it was a pretty great thing
that our meadows flooded with wildflowers and that the long grass would be
waving in the wind. Well, that was because our fields were totally out of control.
Instead of haying consistently since springtime, as is the norm, we'd inadver-
tently let things go. But even though everything was massively overgrown, and
we had to buy hay for our animals instead of cultivating it ourselves, we did
take a moment to enjoy the pleasure of this overabundance.

    I never really expected to love summer as much as I do. I thought I would
hate the humidity, especially being from the desert, but when you feel this
warm mist in the morning that perfumes the air, it's like the land is breathing.
Then there's the garden that's exploding with greens, beans, tomatoes, peppers, and cucumbers; and the market stalls and roadside stands are brimming
with berries, stone fruit, and melons so ripe that you have to inhale them the
moment you get home or bake them into all manner of desserts (or savory
grilled preparations) so they don't go to waste. I already feel a sense of nostalgia
for summer's end even as these things are just coming out of the ground, which
is when I turn to pickling and preserving so I can enjoy these verdant, fresh
flavors well into fall and winter. And in the meantime, I prepare as many dishes
as I can with these ingredients, doing as little to them as possible and spending
as little time at the stove as possible.

RECESPES

SPECIAL PROJECTS

RECIPES

Chilled Elote Soup

12 ears sweet corn, shucked

¼ cup plus 2 tablespoons (90ml) vegetable oil

2 cups (300g) chopped yellow onion

1 teaspoon ground cumin

1 teaspoon kosher salt

1 teaspoon freshly ground black pepper

2 cups (480ml) low-sodium chicken or vegetable stock, plus more as needed

1½ cups (360g) sour cream

1 tablespoon plus 1 teaspoon fresh lime juice

¼ cup (60ml) buttermilk

Fresh cilantro leaves, for serving

Crumbled queso fresco, for serving

Tajin seasoning, for serving

TIPS & TRICKS

Don't be tempted to reach for that convenient bottle of extra-virgin olive oil when making this recipe. Some types of olive oil turn bitter when blended at high speeds, so I recommend just using a simple vegetable oil or something neutral like grapeseed oil.

Cutting the corn off the cobs is an unavoidably messy affair, but there are a few steps you can take to corral the corn clutter. First, place a clean kitchen towel on your work surface and cut downward onto the towel, which will collect the kernels and inhibit their tendency to bounce. When it comes to scraping the cobs, use a shallow bowl to catch all those sweet juices. You don't want to waste a single drop.

When there's an abundance of corn at the market in the summer, and I know it's going to be ridiculously juicy and sweet, I think about all the ways I can cook it. Elote, or Mexican street corn that's slathered with fresh cheese and spices, is one of my favorite preparations. As is silky-smooth corn soup. So I did what any reasonable person would do and combined them. It's all pleasure and flavor, and no greasy hands or kernels stuck in your teeth. SERVES 6 TO 8

Preheat a gas or charcoal grill to medium heat, about 350°F.

Drizzle 3 tablespoons of the oil over the corn and use your hands to coat the corn completely. Grill the corn, covered, until lightly browned and tender, 10 to 15 minutes. Transfer 10 ears to a plate and set aside to cool. Keep 2 ears of the corn on the grill to char, about 5 minutes more. Transfer to the plate with the rest of the corn and let cool.

When the corn is cool enough to handle, cut downward on each cob to strip the kernels from the 2 charred ears. Gather the corn into a bowl and refrigerate until ready to serve. Cut the corn off the remaining cobs and set aside. Working over a plate or a bowl, run the knife one more time down the cobs to extract any extra pulp and juices and set aside separately.

Heat the remaining 3 tablespoons of oil in a large skillet over medium heat. Add the onion, cumin, salt, and pepper and cook, stirring occasionally, until the onion is tender, 8 to 10 minutes.

In a blender, add all but 1½ cups of the corn, plus the reserved pulp, the onion mixture, chicken stock, 1 cup of the sour cream, and 1 tablespoon of the lime juice. Blend until smooth, adding more stock ¼ cup at a time to thin the soup if needed. Taste and adjust seasoning as desired. Transfer the soup to a large container and stir in the reserved 1½ cups of corn. Cover and chill for at least 4 hours.

In a medium bowl, whisk together the remaining ½ cup of sour cream, plus the buttermilk and the remaining teaspoon of lime juice.

Divide the soup between bowls and garnish with the reserved charred corn kernels. Drizzle the sour cream mixture on top and finish with cilantro, queso fresco, and Tajin, as desired.

Grilled Halloumi *and* Figs *with* Toasty Pitas

2 (8-ounce/226g) blocks halloumi cheese

⅔ cup (227g/160ml) honey

Zest and juice of 1 lemon

1 heaping tablespoon finely chopped fresh mint, plus more for serving

1 teaspoon freshly ground black pepper

½ teaspoon Aleppo pepper or crushed red pepper

2 pints (450g) fresh figs (I like Black Mission or Brown Turkey)

4 large pitas

¼ cup (60ml) extra-virgin olive oil

1 lemon, halved

TIPS & TRICKS

Although halloumi is a sturdy cheese that resists melting, it's best to keep it in the refrigerator until ready to grill. For best results, be sure the grill is preheated and the grill grates are cleaned of debris to make searing both sides effortless.

To make grilling the figs easy, thread the halved figs onto 10-inch wood or metal skewers. It also makes transporting them to and from the grill effortless. If your figs are on the larger side, cut them into quarters after grilling.

Thanks to the figs I grew up plucking off the tree in our backyard, I've always loved finding ways to use them in the kitchen. While you normally see figs in sweet preparations, I wanted to play off their mild honeyed flavor with a salty cheese like Greek halloumi. The overall effect is a light and fresh yet substantial meal. SERVES 6

Wrap each block of halloumi in a clean kitchen towel or a few paper towels. Let stand for 10 minutes to absorb any extra whey.

In a small bowl, whisk together the honey, lemon zest and juice, 2 teaspoons of the mint, ½ teaspoon of the black pepper, and ¼ teaspoon of the Aleppo pepper. Set aside until ready to use.

Preheat a gas or charcoal grill to medium-high heat, or about 400°F.

Place the dried halloumi, figs, and pitas on a baking sheet, drizzle the olive oil over everything, and turn to coat. Sprinkle the halloumi and figs with the remaining 2 teaspoons of mint, ½ teaspoon of the black pepper, and ¼ teaspoon of the Aleppo pepper. Coat the pitas with any remaining spice and oil mixture on the baking sheet.

Grill the halloumi, figs, pitas, and lemon halves until grill marks form. This should be 2 to 3 minutes per side for the pitas and figs, and 4 to 5 minutes per side for the halloumi and lemon. Remove everything from the grill and let cool slightly. Cut the halloumi into ½-inch slices, halve the figs, and tear the pitas into rustic pieces.

On a serving platter or board, arrange the halloumi, figs, pitas, and lemon halves. Drizzle the halloumi and figs with a tablespoon or so of the spicy lemon honey. Serve with the remaining honey, garnish with the mint, and squeeze the grilled lemon over each serving.

Caprese Mini Pizzas *with* Burrata

I. Love. Burrata. Everyone should. It's got the firm outer skin of mozzarella with the richest, most luscious cream in the middle. When you top a dish with it, it's not dissimilar to adding a dollop of whipped cream to a dessert—a little extra, a little indulgent, yet not too heavy. It's the perfect final touch for these pizzas that come together in about fifteen minutes after you've made the dough and are basically summer on a plate.   SERVES 4

FOR THE PIZZA DOUGH

½ cup (120ml) warm water (110°F to 120°F)

1 teaspoon active dry yeast

½ teaspoon granulated sugar

2 cups (240g) all-purpose flour

1 cup (120g) bread flour

1½ teaspoons kosher salt

½ cup (120ml) lager beer

2 tablespoons extra-virgin olive oil, plus more for the bowl

FOR THE MINI PIZZAS

1 cup (150g) halved cherry tomatoes

1 tablespoon extra-virgin olive oil

½ teaspoon kosher salt

½ cup (120ml) marinara sauce

4 (2-ounce/56g) balls burrata cheese

1 cup (108g) grated Fontina cheese

½ cup (45g) grated Parmesan cheese

Torn fresh basil leaves, for garnish

Crushed red pepper, for serving (optional)

MAKE THE PIZZA DOUGH: In the bowl of a stand mixer, stir together the water, yeast, and sugar. Let stand until mixture is foamy, about 5 minutes.

In a medium bowl, whisk together the all-purpose flour, the bread flour, and salt. Add the flour mixture to the foamy yeast mixture in the mixer bowl. Attach the dough hook to the mixer and turn on low speed. Add the beer and olive oil and mix until a shaggy dough starts to come together. Increase the mixer speed to medium-low and mix until the dough is smooth and elastic and pulls away from the sides of the bowl, about 10 minutes.

Transfer the dough to an oiled bowl and cover with plastic wrap. Let rise in a warm place until just about doubled in size, around 1 hour and 30 minutes.

MAKE THE MINI PIZZAS: Position the oven racks in the top and bottom of the oven. Preheat the oven to 500°F.

On a foil-lined baking sheet, toss the tomatoes with the olive oil and salt. Roast on the bottom rack until tomatoes burst and start to release their juices, about 7 minutes. Set aside to cool slightly.

Divide the pizza dough into four equal portions. Roll or stretch each portion into an 8-inch circle, adding flour as needed to keep the dough pliable and reduce sticking. Use your fingers to press from the center of the dough out to about 1 inch from the sides to create a slightly raised edge around the perimeter. Place the dough rounds on a nonstick rimmed baking sheet. (If you don't have a nonstick baking sheet, sprinkle a regular baking sheet lightly with cornmeal.)

Spread 2 tablespoons of the marinara on each dough round and top each with an even layer of the roasted tomatoes. Cut the burrata into quarters and place four pieces on each pizza. Sprinkle each pizza with ¼ cup of the Fontina and 2 tablespoons of the Parmesan.

Bake the pizzas on the bottom rack until the crust is browned, about 7 minutes. Move the baking sheet to the top rack and adjust the oven to high broil. Broil until the tops of the pizzas are browned or charred to your desired degree of doneness, 2 to 3 minutes. Let the pizzas cool slightly and garnish with the basil and crushed red pepper, if desired.

TIPS & TRICKS

Working with yeast can be intimidating, but this recipe is designed to ease your worries. By proofing the yeast before you begin in warm water with a little sugar, it gives you the chance to see if the yeast is alive and kicking before you commit. If your yeast isn't foamy after 10 minutes, open another packet and try again. I highly recommend using an instant-read thermometer to make sure your water is the right temperature—too hot and it will kill the yeast; too cool and it won't get activated and happy.

If you have a pizza stone, which helps the bottom of the crust get crispy, by all means preheat it in the oven and use it for this recipe.

Chickpea Salad Sandwich

½ cup (110g) full-fat sour cream

2 tablespoons mayonnaise

2 tablespoons brined capers

1 tablespoon caper brine

Zest and juice of ½ lemon

¼ teaspoon kosher salt

¼ teaspoon freshly ground black pepper, plus more for serving

2 (15-ounce/425g) cans chickpeas, drained and rinsed

1 celery stalk and leaves, diced

1 small shallot, minced

2 tablespoons finely chopped fresh dill

8 slices sourdough bread

Dijon mustard, for serving

Fresh lettuce leaves, for serving

Sliced heirloom tomato, for serving

Flaky salt, for serving

TIPS & TRICKS

You can easily adapt this recipe to include any canned white bean; however, chickpeas hold their texture well, so it's my preferred variety.

Want to make this into a tasty bean dip for a party? Just keep mashing! Or place all the ingredients in a food processor and blend until desired consistency is reached. Serve with crackers or salty pita chips.

Summer is the season of picnics, beach visits, al fresco lunches, and road trips, so it only makes sense to have a great sandwich in your repertoire. This mashed chickpea salad with dill, celery, and capers can get piled on toasted sourdough with heirloom tomatoes and lettuce—or just scooped over greens—and is almost magic. It manages to be that elusive vegetarian sandwich that you'd choose regardless of whether you eat meat.   SERVES 4

In a large bowl, whisk together the sour cream, mayonnaise, capers, brine, lemon zest and juice, salt, and pepper. Add the chickpeas and use a fork to mash the chickpeas lightly into the dressing, just until combined and the chickpeas are somewhat broken up. Fold in the celery, shallot, and dill. Cover and chill for 1 hour for the best flavor.

Spread each sourdough slice with Dijon mustard. Top half of the slices with lettuce leaves, a few scoops of the chickpea salad, and sliced tomato. Season the tomatoes with flaky salt and pepper and top with the remaining bread slices.

Mussels in White Wine *with* Herbs

4 pounds (1.8kg) fresh mussels

¼ cup plus 2 tablespoons (85g) unsalted butter

1 leek, sliced

2 shallots, thinly sliced

2 tablespoons minced garlic (about 6 cloves)

2 tablespoons chopped fresh thyme leaves

1 teaspoon kosher salt

¼ teaspoon freshly ground black pepper

2 cups (480ml) dry white wine, such as Sauvignon Blanc

2 tablespoons heavy whipping cream

½ cup (30g) chopped fresh chervil (or flat-leaf parsley, if you can't find it)

¼ cup (15g) chopped fresh tarragon leaves

2 baguettes, sliced, or you can whip up some French fries, if you prefer

TIPS & TRICKS

Choose a wine that you like to drink, because you'll be enjoying the remainder of the bottle with your meal. Go with something that's not too sweet, like a Sauvignon Blanc.

In a pinch, you can substitute onion for the shallots.

I personally think sopping up the sauce is the best part of this dish. Buying par-baked baguettes means you can finish them off in the oven right before you eat so they're perfectly steamy and crispy. Or you can go with French fries, another classic mussel accompaniment that you can also find in the freezer aisle.

When I was younger and a bit more carefree, I loved whiling away a day at the beach with friends. After soaking up our fill of UV A and B, we'd finish off the afternoon with a great meal, my favorite being mussels in white wine with herbs. It was light, it tasted like the sea, and it was basically just a delicious excuse to sop up a whole bunch of buttery, saucy goodness with great bread. Now I love serving my own version in the comfort of my home as the perfect end to the perfect summer day. It's a fresher alternative to anything you could get in a restaurant (no chewy, sandy, or dodgy mollusks here; plus tons of fresh chervil and tarragon), and even though it takes minutes to make, it always feels just the right amount of fancy. Chilled white wine strongly encouraged. SERVES 4

Clean the mussels well by scrubbing their shells to remove any seaweed and beards. (You can also usually have this done at your local fish market. Just ask to have them cleaned and debearded when purchasing.)

Melt the butter in a large pan over medium-low heat. Add the leek, shallots, garlic, thyme, salt, and pepper. Cook, stirring occasionally, until the vegetables are translucent but not browned, 3 to 5 minutes.

Increase the heat to high and add the mussels and white wine. Cover and cook, stirring occasionally, until the mussels are just opened, 5 to 7 minutes. Some mussels might remain closed and should be discarded at this point. Stir in the cream.

Transfer the mussels and that precious liquid to bowls and top generously with the chervil and tarragon. Serve with fresh baguette slices or French fries.

TIPS & TRICKS

To test your fish for doneness, use a fork to gently pierce and pull the flesh in the thickest portion of the fillet. If it easily flakes and is opaque, it should be done.

Fish Tostadas *with* Green Tomato *and* Mango Salsa

My cousin Juanita once visited us from Mexico when we were living in LA, and we—thinking our California restaurants were pretty impressive when it came to offering authentic Mexican food—took her out to eat. After our meal, she said, "I love American food!" And she was totally right. Here in the States, Mexican food is usually cast as dishes that are smothered in beans and cheese and most likely fried—and granted, there are some traditional dishes like that—but authentic Mexican food is usually a lot lighter and, especially along the coast, features fresh seafood simply prepared with lots of bright acid and herbs. These tostadas capture that vibe, making them the perfect refreshing meal for a summer night. **MAKES 6 TO 8 TOSTADAS**

FOR THE GREEN TOMATO–MANGO SALSA

2 ripe honey mangoes or 1 red mango, peeled, seeded, and diced

1 green tomato, diced

¼ small red onion, diced

1 red or green jalapeño, seeded and finely diced (optional)

¼ cup (15g) chopped fresh cilantro

¼ teaspoon kosher salt

1 lime

FOR THE CILANTRO-AVOCADO CREMA

1 small Hass avocado, peeled and seeded

½ small bunch cilantro, roughly chopped

½ cup (110g) sour cream

Juice of 2 limes (about 5 tablespoons)

2 tablespoons cold water

¼ teaspoon kosher salt

FOR THE FISH TOSTADAS

1 pound (450g) skinless white fish fillets, such as snapper, cod, or halibut, deboned

1 tablespoon extra-virgin olive oil

1 teaspoon chipotle powder

½ teaspoon kosher salt

¼ teaspoon garlic powder

¼ teaspoon ground cumin

¼ teaspoon freshly ground black pepper

6 to 8 tostada shells

Fresh cilantro leaves, for garnish

Hot sauce, for serving (optional)

MAKE THE GREEN TOMATO–MANGO SALSA: In a medium bowl, combine the mango, green tomato, red onion, jalapeño (if using), cilantro, and salt. Zest the lime into the bowl. Cut off and discard the remaining lime pith, finely chop the lime, and stir into the mango mixture to combine. Cover and chill the salsa until ready to serve.

MAKE THE CILANTRO-AVOCADO CREMA: In a blender, add the avocado, cilantro, sour cream, lime juice, cold water, and salt and blend until completely smooth. If the mixture seems too thick, you can add an additional tablespoon of water until the desired consistency is reached. Cover and chill until ready to serve.

MAKE THE FISH TOSTADAS: Position an oven rack 6 inches from the top of the oven and preheat to high broil (500°F).

Lay the fish in the center of a small rimmed baking sheet. Rub the olive oil all over the fish to coat.

In a small bowl, stir together the chipotle powder, salt, garlic powder, cumin, and black pepper. Sprinkle the mixture evenly all over the fish.

Broil until the fish is firm and flaky, 12 to 17 minutes, depending on the thickness of the fillets. You can test the fillet by piercing the thickest portion with a fork. It should be opaque and easily flake apart. Break the fish into chunks using a fork.

Top the tostadas with the fish, drizzle with the crema, and top with the salsa and cilantro leaves. Serve with hot sauce, if desired.

Chipotle *and* Honey–Glazed Shrimp *with* Charred Oranges

Shrimp is popular in summer for a reason: it's light yet filling and cooks up in two shakes of a lamb's tail. (The pretty pink color doesn't hurt, either.) I like giving them a thick coating of sweet-spicy-sticky glaze and serving them with oranges that I've charred in order to bring in even more caramelized flavor. I recommend splurging for the best shrimp you can afford. Fresh, wild-caught seafood makes a big difference when it comes to flavor and texture, especially in a dish where it's the main ingredient.   SERVES 6 TO 8

1 cup (340g/240ml) honey

Zest and juice of 1 orange

2 tablespoons soy sauce

2 tablespoons minced chipotle chiles in adobo sauce (see Tips & Tricks)

2 pounds (900g) fresh jumbo shrimp (16 to 20 count), peeled and deveined (see Tips & Tricks)

8 (12-inch) wooden skewers, soaked in water for 30 minutes

3 tablespoons extra-virgin olive oil

2 teaspoons kosher salt

1 teaspoon freshly ground black pepper

1 teaspoon ground cumin

1 orange, halved

Fresh cilantro leaves, for garnish

TIPS & TRICKS

You can ask the folks at the seafood counter to peel and devein the shrimp for you, which will save you about 30 minutes, but it's easy to do it yourself. Simply run a sharp paring knife in between the shell and the flesh of the shrimp, following the curve of the shell and cutting as you go, all the way through the tail. Then you should be able to peel and remove the shell with the legs all at once. Rinse out the little canyon you created on the back of the shrimp, using the tip of your knife to help remove and discard the vein.

In a small bowl, whisk together the honey, orange zest and juice, soy sauce, and chipotles and set aside.

Thread the shrimp onto the prepared skewers, leaving about ¼ inch between each shrimp. You'll end up with about 5 shrimp per skewer. Drizzle the olive oil over the shrimp skewers and season them evenly with the salt, pepper, and cumin.

Preheat a grill to medium-high heat, or about 400°F. Scrub the grill grates clean with a wire brush if needed to keep the skewers from sticking.

Place the skewers and the orange halves, cut side down, on the grill. Cover and cook the shrimp undisturbed for about 4 minutes, until they start to release from the grates. Turn the skewers and brush the tops with the honey-chipotle sauce. Cover and cook the skewers for about 3 more minutes. Turn the skewers once more, brush the other side with the honey-chipotle sauce, and grill uncovered for 1 more minute. Check the orange halves intermittently during this time to make sure they don't burn. You can reposition them if needed, but you still want them to be nicely charred. If they aren't charring, brush the cut sides with a bit of the honey-chipotle sauce and return to the grill.

Transfer the shrimp skewers to a serving platter. Squeeze the charred orange halves over the shrimp, garnish with the cilantro, and serve with the remaining honey-chipotle sauce.

Chicken Legs *with* Smoky Peach Barbecue Sauce

4 bone-in, skin-on chicken leg quarters

1 tablespoon plus 2 teaspoons kosher salt

1 tablespoon freshly ground black pepper

¾ cup (180ml) apple cider vinegar

¼ cup (110g) firmly packed light brown sugar

2 tablespoons Dijon mustard

2½ teaspoons smoked paprika

2 tablespoon extra-virgin olive oil

½ cup (50g) diced red onion

4 cups (620g) peeled and sliced peaches (4 to 5 peaches)

½ cup (120ml) Pilsner or wheat beer

½ teaspoon crushed red pepper

Sliced scallions, for garnish

Peaches are one of my favorite things to grill in the summer because I'm a big fan of how caramelized fruit brings complex, deep flavor to a dish. (Seriously, if all you're making with your peaches—or any other stone fruit—is pie, you're missing out on a whole world of recipes.) I wanted to take that idea and turn it into a glaze for chicken legs, my other summer grilling love, because of how rich and unctuous their meat is under all that crisp tasty skin and how nicely it plays with the sweet, smoky peaches. SERVES 4

Season the chicken pieces with 1 tablespoon of the salt and 2 teaspoons of the pepper. Refrigerate uncovered for as long as you have to let the seasoning penetrate and the skin dry out a bit, up to overnight if possible (see Tips & Tricks).

In a small bowl, whisk together ¼ cup of the apple cider vinegar, the brown sugar, the Dijon mustard, the remaining 2 teaspoons of the salt, 2 teaspoons of the smoked paprika, and the remaining teaspoon of black pepper.

In a large skillet, heat the olive oil over medium heat. Add the onion and cook, stirring occasionally, until the onion has softened, about 7 minutes. Add the peaches and ¾ cup of water and bring to a simmer. Cook until the peaches are tender, about 10 minutes. Reduce the heat to low and use a potato masher to mash the peaches. Stir in the vinegar–brown sugar mixture and another ¼ cup of water. Simmer until thickened, about 10 minutes, adding a small amount of water if needed to loosen the sauce. Remove from the heat and set aside.

Preheat the grill to medium heat, about 350°F.

In a medium bowl, whisk together the remaining ½ cup of apple cider vinegar, the beer, the red pepper, and the remaining ½ teaspoon of smoked paprika. Set aside.

Place the chicken skin side down on the grill and cook undisturbed until the chicken releases from the grill easily, about 15 minutes. Turn the chicken and place it over indirect heat. Cover the grill and cook the

continued

chicken for 10 minutes. Turn the chicken, baste with the beer mixture, and cook for 10 more minutes. Continue turning and basting with the beer mixture every 10 minutes, until an instant-read thermometer registers 165°F when inserted in the thickest portion of the chicken, about 40 minutes total.

Serve the chicken with the peach barbecue sauce and garnish with the scallions.

TIPS & TRICKS

If your schedule allows, I would recommend seasoning the chicken and placing it in your fridge, uncovered, overnight. This not only allows the salt to penetrate the skin and season the meat but it also allows the skin to dry out and become extra crispy on the grill. If you don't have time, no worries; there's plenty of delicious flavor to come. But this extra step is worth the time.

If you've never made a mopping sauce, you're in for a *huge* treat. Mopping sauces are used by the best barbecue pit masters to add moisture and flavor to meat as it cooks. Unlike a marinade that's usually thick and sticky, this mopping sauce (the beer mixture) is mostly liquid, so it soaks in fast and evaporates quickly, adding flavor without making your meat stick to the grill. I like to use a basting brush to apply the mopping sauce, but feel free to purchase a special basting mop.

You may need to use a little extra water or a little less when making the barbecue sauce, depending on the ripeness and moisture content of your peaches. Do this during the initial simmering process. You're looking for the peaches to get tender and mashable. If fresh peaches aren't in season, you can even use thawed frozen peaches for this recipe.

Grilled Garlic–Rosemary Spatchcock Chicken

Butchering a chicken so it lays flat, also known as spatchcocking, is one of the easiest ways to get a perfectly cooked, perfectly crisp bird. It doesn't need much more in the flavor department, but garlic, lemon, and herbs take it to an especially summery, Mediterranean-inspired place. **SERVES 4 TO 6**

1 (4- to 6-pound/1.8 to 2.7kg) whole chicken

1 tablespoon crushed fennel seed

2 teaspoons kosher salt, plus more for sprinkling

¾ teaspoon freshly ground black pepper, plus more for sprinkling

¼ teaspoon crushed red pepper

¼ cup (34g) minced fresh garlic (about 1 head)

2 tablespoons finely chopped fresh rosemary leaves, plus fresh sprigs for garnish

2 lemons, zested and halved

2 tablespoons plus 1 teaspoon grapeseed or vegetable oil

Vegetable oil, for the grill

4 ears sweet corn, shucked

3 large yellow squash or zucchini, halved lengthwise

Place the chicken on a cutting board with the breast side down. Using kitchen scissors, cut along both sides of the backbone to remove it. Discard the backbone. Turn the chicken over, breast side up. Using the heels of your hands, press firmly against the breastbone until it cracks, then flatten the chicken, like opening a book. Using your fingers, gently loosen the skin from the meat around breasts, thighs, and drumsticks.

In a small bowl, combine fennel seed, salt, black pepper, and red pepper. Reserve 2 teaspoons of this mixture in a separate small bowl and set aside. In the remaining mixture, add the garlic, chopped rosemary, lemon zest, and 1 tablespoon of the oil and stir to make a paste. Spread the paste under the chicken skin.

Rub the outside of the chicken skin with 1 teaspoon of oil and sprinkle the reserved fennel seed mixture all over the chicken.

Preheat a gas or charcoal grill to medium heat, or about 350°F. If using a charcoal grill, scoot the coals to one side to create a lower-temperature zone. If using a gas grill, heat only one side of the grill. Thoroughly clean the grill grates with a wire brush if needed.

Brush the grill grates with vegetable oil and place the seasoned chicken on the hot side of the grill with the skin side up. Cover and grill the chicken for 8 to 10 minutes. (If the grill is flaring up too much, carefully move the chicken to the cooler side of the grill sooner or adjust the heat.) Move the chicken to the cooler side of the grill, with the legs closest to the hot side, and cook until the skin is golden brown and a thermometer inserted into the thickest part of the breast registers 160°F, about 50 minutes.

Meanwhile, brush the corn and squash all over with the remaining tablespoon of oil. Sprinkle lightly with salt and black pepper.

continued

Flip the chicken skin side down onto the hot part of the grill and cook for 3 to 5 minutes, just until the skin darkens in color. (The grill may flare a bit here, so just keep an eye on it and pull it if it looks like it's charring.)

Transfer the chicken to a serving platter and let it rest for 10 minutes. While the chicken is resting, place the corn, squash, and halved lemons, cut side down, on the hot side of the grill. Cook for about 5 minutes, until lightly charred. Remove the lemons. Flip the squash and corn. Continue grilling until charred and tender, about 5 more minutes. Carve the chicken as desired and squeeze the grilled lemon over the chicken. Garnish with additional rosemary and serve with the grilled vegetables.

TIPS & TRICKS

Cutting a chicken in half may seem like a daunting task, but it's actually quite easy with a good pair of poultry shears or heavy-duty kitchen scissors, which you can find at any store with kitchen utensils. My favorite pair comes from Williams Sonoma. If you really don't want to spatchcock the chicken yourself, or want to save some time, check with the butcher at your local grocery store. They will likely prepare it for you, or may have some already prepped for sale.

If you're looking to reduce food waste and be a more resourceful cook, don't throw away that chicken backbone or the leftover carcass. Place in a resealable freezer bag, label it (so you remember what it is!), and stash it in your freezer to make a lovely homemade chicken stock.

Chorizo-Beef Burgers *with* Queso *and* Avocado

Just like my favorite flavorful meatball trick is to use sausage instead of ground beef, the same goes for making burgers. In this case, a chorizo-beef mixture adds Mexican-inspired flavor that naturally calls for a mild white Mexican cheese and plenty of avocado. MAKES 8 BURGERS

FOR THE QUESO

1 tablespoon unsalted butter

2½ teaspoons all-purpose flour

½ cup (120ml) whole milk

2 tablespoons heavy whipping cream

6 ounces (2 cups/170g) freshly shredded Havarti cheese

2 tablespoons diced pickled jalapeño peppers

Kosher salt

FOR THE CHORIZO-BEEF BURGERS

1 poblano pepper

1 teaspoon extra-virgin olive oil

1¼ pounds (563g) fresh chorizo, casings removed if using links

1¼ pounds (563g) ground sirloin

2 teaspoons kosher salt

1 teaspoon freshly ground black pepper

1 teaspoon ground cumin

FOR SERVING

2 avocados, sliced

1 lime, halved

Kosher salt and freshly ground black pepper

8 toasted hamburger buns

8 butter lettuce leaves

Fresh cilantro leaves

Pickled jalapeño peppers

MAKE THE QUESO: In a small saucepan over medium heat, melt the butter until foamy. Sprinkle in the flour and cook, whisking constantly, for 1 minute. Slowly whisk in the milk and cream until smooth. Cook for about 2 minutes, until the mixture comes to a simmer. Add the cheese a small handful at a time and slowly whisk until fully incorporated and melted. Stir in the pickled jalapeños and salt to taste. Remove the pan from the heat and cover to keep warm.

MAKE THE CHORIZO-BEEF BURGERS: Preheat a grill to medium-high heat, about 400°F, or turn on the oven broiler.

Coat the outside of the poblano with the olive oil. Grill, covered, until slightly charred and tender, or broil on a baking sheet until blistered, about 4 minutes per side. Let the poblano cool completely. Remove and discard the stem and seeds, finely chop the pepper, and set aside.

In a large bowl, gently break apart the chorizo and sirloin with your fingertips. Add the salt, pepper, cumin, and the chopped poblano. Use your hands to gently mix until well combined.

On a clean work surface, divide the meat mixture in half. Divide each half into quarters to create eight even portions. Gently form each portion into a patty that is slightly larger than the bun. Set aside on a parchment paper–lined baking sheet.

Grill the burgers, covered, until they reach your desired doneness, 4 to 5 minutes per side for medium. Alternatively, heat a cast iron skillet over medium-high heat and cook the patties for the same time per side.

ASSEMBLE THE BURGERS: In a medium bowl, add the avocado and squeeze the lime juice over. Toss to coat and season to taste with salt and pepper.

Spoon 1 tablespoon of the queso on the bottoms of the buns. Top with the lettuce and the burger patties. Top the patties with an additional tablespoon of the queso, plus the dressed avocado and cilantro. Top with the remaining bun tops. Serve with additional pickled jalapeños, if desired.

Blackberry-Balsamic Pork Chops

4 (1½-inch-thick) bone-in pork chops (about 2½ pounds/1,125g)

2½ teaspoons kosher salt, plus more as needed

1 teaspoon freshly ground black pepper

¼ teaspoon crushed red pepper (optional)

2 cups (280g) blackberries

1 cup (240ml) red wine, such as Pinot Noir

¼ cup (60ml) aged balsamic vinegar

3 tablespoons granulated sugar

Zest and juice of 1 lemon

3 cardamom pods, lightly crushed

Extra-virgin olive oil, for brushing

Fresh basil leaves, for garnish

Lemon wedges, for serving

TIPS & TRICKS

Boneless pork chops tend to be super lean and cut thinly, which can translate to dry, tough grilled pork if you're not careful. Opt for thick (at least 1½-inch-thick) chops with the bone in, if you can find them. To make the pork chops even more flavorful, I like to season them and refrigerate them uncovered overnight. This acts like a dry brine, tenderizing and flavoring the pork from the outside in.

This berry sauce is nice with whatever berries you can find at your local farmers' market.

This is a recipe that grew out of necessity—*way* too many berries sitting ripe and ready in my kitchen, and my refusal to allow pork chops to be as bland as they seemingly want to be. By smothering them with fresh blackberries and balsamic vinegar, you infuse the meat with a ton of flavor that manages to be both savory and sweet thanks to the deep caramelization of the fruit. Think of this as giving your Mrs. Dash the night off.   SERVES 4

Season both sides of the pork chops evenly with the salt, pepper, and red pepper, if using. Set aside or refrigerate, uncovered, up to overnight.

Preheat a grill to medium-high heat, or about 400°F.

In a medium saucepan over medium-high heat, add the blackberries, wine, balsamic vinegar, sugar, 1 teaspoon of the lemon zest, the lemon juice, cardamom pods, and a pinch of salt. Bring the mixture to a boil and reduce the heat to medium-low. Cook, stirring occasionally, until reduced by about half, 20 to 30 minutes.

While the blackberry mixture cooks, brush the pork chops lightly with olive oil and grill them over direct heat, uncovered, until grill marks form and the pork is cooked to around 140°F, about 8 minutes per side. Transfer the grilled chops to a serving platter and tent loosely with foil to rest for 10 minutes.

Stir any resting juices from the pork into the blackberry mixture, if desired. Spoon the blackberry mixture over the pork chops. Garnish with the basil leaves and serve with the lemon wedges.

Lemon-Ginger Icebox Cake

1½ (8-ounce/227g) blocks cream cheese, room temperature

12 ounces (340g) mascarpone cheese, room temperature

¾ cup (60g) powdered sugar

5 cups (1,200ml) heavy whipping cream

1¼ cups (300ml) Citrus Curd (page 243), made with lemon juice, or store-bought lemon curd (See Tips & Tricks)

2 (5.25-ounce/150g) boxes ginger cookie thins (about 65 cookies)

6 ounces (168g) fresh raspberries, halved

Lemon zest, for garnish

Thinly sliced candied ginger, for garnish

TIPS & TRICKS

Depending on the brand and size of your ginger thins, you may use more or fewer cookies in each layer. I use Anna's Swedish Ginger Thins and use 7 cookies for each layer. Chocolate or vanilla wafers or thin cookies can also be substituted if ginger thins are not available.

To make this cake well in advance, or if you're planning to serve it outside on a hot day, assemble the cake and freeze for 1 hour. It can then be wrapped in plastic wrap and kept frozen for up to 1 week. Let the frozen cake stand at room temperature for 15 to 20 minutes before slicing with a warm knife and serving.

A 12-ounce jar of store-bought lemon curd can be used in a pinch, but be sure to use a good brand. My preferred brand is Bonne Maman.

An icebox cake is a foolproof homemade dish that's pretty much designed for sweltering afternoons when you want a cool, sweet treat and most definitely do not want to turn on the oven. It is essentially a tower of cookies layered with cool, bright layers of sunshine-bright citrus and a zing of ginger, and also happens to be the perfect project for small hands, if you're looking to get your kids involved.   MAKES 1 (8-INCH) CAKE

In the bowl of a stand mixer fitted with the whisk attachment, whisk the cream cheese and mascarpone at medium speed until smooth and fluffy, about 2 minutes. Sift in the powdered sugar and beat until well combined. Reduce the mixer speed to low and slowly pour in the cream. Scrape down the sides of the bowl and the whisk with a rubber spatula to make sure everything is evenly incorporated. Increase the mixer speed to medium and beat until stiff peaks form, 5 to 6 minutes. Fold in the Citrus Curd with the spatula until it is fully incorporated.

In the center of a large cake stand or serving plate, spread 1 tablespoon of the lemon cream mixture in a 6-inch circle. (An offset spatula works great here, if you have one.) Place a cookie in the center to cover the filling, or if your cookies are small, arrange a few in the center with edges slightly overlapping. Arrange several cookies in a circle with edges touching around the center cookie. Spread another cup of the lemon cream on top, leaving the cookie edges slightly exposed. Scatter 8 to 9 raspberry halves evenly over the lemon cream, pressing them down gently. Repeat this process until you have eight layers of cookies, lemon cream, and raspberries.

Arrange a final layer of cookies on top, followed by the remaining lemon cream. There should be nine total layers of cookies, and you can pipe the lemon cream on top for a pretty finish, if you like.

Refrigerate the cake uncovered for at least 4 hours. Just before serving, garnish the cake with the lemon zest and candied ginger.

Blackberry-Rosemary Hand Pies

As you've seen in other recipes of mine, I'm very fond of steeping fresh herbs into sweet preparations. I love the way they lightly (emphasis on *light*) infuse the overall flavor with something that you can't quite place but makes the whole thing more delicious. These hand pies are the ultimate portable dessert, perfect for packing up for picnics and beach outings. They're also striking when set out on a tray thanks to the beautiful natural purple color of the blackberry glaze.   MAKES 8 (3½-INCH) PIES

FOR THE ROSEMARY PIE DOUGH

3 cups (360g) all-purpose flour, plus more for dusting

2 tablespoons granulated sugar

2 teaspoons minced fresh rosemary

½ teaspoon kosher salt

½ cup plus 6 tablespoons (198g) cold unsalted butter, cubed

¾ cup (180ml) ice water

FOR THE BLACKBERRY FILLING

6 ounces (172g) fresh blackberries, reserve 1 berry for the glaze

¼ cup (50g) granulated sugar

1 fresh rosemary sprig

1 tablespoon fresh lime or lemon juice

1 teaspoon cornstarch

TO ASSEMBLE

1 large egg

1 teaspoon water

1 tablespoon sparkling sugar

1 blackberry

1 tablespoon Chambord, blackberry liqueur, or water

½ cup (60g) powdered sugar

MAKE THE ROSEMARY PIE DOUGH: In a large mixing bowl, whisk together the flour, sugar, rosemary, and salt. Add the butter and toss to coat the pieces with flour. Cut in the butter using a pastry blender or by squeezing the pieces between your fingers until the biggest pieces are the size of almonds and the smallest ones are about the size of peas. Add 6 tablespoons of the water and mix lightly into the flour mixture using a fork or your hands. Add more water as needed, a tablespoon at a time, until a shaggy dough forms and holds together when squeezed. (You may not need all of the water.) Knead the dough a few times in the bowl to bring it together. Shape the dough into a 1-inch-thick square and wrap tightly in plastic wrap. Chill for 2 hours.

On a lightly floured surface, roll the dough into a rectangle with ½-inch thickness. Fold into thirds like a letter, then turn 90 degrees. Repeat the rolling and folding. Rewrap the dough tightly in plastic wrap and chill for another hour or up to 3 days.

MAKE THE BLACKBERRY FILLING: In a small saucepan, add the blackberries and sugar and gently mash a few times with a potato masher or the back of a spoon. Add the rosemary and let stand for 15 minutes.

Place the saucepan over medium-low heat and bring the mixture to a boil. Cook, stirring frequently, until very soft and syrupy, about 10 minutes.

In a small bowl, whisk together the lime juice and cornstarch. Add to the blackberry mixture and stir, cooking for 1 minute or until thickened and translucent. (The mixture should easily leave a clean trail on the bottom of the saucepot when a spoon is dragged through it.) Remove the

continued

TIPS & TRICKS

The hand pie dough is very similar to a classic pie dough, but with a couple of tricks that make it sturdy enough for a handheld treat. The tri-folding of the dough helps build layers while also gently giving the dough a little more structure than you would want in a super flaky pie crust. The butter is also reduced a touch to keep the dough from crumbling too much when biting into it.

When rolling out the dough after the final fold, it may feel harder to roll than a normal pie dough and shrink slightly after each roll. Just keep rolling or let the dough rest for a few minutes. It'll relax as you continue rolling it.

This recipe can easily be used to make two single 9-inch piecrusts or a 9-inch double-crust pie (the rosemary is a perfect pairing for apple pie!). Just add 2 more tablespoons of butter for a full cup, divide the dough into two disks when chilling, and skip the folding process.

If you have any leftover dough, press the scraps back into a disk, wrap, and chill for at least an hour. Roll to ⅛-inch thickness, sprinkle lightly with cinnamon sugar, fold in half, and cut into 1-inch strips. Twist the strips a few times and bake on parchment paper–lined sheets at 400ºF for 15 to 20 minutes, or until golden brown. Enjoy with tea or coffee.

Not a fan of blackberries or have an abundance of other seasonal fruit? This recipe will also work great with strawberries, mulberries, raspberries, blueberries, and plums. Depending on the juiciness of your fruit, you may need to add an additional teaspoon of cornstarch.

rosemary stem. Transfer the mixture to a heatproof bowl and let cool completely.

ASSEMBLE THE PIES: Preheat the oven to 425°F. Line a baking sheet with parchment paper and set aside.

Let the pie dough stand at room temperature until slightly softened, about 10 minutes. Roll the dough to an ⅛-inch thickness. Cut sixteen circles out using a 3½-inch round cutter dipped in flour. Reroll the scraps once, if necessary.

In a small bowl, whisk together the egg and water. Brush the edges of eight rounds with the egg wash. Spoon 1 tablespoon of the filling into the center of each brushed round. Place the remaining plain rounds on top and press the edges to seal. Crimp as desired and place on the prepared pan 2 inches apart. Brush the tops with the egg wash and cut a small slit in the top of each hand pie. Sprinkle with the sparkling sugar. Freeze for 10 minutes or refrigerate for 30 minutes.

Bake until the crusts are golden brown and the sides are puffed and flaky, 20 to 25 minutes. Let cool completely on a wire rack.

In a small bowl, muddle the blackberry and liqueur or water until the berry is well mashed. Whisk in the powdered sugar until smooth. Drizzle the glaze over the hand pies before serving.

Lemon-Berry Meringue Pie

FOR THE PIE CRUST

1½ cups (180g) all-purpose flour, plus more for dusting

1 tablespoon granulated sugar

½ teaspoon kosher salt

½ cup (1 stick/113g) cold unsalted butter, cubed

4 to 6 tablespoons (60 to 90ml) ice water

1 large egg white, lightly beaten

FOR THE LEMON FILLING

6 large egg yolks, room temperature

¾ cup (180ml) fresh lemon juice

1⅓ cups (266g) granulated sugar

⅓ cup (40g) cornstarch

½ teaspoon ground cardamom

¼ teaspoon kosher salt

¼ cup (57g) cold unsalted butter, cubed

FOR THE MERINGUE

4 large egg whites, room temperature

¾ cup (150g) granulated sugar

2 to 3 tablespoons seedless berry jam or fruit spread, warmed slightly

Lemons and berries make the perfect marriage, each balancing the flavor of the other to create a zingy filling that I like to delicately perfume with floral cardamom. And while most meringue pies require you to fish through the whipped topping to get to the filling, this version calls for swirling berry jam through the meringue, which takes things to a whole new level of flavor and brightness. Not only do you get that signature dramatic top but it also happens to rest on one of my favorite pie crusts.

MAKES 1 (9-INCH) DEEP-DISH PIE

MAKE THE PIE CRUST: In a large bowl, add the flour, sugar, and salt and whisk to combine. Add the butter and toss to coat it with the flour mixture. Cut in the butter using a pastry blender or by squeezing the pieces between your fingers until the biggest pieces are the size of almonds and the smallest ones are about the size of peas. Add half of the water and fold in with a fork. Continue adding the water 1 tablespoon at a time until the mixture forms a shaggy dough. Gently knead it together in the bowl until the dough clumps together. Shape the dough into a disk and wrap tightly in plastic wrap. Refrigerate for 1 hour or up to 3 days.

Preheat the oven to 400°F.

On a lightly floured surface, roll the chilled pie dough into a 12-inch circle. Transfer to a 9-inch deep-dish pie pan. Trim the dough to a 1-inch overhang, tuck the excess under, and crimp around the edge as desired. Poke the bottom of the crust all over with a fork and freeze for 15 minutes.

Brush the edges with the egg white. Place a piece of parchment paper inside the pie crust and fill it with pie weights or dried beans. Place the pie pan on a rimmed baking sheet. Bake for 25 minutes. Reduce the temperature to 375°F and carefully remove the parchment and weights. Continue baking until the crust appears dry on the bottom and is golden brown on the edges, 12 to 15 minutes more. Transfer the pan to a wire rack to let the crust cool completely.

MAKE THE LEMON FILLING: Add the egg yolks to a medium heatproof bowl and whisk until smooth. Set aside.

continued

In a medium saucepan over medium heat, whisk together the lemon juice, sugar, cornstarch, cardamom, and salt with 1¾ cups of water. Cook, whisking frequently, until the mixture starts to bubble and thicken, 3 to 7 minutes. (The whisk should leave a trace in the custard and the custard should register about 175°F.) Remove the pan from the heat and slowly whisk 1 cup of the hot lemon mixture into the egg yolks.

Return the pan to medium heat and slowly whisk the yolk mixture into the pan. Cook, whisking constantly, until the mixture starts to bubble and thicken, about 3 minutes. (The whisk should leave a defined trace in the mixture.) Remove the pan from the heat and whisk in the cold butter until fully incorporated.

Pour the lemon curd into the cooled pie crust. Press a sheet of plastic wrap directly onto the surface of the lemon curd and let cool at room temperature for 1 hour. Chill for at least 3 hours or overnight.

MAKE THE MERINGUE: Fill a small saucepan with 2 inches of water and set over medium heat. Bring to a simmer.

In the bowl of a stand mixer fitted with the whisk attachment, add the egg whites and sugar and beat on medium-low speed until combined. Set the mixing bowl over the simmering pot and cook, stirring frequently, until the mixture reaches 160°F, about 6 minutes. (If you don't have a thermometer, you can rub the mixture between your fingers. It should feel smooth and warm to the touch.)

Return the bowl to the mixer and reattach the whisk. Beat the mixture on medium-high speed until the bowl feels slightly warm and the meringue has thick, glossy peaks, about 10 minutes. Remove the plastic from the lemon curd and top with the meringue, making sure to spread it to the edge so it's touching the crust.

Drop teaspoonfuls of the fruit jam over the meringue and swirl in using the tip of a knife. If desired, toast the meringue with a kitchen torch before slicing. Refrigerate any leftover pie by pressing a piece of plastic wrap against the cut edge, and enjoy within 3 days.

Stonefruit *and* Berry Dacquoise

FOR THE MERINGUE

1 cup (96g) blanched almonds

6 large egg whites, room temperature

¼ teaspoon cream of tartar

⅜ teaspoon fine sea salt

1 cup (200g) superfine granulated or caster sugar

¼ teaspoon almond extract

FOR THE FRENCH BUTTERCREAM

8 large egg yolks, room temperature

¾ cup plus 2 tablespoons (180g) granulated sugar

½ vanilla bean, seeds scraped, or 2 teaspoons vanilla bean paste

1 cup plus 5 tablespoons (298g) salted European-style butter, softened and cubed

FOR THE FILLING

1 purple plum, halved, pitted, and sliced into ¼-inch slices

1 yellow nectarine, halved, pitted, and sliced into ¼-inch slices

1 teaspoon fresh lemon juice

1 cup (240ml) heavy whipping cream

2 tablespoons powdered sugar, plus more for dusting

6 ounces (170g) fresh raspberries

6 ounces (170g) fresh blueberries

In some ways, this cakey version of a pavlova reminds me of the Swedish *äppelkaka* my mom would always make in that it's super light and typically served with some kind of boozy whipped cream. Here, though, instead of showcasing apples, it's all about the season's stone fruit, especially plums and nectarines. And instead of just whipped cream, there's a custardy French buttercream between the layers. This dessert checks all the boxes of the ideal summer dessert: refreshing, creamy, and bursting with seasonal fruit.   MAKES 1 3-LAYER (8-INCH) CAKE

MAKE THE MERINGUE: Preheat the oven to 225°F. Position two oven racks near each other in the middle third of the oven. On two sheets of parchment paper, trace three 8-inch circles. Place the parchment ink side down on two baking sheets and set aside.

Place the almonds in a food processor and pulse until very finely ground, about 1 minute.

In a stand mixer fitted with the whisk attachment, add the egg whites, cream of tartar, and salt. Beat on medium speed until foamy and doubled in size, about 2 minutes. With the mixer running, very slowly add the sugar and continue beating until stiff and glossy, about 8 minutes. Add the almond extract and beat until just combined.

Sprinkle half of the ground almonds over the meringue and use a silicone spatula to fold them in until fully combined. Fold in the remaining almonds. At this point, the meringue should be thick but may have lost its stiff peaks. Fill a large piping bag with the meringue and snip about 1 inch off the tip. Pipe the meringue into three disks onto the prepared baking sheets, using the traced circles as a guide. Gently smooth the tops with a spatula.

Bake the meringues for 2 to 2½ hours or until dry to the touch in the center. Turn the oven off and leave the meringues inside with the door closed for at least 3 hours, or up to overnight, to cool and dry out.

MAKE THE FRENCH BUTTERCREAM: Fill a medium saucepan with 2 inches of water. Set the pan over medium-high heat and bring to a boil.

continued

In the bowl of a stand mixer fitted with the whisk attachment, add the egg yolks, sugar, and vanilla seeds, and beat on low speed until just combined, about 1 minute. Remove the bowl from the mixer and place it on top of the pot of water, making sure the bowl isn't touching the water. Reduce the flame to medium-low and cook the egg yolk mixture, stirring constantly with a spatula, until the mixture reaches 150°F to 160°F or is warm to the touch and smooth when rubbed between your fingers, 3 to 5 minutes.

Return the bowl to the stand mixer with a clean whisk attachment and beat the egg yolk mixture on medium-high speed until very stiff and gathering around the beater, and the outside of the bowl is barely warm to the touch, about 7 minutes. Add the butter 1 tablespoon at a time, waiting a few seconds between each addition. Beat until the buttercream is thick and spreadable and holds its shape, about 3 minutes. Transfer the buttercream to a piping bag fitted with an open star tip and chill until ready to use.

MAKE THE FILLING: In a medium bowl, toss the sliced plum and nectarine with the lemon juice and set aside.

In a stand mixer fitted with the whisk attachment, beat the cream and powdered sugar on medium-high speed until stiff peaks form, 3 to 5 minutes. Chill until ready to use.

ASSEMBLE THE DACQUOISE: Carefully remove the meringue disks from the parchment paper using a long, thin knife or offset spatula underneath them to help release from the paper. Place one of the meringues on a cake plate and pipe dots of the buttercream in a single layer over the meringue. Arrange half of the plums, nectarines, and berries over the buttercream. Place another meringue on top and repeat with the buttercream and fruit. Top with the remaining meringue. Dot with the remaining buttercream, and pile the whipped cream on top. Serve immediately.

Brambleberry Icebox Pie *with* Biscoff-Almond Crust

1½ cups (225g) fresh mixed berries, such as blackberries and raspberries, plus more for garnish, or use frozen and thawed berries

Zest and juice of 1 lemon

1 tablespoon granulated sugar

20 Biscoff cookies

½ cup (46g) sliced almonds

6 tablespoons (85g) unsalted butter, melted

2 tablespoons firmly packed light brown sugar

¼ teaspoon kosher salt

1 cup (248g) whole-milk ricotta cheese

1 (8-ounce/227g) block cream cheese, room temperature

1 cup (120g) powdered sugar

1¼ cups (300ml) heavy whipping cream

Fresh mint leaves, for garnish

Summertime screams for cool, creamy, no-bake delights. That's how I came up with this dreamboat of a dessert—I wanted a crunchy cookie crust without needing to turn on my oven. The trick is using just a little extra butter, which helps the crumbs stick together. It's also the perfect way to use up all those peak-season berries. You can use whatever kind of berry you like in this recipe, though I love blackberries and raspberries, aka "bramble" berries, for their juiciness and tart-sweet flavor.

MAKES 1 (9-INCH) PIE

In a medium bowl, mash 1 cup of the berries with a fork. Gently stir in the remaining ½ cup of berries, plus the lemon juice and granulated sugar. Set aside.

In the bowl of a food processor, add the cookies and pulse until they are broken into small bits. Add the almonds, melted butter, brown sugar, and salt and pulse until the mixture is mostly fine crumbs that hold together when pinched.

Transfer the mixture to a 9-inch pie dish. Use the bottom of a glass or a small spatula to firmly press the mixture into the bottom and up the sides of the dish. Freeze until firm, about 15 minutes.

In a large bowl, add the ricotta, cream cheese, and lemon zest. With a handheld electric mixer, beat the mixture on medium speed until smooth. Add ¾ cup of the powdered sugar and beat on low speed until combined.

In another large bowl, add ½ cup of the cream and use the electric mixer to beat on medium-high speed until soft peaks form. Add the whipped cream to the ricotta mixture and gently fold until combined.

Drain the berry mixture over a bowl to reserve any excess juice. Very gently, fold the berry mixture into the filling. Refrigerate the reserved juice for topping.

Gently spoon the ricotta-berry filling into the frozen crust and smooth the top with an offset spatula. Freeze until firm, about 3 hours.

continued

When almost ready to serve, remove the pie from the freezer to thaw slightly, about 20 minutes.

In a medium bowl, add the remaining ¾ cup cream and the remaining ¼ cup powdered sugar. Use a handheld electric mixer on medium speed to beat until soft peaks form. Spread the freshly whipped cream on top of the pie and drizzle with 1 tablespoon of the reserved berry juice. Garnish with the fresh berries. Keep any leftovers covered and frozen for up to 1 month.

Raspberry-Rose Sheet Cake

FOR THE RASPBERRY CAKE

1 cup (2 sticks/226g) unsalted butter, softened, plus more for the pan

3 cups (360g) all-purpose flour, plus more for the pan

1½ teaspoons baking powder

¼ teaspoon kosher salt

¼ teaspoon baking soda

1⅔ cups (333g) granulated sugar

4 large eggs, room temperature

2 teaspoons vanilla extract

1 cup (240ml) whole milk, room temperature

8 ounces (225g) fresh raspberries

FOR THE ROSE WATER SWISS MERINGUE BUTTERCREAM

6 large egg whites

1¾ cups (350g) granulated sugar

4 teaspoons (20ml) rose water

2 cups (4 sticks/452g) unsalted butter, softened (see Tips & Tricks)

Most people associate rose water with Middle Eastern cuisine, as I did for a long time after enjoying rose water ice cream at Mashti Malone's, the Iranian ice cream shop in LA. Then I learned that in traditional English baking, rose water was vanilla's early predecessor—something I find to be as charming as it is interesting. I happen to love the subtle perfume of rose water in baked goods, which when used with a sparing hand adds a lovely aroma and flavor to whatever it's paired with. I think it works especially well with raspberries by complementing their natural floral bouquet—a pretty elegant pairing for a humble sheet cake. But as fancy as it may sound, rose water is actually quite easy to come by in the grocery store.   MAKES 1 (9X13-INCH) CAKE

MAKE THE RASPBERRY CAKE: Preheat the oven to 350°F. Butter a 9x13-inch cake pan and fully line with parchment paper. Set aside.

In a large bowl, whisk together the flour, baking powder, salt, and baking soda. Set aside.

In the bowl of a stand mixer fitted with the paddle attachment, beat the butter and sugar on medium speed until light and fluffy, about 3 minutes. Add the eggs one at a time, beating until fully combined after each addition and scraping down the sides of the bowl as needed. Add the vanilla and beat for a few more seconds to combine.

Reduce the mixer speed to low and add the flour mixture, alternating with the milk, beginning and ending with the flour. Stop to scrape down the sides of the bowl as needed. Fold in the raspberries. Gently transfer the batter to the prepared pan.

Bake until a wooden pick inserted in the center comes out clean, 35 to 40 minutes. Let the cake cool completely on a wire rack.

MAKE THE ROSE WATER SWISS MERINGUE BUTTERCREAM: Fill a small saucepan with 2 inches of water and set over medium-high heat to bring to a simmer.

In a medium heatproof bowl, whisk together the egg whites and sugar. Set the bowl over the simmering water, making sure the bowl doesn't touch the water, and whisk constantly until the sugar is dissolved and the

continued

Make sure your raspberries have been washed and thoroughly dried before adding them to the cake batter. The centers can trap water adding extra moisture to the cake and causing it to not bake properly.

For the frosting, butter that is between 60°F and 65°F works best. Remove butter from the fridge about 30 minutes before starting your meringue. If the frosting is still runny and not thickening up after several minutes, place an ice bag or something cold on the outside of your mixer bowl to cool the frosting down. You can also put the bowl in the fridge for a few minutes and then continue beating. It should thicken up shortly!

Not a fan of rose water? Leave it out entirely or swap it for orange blossom water, 2 teaspoons vanilla extract, or 1 teaspoon almond extract.

mixture reaches 160°F, about 8 minutes. (The mixture should feel warm to the touch and smooth when rubbed between your fingers.)

Transfer the mixture to the bowl of a stand mixer fitted with the whisk attachment. Beat on high speed until thick and glossy and the sides of the bowl are barely warm to the touch, about 8 minutes. Add the rose water and beat until just combined.

Switch to the paddle attachment and reduce the mixer speed to medium. Add the butter 1 tablespoon at a time, beating until fully combined after each addition. Return the mixer speed to high and beat until the frosting is very thick and fluffy, 5 to 10 minutes. (If the frosting looks runny or curdled after adding the butter, keep beating it until it's stiff and spreadable. This may take several minutes.)

Remove the cake from the pan, discarding the parchment paper, and place on a serving platter. Spread 3 cups of the buttercream evenly over the top of the cake. Divide the remaining frosting between separate bowls and color as desired with gel food coloring. Transfer the colored buttercream to piping bags fitted with decorative tips. Pipe in a decorative pattern or make buttercream roses and place them on top of the cake (see box below). Serve immediately or refrigerate for up to 2 days.

Buttercream Roses

I prefer using a classic American buttercream for these, as it holds its shape well when piping and dries into crisp, sugary flowers. You can halve the recipe for the frosting from the Chocolate Peppermint Bark Cake (page 159)—just swap out the peppermint extract for vanilla or your favorite flavoring. Because buttercream flowers work best when the frosting is on the firmer side, you can add more powdered sugar to stiffen things up if the frosting seems too soft. Lastly, the cake will look its best when the flowers are varying shades of color and different sizes. Mix up several shades you love and pipe away!

Cut 2-inch squares of parchment paper for each rose you want to make and set aside. Transfer the frosting to a piping bag fitted with a petal tip, such as an Ateco 126.

Place a dab of buttercream on the flat surface of a piping or flower nail and press a parchment square on top. Use a small spatula to create a roughly ½-inch-high cone of buttercream in the center of the square.

Pipe a spiral onto the tip of the cone (with the narrow side of the piping tip facing up). This will be the center of the rose. Create the petals by making small arcs with the piping tip, working your way outward from the center of the flower. Gradually make the arcs larger as you get closer to the outer edge of the flower.

Use a pair of sharp scissors to cut off the rose at the base and transfer it to the cake. Repeat for as many roses as desired, making sure to pipe some of varying sizes.

Arrange the flowers on the cake and pipe the leaves using a leaf tip.

Pressed Flower Shortbread Cookies

I love shortbread cookies, and I grew up pressing flowers from the garden in massive history books from my dad's library, so I combined the two to give this simple, classic treat an extra-special touch. While it's exciting to make these in the spring with all the blooms that are reawakening, if you store the pressed flowers properly, you'll be able to bake with them in the fall and winter as well—the perfect reminder that spring is just around the corner.   MAKES ABOUT 20 COOKIES

FOR THE SHORTBREAD COOKIES

2 cups (240g) all-purpose flour

⅓ cup (40g) cornstarch

½ cup (100g) granulated sugar

Zest of 1 orange (peeled with a vegetable peeler)

½ teaspoon kosher salt

1 cup (2 sticks/226g) unsalted butter, cubed and softened

1 teaspoon vanilla bean paste or extract of choice

FOR THE GLAZE

1 cup (120g) powdered sugar

1 to 2 tablespoons fresh orange juice or water

24 to 36 pressed edible flowers or flower petals (see Pressed Flowers project, page 307)

TIPS & TRICKS

This dough can easily be flavored with any citrus zest and extract you'd like. Or swap the zest for ½ cup of fresh mint leaves for a bright spring green color and delicious minty-fresh flavor.

Thanks to slowly dehydrating the flowers by pressing them between sheets of paper, these cookies will keep their taste and beauty for up to 2 weeks if stored in an airtight container.

MAKE THE SHORTBREAD COOKIES: In a small bowl, whisk together the flour and cornstarch. Set aside.

In the work bowl of a food processor, combine the sugar, strips of orange zest, and salt. Process until the zest is very fine and the mixture feels like wet sand. Add the butter and vanilla. Process until smooth and fluffy, about 30 seconds, stopping to scrape the sides of the bowl as needed. Add the flour mixture and pulse until the dough starts to clump together. Stop and scrape the sides of the bowl and pulse 3 to 4 more times until fully combined. Dump the dough out onto a lightly floured surface and knead a few times until the dough comes together. Shape the dough into a disk and wrap tightly in plastic wrap. Chill for 1 hour.

Preheat the oven to 350°F. Line two baking sheets with parchment paper and set aside.

On a lightly floured surface, roll out the dough to ¼-inch thick. Using a 2½-inch-round cookie cutter dipped in flour, cut the cookies out of the dough and place them on the prepared pans, 1 inch apart.

Bake one sheet at a time for 14 minutes, or until the cookies are firm and the bottoms are just starting to brown. Let them cool on the baking sheet for 5 minutes. Allow them to finish cooling on a wire rack.

MAKE THE GLAZE: In a small bowl, whisk together the powdered sugar and enough orange juice or water to reach the desired thickness, about the consistency of room-temperature honey. Spoon the glaze over each cookie, using the back of the spoon to spread it into a thin layer. Adhere the pressed flowers immediately. Use a small, clean paintbrush to paint a thin coating of glaze over the flowers. Let the cookies dry completely, about 1 hour. The cookies will keep in an airtight container for up to 2 weeks.

Summer Trifle *with* Grilled Peaches, Cherries, *and* Boozy Pound Cake

The first time I had a trifle was at a brunch at the incomparable Inn of the Seventh Ray. It was a magical Topanga Canyon moment made even more so by this bounty of fresh fruit layered with heaps of whipped cream and perfectly moist pound cake. Ever since, I've made it a point to work trifles into my summer dessert rotation, what with their being generously laden with all the fruit. For this version with peaches and cherries, we're grilling the peaches, which as you might know, is the secret to imbuing them with a delectable burnt-sugar flavor.

SERVES 14 TO 16

FOR THE VANILLA BEAN CAKE

Nonstick baking spray, for the pan

3¼ cups (390g) all-purpose flour

2¼ cups (450g) granulated sugar

2½ teaspoons baking powder

¼ teaspoon baking soda

¼ teaspoon kosher salt

1 cup (2 sticks/226g) unsalted butter, melted

1 cup (240ml) whole milk, room temperature

4 large eggs, room temperature

1 vanilla bean, seeds scraped, or 1 tablespoon vanilla bean paste

FOR THE TRIFLE

2¼ pounds (1,013g, about 6) slightly firm peaches, halved and pitted

1 tablespoon unsalted butter, melted

1 pound (450g) sweet cherries, halved and pitted

1½ cups (360ml) Lillet Blanc or sweet white wine

¼ cup plus 2 tablespoons (90ml/from about 1 orange) fresh orange juice

¼ cup plus 2 tablespoons (85g) granulated sugar

2 cups (480ml) heavy whipping cream

2 cups (450g) whole-milk Greek yogurt

½ vanilla bean, seeds scraped

MAKE THE VANILLA BEAN CAKE: Preheat the oven to 350°F. Butter and flour a 9x13-inch cake pan or spray with baking spray and set aside.

In a large bowl, sift together the flour, sugar, baking powder, and baking soda and whisk in the salt. In another large bowl, whisk together the melted butter, milk, eggs, and vanilla seeds. Add the butter mixture to the flour mixture and whisk until the batter is just combined.

Pour the batter into the prepared cake pan and bake for 35 to 40 minutes, until a wooden pick inserted in the center comes out with a few moist crumbs. Let the cake cool completely in the pan.

MAKE THE TRIFLE: Preheat the grill to medium-high, or about 400°F.

Brush the cut sides of the peaches lightly with the melted butter. Grill the peaches cut side down for 5 minutes, or until dark grill marks appear. Transfer the peaches to a sheet tray and let cool.

In a medium bowl, toss the cherries with 3 tablespoons of the Lillet Blanc, 3 tablespoons of the orange juice, and 1 tablespoon of the sugar. Set aside.

Slice the grilled peaches into ½-inch slices and place in a large bowl. Toss with 3 tablespoons of the Lillet Blanc, the remaining 3 tablespoons of orange juice, and 1 tablespoon of the sugar. Set aside.

In the bowl of a stand mixer fitted with the whisk attachment, add the cream and the remaining ¼ cup of sugar. Beat on medium speed until

continued

The Vanilla Bean Cake makes a great sheet cake! You can top it with any of the frosting recipes in the book, but the Rose Water Buttercream (page 290) and the orange cream cheese frosting (page 236) are my favorites.

If your trifle dish is less than 4 quarts, you may have some cake cubes left over. They can be frozen in a freezer container for up to 2 months for long-term storage. Use them to make a quick dessert by placing a few cubes each in individual serving bowls, topping with fresh fruit or preserves, and serving with whipped cream or ice cream.

Baking the cake with a cake strip around the pan will keep the cake soft on the edges, keeping the trifle moist. If you don't have cake strips and your cooled cake has crusty edges, just trim them off. You can crumble the trimmings over ice cream for an easy treat.

If you don't have or want to fire up the grill for the peaches, heat a nonstick skillet over medium-high heat. Cook as directed in step 5 until they are dark brown and caramelized, about 5 minutes.

stiff peaks form, about 5 minutes. Add the Greek yogurt and vanilla and beat just until combined.

Cut the cake into 1-inch cubes. Spread 1½ cups of the whipped cream on the bottom of a 3- or 4-quart trifle dish. Tightly pack the cake cubes over the whipped cream in a single layer. Drizzle about ½ cup of the Lillet Blanc over the cake cubes. Layer a little less than half of the peach slices over the cake, drizzling with some of the juices from the bowl. Spoon a little less than half of the cherries over the peaches along with some of the juices from the bowl. Top with half of the remaining whipped cream and repeat the layers, leaving some of the fruit for the top. (You may have some cake cubes leftover if your trifle dish is smaller than 4 quarts; see Tips & Tricks.)

Top with the remaining whipped cream and remaining peaches and cherries. Serve immediately or refrigerate for up to 6 hours before serving.

Tipsy Caramelized Banana Pudding

This mash-up of banana pudding, a classic summer potluck staple, with Bananas Foster is a fun way to serve a nostalgically familiar dessert but with a decidedly adult twist. Traditionally, banana pudding doesn't have banana-flavored pudding (just vanilla and sliced bananas), but here we're introducing a banana caramel and burnt-sugar-flavored Biscoff cookies instead of Nilla Wafers for dramatically intensified richness.

SERVES 6

FOR THE CUSTARD

6 large egg yolks

1 tablespoon vanilla extract

1¼ cups (250g) granulated sugar

¼ cup (28g) cornstarch

½ teaspoon kosher salt

4 cups (960ml) whole milk

3 tablespoons bourbon or whiskey

¼ cup (57g) cold unsalted butter, cubed

FOR THE BANANA CARAMEL

2 cups (400g) granulated sugar

1 very ripe banana, mashed

¼ cup (60ml) bourbon or whiskey

¼ teaspoon kosher salt

¾ cup (180ml) heavy whipping cream, warmed

FOR THE BANANA PUDDING

5 large ripe bananas (about 2 pounds/900g), peeled and sliced into ¼-inch rounds

1 (8-ounce) package Biscoff cookies

1 cup (240ml) heavy whipping cream

2 tablespoons powdered sugar

MAKE THE CUSTARD: In a large heatproof bowl, whisk together the egg yolks and vanilla and set aside.

In a large saucepan, whisk together the sugar, cornstarch, and salt. Slowly whisk in the milk until combined. Place the pan over medium-high heat and cook, whisking frequently, until the mixture is thickened and starts to bubble, 12 to 15 minutes. Remove the pan from the heat.

Slowly whisk about 2 cups of the hot milk mixture into the egg yolk mixture. Slowly whisk the egg yolk mixture back into the saucepan. Cook over medium heat, whisking constantly but gently, until the mixture is thickened and the whisk leaves a defined trace, 3 to 5 minutes. Whisk in the bourbon and remove the pan from the heat. Add the cold butter and whisk until melted and well combined. Immediately transfer the custard to a large bowl. Press a sheet of plastic wrap directly over the surface of the custard and let cool for about an hour. At this point, the custard can be chilled for up to 2 days.

MAKE THE BANANA CARAMEL: In a large saucepan, add the sugar and 1 cup water and gently stir just until the sugar is moistened. Set the pan over medium-high heat and bring to a boil. Reduce the heat to medium and boil until the sugar is amber in color, about 20 minutes.

Remove the pan from the heat and carefully whisk in the mashed banana, bourbon, and salt. Return the pan to medium heat and cook, whisking constantly, until deep golden brown and a candy thermometer reaches 230°F to 235°F, 2 to 5 minutes.

Whisking constantly, carefully add the cream in a very slow, steady stream. The mixture will vigorously bubble up so be careful. Remove the

continued

The caramel sauce and custard can be made in advance for easy assembly. The caramel sauce can be cooled and then refrigerated for up to 1 week. When ready to assemble the pudding, reheat the sauce just until warm, then stir in the banana slices. The custard can be made and chilled for 2 days before assembling.

pan from the heat. Once the bubbles subside, pour $\frac{1}{2}$ cup of the caramel into a heatproof container and set aside. Pour the remaining caramel sauce into a large heatproof bowl.

MAKE THE BANANA PUDDING: Add the bananas to the large bowl with the hot caramel sauce and stir gently to combine. Let the mixture stand until just warm to the touch, about 20 minutes.

Place $\frac{1}{4}$ cup of the chilled custard in the bottoms of six (12-ounce) low-ball glasses or parfait dishes. Crumble 2 Biscoff cookies over the top, followed by $\frac{1}{3}$ cup of the banana-caramel mixture. Repeat the layers and top off with more custard. Chill the parfaits for 2 hours or until ready to serve.

In a large mixing bowl, add the cream and powdered sugar and beat with a handheld electric mixer on medium speed until soft peaks form. Top the pudding cups with the whipped cream. Garnish with additional banana slices and cookies, and serve with the reserved caramel sauce.

Key Lime Coconut Cream Pie

This is a tropical-dream mash-up of key lime and coconut cream pies that will have you thinking pink-sand beaches and slushy cocktails. To achieve this beautifully balanced flavor, we're using toasted coconut flakes. Because I firmly believe that the only place for artificial coconut is in sunscreen.

MAKES 1 (9-INCH) DEEP-DISH PIE

FOR THE CRUST

6 sheets honey graham crackers, broken up into rough pieces

½ cup (50g) shredded sweetened coconut

¼ cup (55g) firmly packed light brown sugar

¼ cup (57g) unsalted butter, melted

FOR THE FILLING

1 (14-ounce/397g) can sweetened condensed milk

2 large eggs

½ teaspoon vanilla extract

⅛ teaspoon kosher salt

½ cup (120ml) fresh key lime juice

1½ cups (360ml) heavy whipping cream

¼ cup (30g) powdered sugar, sifted

TIPS & TRICKS

If you don't have access to fresh key limes, regular lime juice can be substituted. Or use Nellie and Joe's Famous Key West Lime Juice, which can be found with the shelf-stable juices in your local grocery store. For a hint of glowing lime beauty, add a small drop of green food coloring to the filling, if desired.

MAKE THE CRUST: Preheat the oven to 350°F.

In the bowl of a food processor, add the graham crackers, shredded coconut, and brown sugar and process into very fine crumbs, about 1 minute. With the processor running, drizzle in the butter. Continue processing until the mixture is the texture of wet sand, about 1 minute. Pour the mixture into a 9-inch pie pan and use the bottom of a glass or silicone spatula to press into the bottom and up the sides of the pan.

Bake for 10 minutes or until fragrant and just starting to darken on the edges. If the crust puffs anywhere, gently press it smooth with the back of a spoon. Set aside to cool.

MAKE THE FILLING: In a large bowl, whisk together the condensed milk, eggs, vanilla, and salt. Whisk in the key lime juice and pour the mixture into the pie crust.

Bake for 10 to 15 minutes or until the center is jiggly and the edges are just set. Let the pie stand at room temperature for 30 minutes, then refrigerate for at least 4 hours or overnight.

In the bowl of a stand mixer fitted with the whisk attachment, beat the heavy cream and powdered sugar on medium until the mixture forms stiff peaks, about 4 minutes.

Using a small spring-loaded scoop, dollop the whipped cream over the top of the chilled pie. Keep the pie refrigerated until ready to serve or up to 3 days.

Cherry *and* Apricot Clafoutis

1 tablespoon unsalted butter, softened

Powdered sugar, for dusting

3 large eggs

½ cup (100g) granulated sugar

Zest of 1 lemon

1 teaspoon vanilla extract

⅛ teaspoon kosher salt

½ cup (60g) all-purpose flour

⅔ cup (160ml) whole milk

⅓ cup (80ml) heavy whipping cream

½ pound (225g) fresh cherries, pitted

½ pound (225g) apricots, pitted and sliced

Whipped cream or vanilla ice cream, for serving (optional)

TIPS & TRICKS

To make this clafoutis throughout the year, swap cherries and apricots for other seasonal fruits like blueberries, sliced peaches, chopped soft pears, halved figs, or sautéed apples. You can also add your favorite baking spices or a flavoring like almond extract for additional flavor.

Clafoutis is often baked in a cast iron skillet. My recipe was developed for any 2-quart baking dish, so feel free to use your favorite skillet if you'd like.

The edges of the custard may puff up above the sides of the dish (like a Dutch baby) while baking, but it will settle as it cools.

My mom had a clafoutis in her baking repertoire, so while I'm very familiar with this gooey, fruit-studded cake, I realize that not many others might be. I like to think of a clafoutis (pronounced clah-foo-tee) as a cross between a custard and a Dutch baby (essentially a giant pancake). All there is to it is making a batter and lacing it with whatever seasonal fruit is available, summertime or otherwise. The pop of bright flavor from tart summer cherries and sun-sweetened apricots against the custard is basically magic. SERVES 6 TO 8

Preheat the oven to 375°F. Coat the bottom and sides of a deep 2-quart baking dish with the softened butter and dust lightly with powdered sugar. Set aside.

In a large mixing bowl, combine the eggs, sugar, lemon zest, vanilla, and salt. Whisk until well combined and smooth. Sift in the flour and whisk until smooth. As you whisk, stream in the milk and cream and mix until smooth. Pour the batter into the prepared baking dish and gently set the cherries and apricots on top.

Bake for 40 to 45 minutes, until puffed, and a toothpick inserted in the center comes out clean. Let the clafoutis cool for 15 minutes and dust with powdered sugar. Serve with whipped cream or ice cream, if desired. The clafoutis can be served warm, room temperature, or cold and refrigerated for up to 2 days.

SPECIAL
PROJECTS

PRESSED FLOWERS

When we were little, my brother and I were always picking flowers and pressing them between the pages of the books in our family's library. Even now, you can pick up almost any one of them and find a small treasure that we snuck in there. So when the frost melted after our first Connecticut winter and the open fields exploded with flowers, I taught the boys how to carefully enclose their favorite blossoms in our family's books, knowing that we were creating a time capsule of sorts—a reminder of spring in the depths of winter, a token of the awe-inspiring things the land around our home produces, and a keepsake we'd all be able to revisit as a suspended moment in time.

Pressed flowers are not only beautiful mementos, they're also perfectly suited for adorning the tops of shortbread cookies. You just have to make sure you're using edible varieties of flowers! You can find these at many supermarkets, though you'll get a superior product if you seek them out at your local farmers' market. If someone's not already selling them, ask around if any of the farmers are growing things like pansies, chamomile, nasturtiums, or violas. They might just be willing to share their secret stash.

Start by gathering clean flowers free of marks and blemishes. This is a perfect activity for a sunny morning, as the flowers should be dry when picked but still full of water inside. Delicate flowers work best, so if you have a large one to press, you'll want to cut it down the middle.

Prepare the flowers by removing their leaves then giving them a fresh cut at the stem. Place them in a glass of water to plump up.

Place the flower between two pieces of printer paper. Ideally your paper would have some wicking quality to pull moisture away from the flowers. Coffee filters work well, too. Choose your favorite large book and carefully sandwich the paper and flowers inside. Close the book and add another book or two on top for additional weight.

When I pressed flowers as a child, I would just leave the flowers in the books for a while, but it's actually best to switch out your papers every couple of days so more water is wicked away from the flower.

After 2 to 3 weeks, depending on the size and thickness of your flower, they will be desiccated and ready to leave their books—and maybe top some cookies!

Pickling

FOR THE PICKLING SPICE MIX

1 tablespoon mustard seeds

1 tablespoon fennel seeds

1 tablespoon black peppercorns

2 teaspoons juniper or allspice berries

FOR THE PICKLES

4 cups (960ml) distilled white vinegar

½ cup (120ml) white wine vinegar

½ cup (100g) granulated sugar

1 tablespoon non-iodized kosher or pickling salt

5 bay leaves

Fresno, jalapeño, or Thai red or green chile peppers (optional)

2 to 3 pounds (900 to 1,350g) pickling vegetables, such as cucumbers, sweet peppers, or onions, trimmed and cut as needed

Not only does pickling help preserve the freshness of spring and summer all winter long, it also gives you another briny, crunchy element to play with in your cooking. I like to offer pickles as finger foods along with cheese and bread, or make the very same as a snack. I chop them into salads, mince them into relishes, and toss them alongside any dish that needs a little extra acid and brightness. To make sure I'm capturing the produce at its peak freshness, I set aside a day devoted to pickling and then basically work my way through the garden. It's a fun task that the whole family can get into and makes it even more special when you tuck into that first jar and remember the fresh abundance of the season as you slip into winter.   MAKES 5 (16-OUNCE) JARS

MAKE THE PICKLING SPICE: In an airtight container, combine the mustard seeds, fennel seeds, peppercorns, and juniper berries.

MAKE THE PICKLES: In a medium pot over medium-high heat, whisk together the white vinegar, white wine vinegar, sugar, and salt and bring to a simmer. Cook, stirring, until the sugar and salt have dissolved. Remove the pot from the heat and cover to keep warm.

Sterilize the jars: Fill a large canning pot with enough water to cover the empty glass canning jars by 2 inches. Set the pot over medium-high heat to bring to a boil.

Use canning tongs to gently lower five pint-size canning jars, without the lids, into the boiling water, making sure to tilt the jars to fill them with water. Cover the pot and let the jars boil for 15 minutes. Carefully remove the jars with canning tongs, emptying any water back into the pot. Place the jars upside down on a clean dish towel.

ASSEMBLE THE PICKLES: Add 1 teaspoon of the pickling spice mix to the sterilized jars. Add 1 bay leaf and a spicy pepper, if using, to each jar. Loosely pack each jar with the vegetables to the bottom lip of the lid threads. Pour the warm brine over the jars, just enough to cover the vegetables. There should be about ½ inch of space left from the top of the pickling mixture to the top rim of the jar.

continued

TIPS & TRICKS

If for some reason you don't have enough brine to cover the vegetables in each jar, top off the jar with more vinegar, making sure to leave ½ inch of space at the top.

You can use this recipe to pickle all types of vegetables throughout the year. Boiled, peeled, and sliced beets work great, as do carrot sticks or rounds, garlic scapes, or cauliflower florets.

For a sweet and tangy twist, replace the mustard seeds with 1 tablespoon dried tarragon and fill the jars with hulled strawberries, sliced firm peaches, or blueberries. Pickled fruits make an excellent addition to cheese boards.

If following this water-bath canning method for other recipes, the processing time of the filled jars will vary by size. For jars smaller than 1 pint, process for 10 to 12 minutes. For pint-size jars, process for 15 to 20 minutes. You can also refer to processing times recommended by the jar manufacturer.

Wipe the rim of each jar with a clean damp towel and secure the lids. Give each jar a gentle shake to distribute the brine among the vegetables—they should have some wiggle room. If they do not, remove some from the jar.

Process the jars: Lower the lidded jars back into the canning pot, making sure they're covered with at least 1 inch of water. Cover the pot and return to medium-high heat. Bring the water to a boil and continue boiling for 15 minutes. Remove the jars using the canning tongs and place on a kitchen towel. Let cool, undisturbed, for 12 hours. You should hear the lids pop as they cool. After 24 hours, press the center of the lids with your finger. If any lid springs back, it means it did not seal properly.

Pickles are best if left to rest for 48 hours before consuming. Processed jars can be stored in your pantry for up to a year. You can also skip the processing and refrigerate the pickles for up to 3 months.

WILDFLOWER ARRANGEMENTS

When we were living in LA, Brian would always pro-claim that he was going to take up a hobby. It would change from time to time, but eventually it settled on arranging flowers. So we went down to the flower district in downtown LA, which is not just some little neighbor-hood flower shop. There are upwards of fifty vendors and 125 different varieties of cut flowers on any given day. We came home with piles and piles of flowers, and let's just say that it became *John* arranging flowers as a hobby now.

At first, I thought it would come naturally to me—after all, I was an art major *and* type A, so it seemed like the right fit. But it took me some time to figure it out. Luckily, there's just a few basics to know before you can make your own beautiful arrangements. This is now something I do any chance I can get—in the spring when the bulbs are coming up, and in the summer when our pastures and the farmers' markets are full of wildflowers. With the help of the boys, I love bringing that life into the house, especially by the front door or on bedside tables. Looking at a vase of flowers that I've arranged is the ultimate reminder to soak in this ephemeral moment in the seasons, not unlike eating asparagus or raspberries.

Here are a few easy tips for getting started:

- Remember that it doesn't have to be perfect—it's okay to make a beautiful mess.
- Start with *one* type of flower that you love instead of diving into the deep end with multiple varieties. You can still play around with the height you cut the flowers, as in whether you want them all uniform, tightly clustered in a pavé dome, or bursting in beau-tiful chaos.
- When graduating to more than one type of flower, start with your biggest blooms. Then gradually build with smaller pieces to add more detail. Remember, there's something naturally beautiful in odd numbers and asymmetry.

- Experiment with vases in different shapes and sizes. Pretty much anything can function as a vase so long as it won't be damaged by water, such as Mason jars, milk jugs, teacups, pitchers, bowls, and urns.

ACKNOWLEDGMENTS

I would like to send my heartfelt thanks and gratitude to those who made this book possible:

My husband, Brian Dow, for his encouragement, support, and guidance in all things.

My sons, Lachlan and George; thank you for being my constant inspiration every day. Your Papa and Dada love you to the moon and back!

My lovely mother, Rita, for teaching me all my cooking skills and instilling in me a love of gardening, learning, sharing, and teaching.

My late father, John, for nurturing my love of art and always encouraging me to pursue my passions.

My little brother, Eric, for putting up with me all these years.

Janis Donnaud, for believing in this project and helping to make it happen.

Justin Schwartz, Richard Rhorer, and the entire team at Simon Element for your faith in this book from day one and your guidance through this process.

Rachel Holtzman, for capturing my story so beautifully.

Sarah Ward, who touched every part of this book and made it all come together. I could not have done it without you.

Nicole Perez, Caroline Holmberg, Alec Huerta, Taylor Rodriguez, and the rest of the team at Align. I truly can't thank you enough for all that you've done.

David Malosh, for the beautiful photography, and Simon Andrews, for making my recipes look so delicious.

Spencer Richards and Philip Nix, for helping our marathon photo shoots go so smoothly.

Beth Seeley, for her lovely prop styling.

My Preppy Kitchen team—Jed Rullman, Sarah Ward, Noelle "Elle" Lease, and Steve Fitzgerald—for keeping it all running.

Megan Brown and the team at Underscore, for all your support.

Aliza Simons and her mother, Loren, of Henry Street, for saving the day with the perfect table.

Josh Miller, Erin Merhar, and Taylor Wann, for all their help making sure these recipes are perfect.

Amy Beth Cupp, for sharing her amazing style and being so generous with her many whispers.

And to all the millions of Preppy Kitchen readers and viewers around the world, whose support and encouragement are what truly made this book possible. Thank you for trusting me and my recipes for the special moments in your lives. You all have made my dreams come true, and words can never describe the full measure of my gratitude. THANK YOU!

INDEX

A

Afternoon Tea, 247
aioli, 112, 113
almonds, 85, 115, 286
apples
  Apple Butter, 32
  Apple Butter and
    Marzipan Bread, 55–56
  Apple Cake with Maple
    Buttercream, 61–62
  Browned Butter Apple-
    Pecan Crostata, 68–69
  decorating with, 89
  Gingery Apple and
    Cucumber Slaw, 204
  Poached Apples, 85
  Spiced Apple Pie with
    Brandy Crème Anglaise,
    65–66
  Swedish Apple Cake, 85
  Tips & Tricks, 32, 62, 66,
    69, 85
Arugula-Avocado Ranch,
  192
asparagus
  Asparagus Spears with
    Poached Eggs and
    Butter-Fried Bread
    Crumbs, 188–89
  Breakfast-for-Dinner Tart
    with Farm Eggs,
    Asparagus, and Radishes,
    210
  Pan-Roasted Chicken with
    Mushrooms, Asparagus,
    and Champagne Beurre
    Blanc, 218
  Tips & Tricks, 189
Avgolemono (Greek Chicken
  Soup), 127
avocado
  Arugula-Avocado Ranch,
    192
  Chorizo-Beef Burgers with
    Queso and Avocado,
    272, 273

Cilantro-Avocado Crema,
  263

B

Banana Caramel, 299–300
Banana Pudding, 299, 300
beans
  Chickpea Salad Sandwich,
    259
  Garlicky White Beans and
    Rainbow Chard, 116
  Tips & Tricks, 116, 259
beef
  Beef Tenderloin with
    Miso-Honey Caramel,
    139
  Chorizo-Beef Burgers with
    Queso and Avocado,
    272, 273
beets
  Beet and Grapefruit Salad,
    203
  Tips & Tricks, 203
Blackberry-Balsamic Pork
  Chops, 274
Blackberry-Rosemary Hand
  Pies, 278, 280
Black Bottom Cranberry
  Tart, 151–52
Black Pepper–Herb Goat
  Cheese, 178–79
Black Pepper Pie Dough, 98
Blueberry-Honey Goat
  Cheese, 178–79
Boozy Cherries, 147
Brambleberry Icebox Pie
  with Biscoff-Almond
  Crust, 287, 289
branches, brush, and
  greenery, 89, 247
Brandy Crème Anglaise, 65
breads
  Apple Butter and
    Marzipan Bread, 55–56
  Browned Butter and Sage
    Cornbread, 109
  Butter-Fried Bread
    Crumbs, 188

Chai Babka, 25–26
Chive and Parmesan
  Buttermilk Biscuits, 52
Crispy Flatbread with
  Spring Herbs, Radishes,
  and Whipped Feta, 195
Mini Seafood Gratins with
  Garlic Bread Crumbs,
  119
Orange Pecan Cinnamon
  Rolls, 102, 105
Tips & Tricks, 119, 137,
  260
White Cheddar and
  Rosemary Dinner Rolls,
  110
Breakfast-for-Dinner Tart
  with Farm Eggs,
  Asparagus, and Radishes,
  210
broth, Tips & Tricks, 41, 127
Brown Butter, 87
Browned Butter and Sage
  Cornbread, 109
Browned Butter Apple-Pecan
  Crostata, 68–69
Brûléed Blood Orange
  Cheesecake, 145–46
butter
  Apple Butter, 32
  Brown Butter, 87
  Browned Butter and Sage
    Cornbread, 109
  Browned Butter Apple-
    Pecan Crostata, 68–69
  Butter-Fried Bread
    Crumbs, 188
  European-style butter, 81
  grating frozen butter, 72
Buttercream Roses, 293
buttermilk
  Buttermilk Shortcakes,
    237–38
  Chive and Parmesan
    Buttermilk Biscuits, 52

C

Cacio e Pepe with Cavatelli
  Pasta, 124

cakes
  Apple Cake with Maple
    Buttercream, 61–62
  Chocolate Carrot Cake,
    235–36
  Chocolate Peppermint
    Bark Cake, 159–60
  Lemon-Elderflower Tea
    Cake, 222
  Lemon-Ginger Icebox
    Cake, 277
  Raspberry-Rose Sheet
    Cake, 290, 293
  Strawberry-Lavender
    Victoria Sponge, 156–57
  Summer Trifle with Grilled
    Peaches, Cherries, and
    Boozy Pound Cake,
    297–98
  Swedish Apple Cake, 85
  Tips & Tricks, 14, 62, 157,
    235, 238, 298
  Vanilla Bean and Fresh Fig
    Cake, 81
  Vanilla Bean Cake, 297,
    298
Candied Carrots, 235, 236
Candied Kumquat Flan,
  153–54
Caprese Mini Pizzas with
  Burrata, 256–57
caramel
  Banana Caramel, 299–300
  Miso-Honey Caramel, 139
  Mulled Wine Caramel
    Sauce, 71, 72
  Pecan Shortbread and
    Rosemary Caramel Bars,
    57–58
  Rosemary Caramel, 57
  Tips & Tricks, 300
Caramelized Garlic and
  Chard Quiche, 98–99
Chai Babka, 25–26
Champagne-Butter Clams
  with Herby Sourdough
  Toasts, 213
Champagne-Shallot
  Vinaigrette, 200